"This book is extremely impressive. It presents a new and original approach to the issue of the role of voluntariness in valid consent, one emerging from and informed by a thorough knowledge of the extensive literature in the field and in a wide array of different debates. The presentation is very well organized, and the overall strategy is powerfully and clearly articulated. At the same time, it contains a remarkable number of fruitful and suggestive arguments."

Roger Crisp, *St Anne's College, University of Oxford, UK*

"Max Kiener proposes a radical, novel account of when consent is voluntary: consent is voluntary by default and becomes involuntary when motivated by influences that cannot be interpersonally justified. His account has striking implications for organ donation, payment in clinical trials and nudging, and also extends to sexual relations. The most significant and original contribution to consent in the last 20 years."

Julian Savulescu, *Chen Su Lan Centennial Professor in Medical Ethics and Director of the Centre for Biomedical Ethics, National University of Singapore*

Voluntary Consent

Voluntariness is a necessary condition of valid consent. But determining whether a person consented voluntarily can be difficult, especially when people are subjected to coercion or manipulation, placed in a situation with no acceptable alternative other than to consent to something, or find themselves in an abusive relationship.

This book presents a novel view on the voluntariness of consent, especially medical consent, which the author calls Interpersonal Consenter–Consentee Justification (ICCJ). According to this view, consent is voluntary if and only if the process by which it has been obtained aligns with specific principles of interpersonal justification. ICCJ is distinctive because it explains voluntary consent neither as a 'psychological' concept indicative of the inner states of a person's mind (e.g. willingness or reluctance) nor as a 'circumstantial' concept indicative of a person's set of options. Rather, ICCJ explains the voluntariness of consent as an 'interpersonal' concept focusing on the interaction between the person giving consent and the person receiving it and requiring the absence of illegitimate control by the consent-receiver. In so doing, ICCJ further develops the notion of interpersonal justification, known from contractualist theories in moral philosophy, and introduces it to the debate on consent. The author employs a top-down approach, defending ICCJ's key characteristics on the basis of general theoretical arguments, as well as a bottom-up approach, supporting ICCJ in its application to clinical challenges such as nudging and manipulation, living organ donation, and clinical trials.

Voluntary Consent will appeal to researchers and advanced students in normative ethics, bioethics, philosophy of law, behavioural psychology, and medicine.

Maximilian Kiener is a Leverhulme Early Career Fellow in Philosophy at the University of Oxford, UK. He is also an associate research fellow of The Institute for Ethics in AI at Oxford, of the ERC project Roots of Responsibility, based at UCL, and of the Oxford Uehiro Centre for Practical Ethics. His published work has appeared in journals including *Philosophical Studies*, the *Journal of Moral Philosophy*, and the *Journal of Medical Ethics*.

Routledge Annals of Bioethics
Series Editors: Mark J. Cherry
St. Edward's University, USA

Ana Smith Iltis
Wake Forest University, USA

Care Ethics and Social Structures in Medicine
Ruth E. Groenhout

Uncertain Bioethics
Moral Risk and Human Dignity
Stephen Napier

A Virtue-Based Defense of Perinatal Hospice
Aaron D. Cobb

A New Theory of Conscientious Objection in Medicine
Justification and Reasonability
Robert F. Card

The Limits of Parental Authority
Childhood Wellbeing as a Social Good
Johan Bester

Bloody Bioethics
Why Prohibiting Plasma Compensation Harms Patients and Wrongs Donors
James Stacey Taylor

Agency, Pregnancy and Persons
Essays in Defense of Human Life
Edited by Nicholas Colgrove, Bruce P. Blackshaw, and Daniel Rodger

Voluntary Consent
Theory and Practice
Maximilian Kiener

For more information about this series, please visit: https://www.routledge.com/Routledge-Annals-of-Bioethics/book-series/RAB

Voluntary Consent
Theory and Practice

Maximilian Kiener

Routledge
Taylor & Francis Group
NEW YORK AND LONDON

First published 2023
by Routledge
605 Third Avenue, New York, NY 10158

and by Routledge
4 Park Square, Milton Park, Abingdon, Oxon, OX14 4RN

Routledge is an imprint of the Taylor & Francis Group, an informa business

ISBN: 978-1-032-29388-2 (hbk)
ISBN: 978-1-032-29389-9 (pbk)
ISBN: 978-1-003-30141-7 (ebk)

DOI: 10.4324/9781003301417

Typeset in Sabon
by Newgen Publishing UK

Contents

Acknowledgements

Voluntary Consent is an updated version of my doctoral thesis at the University of Oxford. I am, therefore, particularly indebted to my doctoral supervisors Prof John Hyman and Prof Dominic Wilkinson for their outstanding academic support as well as to my examiners Prof Roger Crisp and Prof Erasmus Mayr for their excellent criticisms and constructive suggestions. Working with John and Dominic as my supervisors was a unique opportunity and I am very grateful for how much I have learnt from them and still do. I also wish to thank the *German National Academic Foundation (Studienstiftung des deutschen Volkes e.V.)*, the *Arts and Humanities Research Council UK*, the *European Research Council*, and the *Leverhulme Trust* for their generous funding of my work culminating in this book.

In addition, I benefitted considerably from the discussion with colleagues at the Oxford Uehiro Centre for Practical Ethics, the ERC-project *Roots of Responsibility*, and the various conferences and workshops, where I had to the opportunity to present my work, including the Joint Session at the University of Hertfordshire (2021), the Oxford Jurisprudence Discussion Group (2021), the XXV. Congress of the German Society for Philosophy (2021), and the 10th Congress of Analytic Philosophy (ECAP 2020). A special thanks goes to David Campbell, Karamvir Chadha, Simon-Pierre Chevarie-Cossette, Thomas Douglas, Michael Dunn, David Enoch, Kim Ferzan, Claire Field, Lisa Forsberg, Mollie Gerver, Alexander Greenberg, Viktor Ivanković, Chloë Kennedy, Felix Koch, Neil Levy, Sebastian Lewis, Christian List, Andrew Lloyd, Gabriel de Marco, Crescente Molina, Yuuki Ohta, Dennis Patterson, Peter Schaber, Mark Sheehan, Patrick Tomlin, Laura Valentini, and the anonymous referees whose thorough feedback prompted me to refine many parts of this book. I am also grateful for the permission to reprint content from Chapters 6, 7, and 9 which were previously published, respectively, in the *Journal of Moral Philosophy*, *Philosophical Studies*, and the *Journal of Medical Ethics*. But the list of my academic supporters will not be complete until I mention the person who first encouraged me to think about consent, Prof Les Green. Les supervised me during my time on the BPhil at Oxford and his exceptional breadth of knowledge and own fascination for ethics and jurisprudence have influenced me up to this day.

Finally, I wish to thank my family, especially my parents Elvira and Siegfried, my sister Stefanie with her family, and my partner Antonia, for their endless support and encouragement.

Part 1

A Novel Account of Voluntary Consent

1 Introduction

Rambha Gajre is a young mother from India who is worried about her son. He is seriously ill and needs life-saving treatment, but Rambha cannot pay for it. She has so little money that she struggles to pay her rent and has been threatened with eviction. To earn enough money for the rent and her son's treatment, Rambha consents to paid participation in a clinical trial. Such participation may be highly intrusive, involve exploitation and even threats, and be the consequence of unjust circumstances. Yet, Rambha enrols and explains her situation as follows:

> Many people commit suicide and I didn't want to become one of those and I didn't want people to think I did it to avoid repaying [i.e. paying the rent]. I have two young kids, 10 and 12 years old. What would become of them? .... I am helpless, I have to do this [i.e. paid trial participation] .... I don't have a choice.[1]

Is Rambha's consent to trial participation *voluntary*? It is true that she deliberately chose to consent. But she is also highly reluctant to undergo the medical procedures, lacks any other option to earn the money for the rent and her son's treatment, and may have even been threatened or manipulated.

In medical ethics, people are acknowledged to have a right of self-determination, that is, a right to decide how their own body will be treated. This means that competent individuals, that is, individuals possessing the required mental capacities, have the right to decide which available medical procedures to undergo. Consent is a tool for exercising such a right and one by which individuals grant their physicians or clinical investigators permission to perform a medical procedure, which would otherwise be illegitimate to perform.

But in order for a competent person's consent to be valid and thereby make an otherwise impermissible procedure permissible, it has to be both informed and voluntary. Consent is *informed* if the individual knows the relevant facts about the medical procedure. The quantity and nature of these facts has been the focus of a large and still rapidly growing debate (Beauchamp & Childress, 2013; Berg, Appelbaum, Lidz, & Parker, 2001;

DOI: 10.4324/9781003301417-2

Bromwich & Millum, 2015; Dougherty, 2020; Manson & O'Neill, 2007). *Voluntariness*, on the other hand, requires that a person be able to give her consent freely and not be subject to constraints that impair her self-determination. But what exactly does it mean for a person to consent freely in the relevant sense?

Unfortunately, the voluntariness of consent faces numerous difficult challenges. Being subjected to coercion or manipulation, being placed in a situation with no acceptable alternative other than to consent to a procedure, or being in an abusive relationship are all potential obstacles to self-determination and voluntariness. In fact, Rambha's case is only one among very many where people consent under pressure. For this reason, clarity about the voluntariness of consent is urgently needed. It is impossible to understand consent as a tool for self-determination without understanding voluntariness.

In this book, I will present a novel account on the voluntariness of medical consent. I will argue that consent to a medical procedure is voluntary unless it is motivated by an influence that cannot be 'interpersonally justified', and I will call this view *Interpersonal Consenter–Consentee Justification* (ICCJ).

ICCJ is distinctive in that it claims that voluntary consent is neither a 'psychological' concept indicative of the inner states of a person's mind (e.g. willingness or reluctance) nor a 'circumstantial' concept indicative of a person's set of options. Rather, it is an 'interpersonal' concept focusing on the interaction between the person *giving* consent and the person *receiving* consent and requiring the absence of illegitimate control by the consent-receiver. So understood, ICCJ differs from other views in the literature by focusing on the reasons or motivation for which a person consents, instead of mere causal links or counterfactuals, allowing a specific form of moral legitimacy, and not just the strength of an influence, to have a bearing on the voluntariness of consent and making the behaviour of the person receiving consent (the consentee) central to its approach.

My plan in this book is as follows. The rest of Part One outlines my core proposal, ICCJ, after providing some historical background and terminological precision. Parts Two and Three then build the double support for ICCJ. Part Two, 'The Theory of Voluntary Consent', provides a *Top-Down* defence of ICCJ, defending ICCJ on the basis of general theoretical considerations, whereas Part Three, 'The Practice of Voluntary Consent', provides a *Bottom-Up* defence of ICCJ, defending ICCJ on the grounds that it successfully deals with key challenges from clinical practice, including Rambha's case. Finally, I conclude by looking beyond medical consent and generalising my result.

Note

1 Reference from Wertheimer (2014, pp. 280–281). Wertheimer listed the NBC News Open Channel (2012) as the source, which no longer makes Rambha's

story available. Here are two further websites giving information about Rambha: https://mcquaig.typepad.com/blog/2012/03/in-india-oversight-lacking-in-outsourced-drug-trials.html and www.firstpost.com/living/indias-poor-pharma-industrys-favourite-guinea-pigs-537682.html

References

Beauchamp, T. L., & Childress, J. F. (2013). *Principles of biomedical ethics.* New York: Oxford University Press.

Berg, J. W., Appelbaum P. S., Lidz, C. W., & Parker, L. S. (2001). *Informed consent: Legal theory and clinical* practice. Oxford; New York: Oxford University Press.

Bromwich, D., & Millum, J. (2015). Disclosure and consent to medical research participation. *Journal of Moral Philosophy, 12*(2), 195–219.

Dougherty, T. (2020). Informed consent, disclosure, and understanding. *Philosophy & Public Affairs, 48*(2), 119–150.

Manson, N. C., & O'Neill, O. (2007). *Rethinking informed consent in bioethics.* Cambridge: Cambridge University Press.

Wertheimer, A. (2014). Poverty, voluntariness, and consent to participate in research. In T. Meyers (Ed.), *Poverty, agency, and human rights* (pp. 272–298). New York: Oxford University Press.

2 The History and Definition of Voluntariness and Consent

Introduction

Today's debate about voluntary *consent* is far from being an ahistorical episode in practical ethics. Many of its key assumptions, questions, and challenges come from a wider discussion about voluntary *action*. Thus, if we are to understand consent, we have to take a step back.

In early modern philosophy, voluntary action was widely understood as action that had a particular cause, namely a volition or act of will. A paradigmatic defender of such theories was John Locke, who argued that

> we find in ourselves a *power* to begin or forbear, continue or end several actions of our minds and motions of our bodies, barely by a thought or preference of the mind ordering or, as it were commanding, the doing or not doing such or such a particular action. This *power* ... is that which we call the *will*. The actual exercise of that power, by directing any particular action, or its forbearance, is that which we call *volition* or *willing*. The forbearance of that action, consequent to such order or command of the mind, is called *voluntary*. And whatsoever action is performed without such a thought of the mind is called *involuntary*.
>
> (2008, 2.21.5, original emphasis)

Thus, according to Locke, voluntary action requires the presence of a 'volition' or 'willing', which he explains as 'nothing but that particular determination of the mind, whereby, barely by a thought the mind endeavours to give rise, continuation, or stop, to any action which it takes to be in its power' (2.21.30). Although Locke says that acts are voluntary if they are 'consequent to' a volition, his view requires a *causal* rather than merely *temporal* relation between volitions and voluntary action, as becomes clear from the following passage:

DOI: 10.4324/9781003301417-3

> My right Hand writes, whilst my left Hand is still: What *causes* rest in one, and motion in the other? Nothing but my Will, a Thought of my Mind, [a volition].
>
> (4.10.19, emphasis added)

Hence, on Locke's view, action is voluntary if it is *caused by* a volition, and involuntary otherwise. Thus, blinking, reflexes, or digestion will be involuntary because these bodily movements are not caused by a volition. But deliberately handing over one's wallet to a robber will still be caused by a volition and therefore voluntary on Locke's view.[1]

Locke's view is a paradigmatic example of theories postulating volitions because, firstly, he assumes that voluntary action is action that has a particular type of cause and, secondly, because he does not distinguish between volition and intention, or between voluntary action and intentional action. In fact, Locke seems to think that all human action is caused by a volition.

However, during the twentieth century, theories postulating volitions came under severe attack. Especially the criticisms from Ryle and Wittgenstein were so influential that the rejection of 'volitions' became common ground in twentieth-century philosophy of action and the treatment of voluntariness mainly a *post-volitional* project.[2] And once philosophers rejected theories postulating volitions, they could suddenly reconsider several questions that had seemingly received fixed answers, for example, whether voluntary action requires causation by some distinctive mental event, or whether there are differences between intentional action, voluntary action, and action as such.

These historical developments in the explanation of voluntary action are important because today's questions about voluntary *consent* stem from the twentieth-century debate on voluntary *action,* inheriting the latter's key assumptions, questions, and challenges. Unfortunately, scholars have neglected the important connections between these two philosophical areas and thereby missed out on an important resource for the investigation into voluntary consent. In this chapter, I want to fill this historical blind spot in the debate about voluntary consent, outlining how the two key approaches to voluntary action in the twentieth century shaped our thinking about voluntary consent today.

2.1 Two Main Approaches to Voluntary Action in the Twentieth Century

Ethical Models

The first approach in the twentieth century can be called *Ethical Models* as its proponents considered voluntariness to be of general relevance to ethical questions and were interested in voluntariness precisely for that reason. For instance, Feinberg claimed that voluntariness was generally relevant when considering whether one may paternalistically interfere with a person's action. Feinberg, defending soft paternalism, argued that 'the state has the right to prevent self-regarding harmful conduct ... *when but only when* that conduct is substantially nonvoluntary, or when temporary intervention is necessary to establish whether it is voluntary or not' (1986, p. 12, original emphasis). Voluntary conduct, on the other hand, 'preclude[s] interference' (p. 143).

Ryle claimed that voluntariness was generally relevant to the question of whether someone can be excused for his wrongdoing. He argued: '[A person] is accused of making a noise, and the guilt is his, if [and only if] the action was voluntary, like laughing; he has successfully excused himself, if he satisfies us that it was involuntary, like a sneeze' (Ryle, 2009, p. 56). Ryle argued that 'in their most ordinary employment "voluntary" and "involuntary" are used, with a few minor elasticities, as adjectives applying to *actions which ought not to be done*' (p. 56, emphasis added) and thereby tied the concept of voluntariness closely to the ethical context of guilt. Outside of this context, he considered it 'absurd to discuss whether *satisfactory, correct or admirable performances* are voluntary or involuntary' (p. 56).

Finally, Nozick claimed that voluntariness is generally relevant to the validity of contracts and whether the transfer of goods satisfies principles of justice. He argued that contracts are valid, and 'justice in transfer' (1974, p. 150) is obtained if and only if there was a '*voluntary* exchange' (p. 262, emphasis added). And like Ryle, Nozick ties the concept of voluntariness tightly to the ethical context under consideration.

On this basis, *Ethical Models* were able to reconsider questions to which theories postulating volitions had provided seemingly fixed answers. *Ethical Models* rejected the view that voluntary action is action caused by a particular mental event. However, they retained a *negative causal* proposal, that is, the view that voluntary action is any action *not* caused by certain influences, for example, coercion.

This negative causal proposal made the voluntariness of a person's behaviour the default: unless a person was under the influence of coercion or a similarly controlling influence, his action would be voluntary, and making voluntariness the default assumption was used to explain other default assumptions made by proponents of *Ethical Models*, for example, the assumptions that, due the voluntariness of a person's behaviour, (1) it is illegitimate to interfere with his acts on paternalistic grounds (Feinberg), (2) this person can be blamed for his wrongdoing (Ryle), and (3) a transaction with this person is valid (Nozick).

Furthermore, *Ethical Models*, unlike theories postulating volitions, distinguished between intentional action and voluntary action. Almost all of them accepted the following two claims:

(1) **Intention without Voluntariness:** One can act intentionally without acting voluntarily.

(2) **Voluntariness without Intention:** One can act voluntarily without acting intentionally.

Nozick, Ryle, and Feinberg supported (1) *Intention without Voluntariness* with reference to cases of coercion: if someone is severely coerced into handing over his wallet to a robber, he may do so intentionally. Yet, coercion negates the voluntariness of his acts. Hence, according to *Ethical models*, voluntary action and intentional action are different: whereas 'intentional action' is about the beliefs and desires of an agent, the voluntariness of an action depends on whether the agent was forced to act as he did.

On the other hand, Nozick, Ryle, and Feinberg supported (2) *Voluntariness without Intention* in two types of cases. Firstly, there are cases of smiling or frowning, that is, acts that people do not do intentionally, yet do voluntarily.[3] Secondly, there are cases of negligence where a person neither intends nor foresees that his acts harm someone else, but they do. If the person was not forced to act as he did, he acted voluntarily but not intentionally.[4]

In addition, almost all *Ethical Models* claimed that voluntariness requires the absence of force *and ignorance* and thereby adopted a broadly Aristotelian view.[5] According to Aristotle's account, only voluntary acts warrant praise or blame, and force as well as ignorance can render these inappropriate. Just as a person may not be blamed for what she was forced to do, a person revealing a secret while being ignorant that it is a secret may also be immune from blame if her ignorance was non-culpable. Thus, voluntariness requires the absence of force and ignorance.[6]

However, *Ethical Models* were divided over whether the voluntariness of one person's action depends on the morality of another person's action. Nozick answered affirmatively:

> Whether a person's actions are voluntary depends on what it is that limits his alternatives. If facts of nature do so, the actions are voluntary .... Other people's actions place limits on one's available opportunities. Whether this makes one's resulting action non-voluntary depends upon whether these others had the *right to act as they did.*
> (1974, p. 262, emphasis added)

Nozick claims that there are only certain limitations that negate the voluntariness of action, that is, those which have been imposed by *other people*, as opposed to natural limitations, and which are illegitimate because the people imposing them *did not have the right to do so*. Thus, on Nozick's view, the voluntariness of one person's action depends on the morality of other people's action: only morally illegitimate, that is, limitations that exceed rights, negate voluntariness. Natural facts and legitimate constraints do not negate voluntariness, however great their impact.

On the other hand, Feinberg denied that the voluntariness of one person's action depends on the morality of another person's action:

> One can think of voluntariness as a matter of degree. At one end of a spectrum are the acts ... which I shall call ... perfectly voluntary: actions of normal adult human beings *in full control* of their deliberative faculties ... fully informed of all relevant facts and contingencies, with their eyes wide open, so to speak, and in the absence of all coercive pressure. In the ideal case, there must be calmness and deliberateness ... no distracting or unsettling emotions, no neurotic compulsion, no misunderstanding .... At the very opposite end of the spectrum are [situations] ... when one *lacks all muscular control*, or when one is knocked down, or pushed, or sent reeling by a blow or an explosion – or when through ignorance one chooses something other than what one means to choose, for instance thinking arsenic powder is table salt, and thus choosing to sprinkle it on one's scrambled eggs.
>
> (1986, p. 104, emphasis added)

On Feinberg's view, the voluntariness of a person's action depends on how much control he has over it, that is, the extent to which he can exercise the physical and mental power required to determine his action and the extent to which he is free of pressure from others. As a person can have more or less control over his action, voluntariness becomes a matter of degree too. Thus, Feinberg thinks that something diminishes voluntariness *to the extent to which* it reduces a person's control and he understands control as a morally neutral concept. Therefore, the moral legitimacy of an influence lacks independent significance. Accordingly, and *pace* Nozick, Feinberg holds that something can undermine the voluntariness of a person's action even if it was *not* imposed by other people and therefore *cannot* be assessed in terms of rights or moral legitimacy, and something can fail to undermine voluntariness even if it was the influence of someone exceeding his rights.

However, Feinberg believes that moral considerations play a role in the *application* of voluntariness. For instance, 'depending on ... the moral or legal purpose to be served' (1986, p. 117), Feinberg explains, we need to make a moral judgement about whether an act was '"voluntary enough" to be immune from [paternalistic] restriction' (p. 118), that is, whether a person was sufficiently in control of his action, or whether '"consent" is ... "voluntary enough" to be valid' (p. 174). In each context, a different degree of voluntariness may be required, and moral considerations may help determine which degree is the correct one.

Ryle seems to be closer to Feinberg than Nozick on the question of whether the voluntariness of one person's action depends on the morality of another person's action. Claiming that someone acts involuntarily if he 'could not help doing it' (Ryle, 2009, p. 56) or was 'trying hard enough'

(p. 57) to avoid the performance of the act, Ryle – like Feinberg – refers to the control of the agent and refrains from any reference to the morality of other people's behaviour. However, when Ryle talks about 'external coercion and ... duress' (p. 58), he seems to allow for the possibility that the illegitimacy of creating coercion or duress is relevant to whether doing so negates the voluntariness of another person's action.

Anscombian Models

The second main approach to voluntariness in the twentieth century I will term *Anscombian Models* after their most prominent proponent, G. E. M. Anscombe. Anscombe and her followers[7] focused on voluntariness to provide a comprehensive understanding of human agency rather than to answer ethical questions.

Anscombe's objective was 'to delineate such concepts as the voluntary and the intentional' (2000, §5). Concerning the voluntary, Anscombe explicitly rejected theories postulating volitions. She claims that 'a positive act of mine is voluntary, not because it is accompanied or preceded by an act of will' (1981, p. 107).[8] Rather, an act is voluntary if and only if

(i) 'it is in the power of the agent to do it or not ... and this is a matter of physical possibility' (Anscombe, 2008, p. 178),[9] and
(ii) 'it is done ... either for its own sake or for the sake of something else' (Anscombe, 1981, p. 107).

Condition (i) requires the agent's physical control to determine his action, and condition (ii) requires that the agent be in some sense aware of what he is doing, that is, that he is not in complete ignorance about what his bodily movements amount to. Anscombe's condition (ii) may depart slightly from a very similar condition that Kenny defended. Kenny argued that a person acts voluntarily only if he, in a minimal sense, *wants* to act as he did, and added: 'To say that an agent wants to Φ in this sense is merely to say that he knows that it is in his power to refrain from Φ-ing if only he will give up one of his chosen purposes' (1975, p. 58). Fortunately, the potential slight difference between Anscombe's 'doing something for its own sake or for the sake of something else' and Kenny's 'wanting to do something in a minimal sense' will not affect my further arguments. Thus, I will assume that they both embrace roughly the same condition (ii).

Anscombe then explains that intentional actions are

> the actions to which a certain sense of the question 'Why?' is given application; the sense is of course that in which the answer, if positive, gives a reason for acting.
>
> (2000, §5)

For instance, suppose someone orders a taxi and is asked why he did so. If he answers that he needed a taxi in order to arrive at his appointment in time, the aforementioned question 'Why?' is given application and his positive answer provides a reason for his act. Hence, he acted intentionally. By contrast, if he answers that he accidentally dialled the number of the taxi company, the aforementioned question 'Why?' is refused application and his act was therefore unintentional. The question 'Why?' is refused application in cases of doing something accidentally, without control, in ignorance (relative to the relevant description), and when one brings about a foreseen but unintended side-effect. It is not refused application when one simply lacks a specific reason for action as when one does something for no particular reason at all, for example, out of boredom.[10]

On this basis, Anscombe distinguishes between the voluntary and the intentional in two ways. On the one hand, she talks about 'voluntary *rather than* intentional' (2000, §49, emphasis added), thereby indicating an *inclusive* contrast, that is, a contrast in which an act may be both intentional *and* voluntary but still be more appropriately referred to as 'voluntary'. Anscombe explains:

> Mere physical movements, to whose description our question 'Why?' is applicable, are called voluntary rather than intentional when (a) the answer is e.g. 'I was fiddling', 'it was a casual movement', or even 'I don't know why' (b) the movements are not considered by the agent, though he can say what they are if he does consider them.
>
> (§49)

Note that Anscombe here claims that the question 'Why?' remains applicable. Thus, the criterion for intentional action is fulfilled and the contrast between the voluntary and the intentional is *inclusive*, that is, calling an action voluntary does deny that the criterion for intentional action is fulfilled too. Yet, Anscombe suggests that the movements in cases (a) and (b) are more appropriately referred to as voluntary. Unfortunately, Anscombe leaves us without further explanation for why this is so. It seems that she thinks the label 'voluntary' is more appropriate because the person does not act for a reason (as in my taxi example), or because a person does not really *intend* the movements in cases (a) and (b). However, unclarity remains.

On the other hand, Anscombe talks about 'voluntary *though not* intentional' (2000, §49, emphasis added), thereby indicating an *exclusive* contrast, that is, a contrast in which an action is voluntary *but not* intentional. Anscombe elaborates:

> Something is voluntary though not intentional if it is the antecedently known concomitant result of one's intentional action, so that one

> could have prevented it if one would have given up the action; but it is not intentional: one rejects the question 'Why?' in its connexion.
>
> (§49)

Note that Anscombe now claims that one rejects the question 'Why?' in such a case. Thus, the criterion of intentional action is no longer met and the resulting contrast between voluntary and intentional is *exclusive*. However, it remains puzzling why exactly Anscombe thinks one rejects the question 'Why?' in situations of antecedently known concomitant results: after all, for an action to be voluntary, it has to meet the condition (ii), that is, it needs to be done 'either for its own sake or for the sake of something else' (Anscombe, 1981, p. 107). But if this is the case, one seems to have an intelligible answer to the question 'Why?': one brought about the concomitant result for the sake of something else. Hence, it seems the question 'Why' is answered and thereby given application, rather than rejected.[11]

These two contrasts and the unclarity that remains show that Anscombe did not have a precise account of the difference between the voluntary and the intentional. From an exegetical perspective, however, one can state that Anscombe aimed to provide two contrasts between the voluntary and the intentional: there is the inclusive 'rather than' contrast and there is the exclusive 'though not' contrast.

From there, Anscombe then proceeds to *involuntariness* and provides two examples. Firstly, she considers peristaltic movement and reflexes of the knee involuntary, and secondly, she considers certain acts due to ignorance involuntary, giving the following example:

> If I do something out of revenge which is in fact advantageous rather than harmful to my enemy, my action, in its description of being advantageous to him, is involuntary.
>
> (2000, §14)

Peristaltic movement and reflexes of the knee are involuntary because condition (a) of voluntariness is not satisfied: a person cannot directly control these bodily movements. Certain acts done in ignorance, for example, benefitting my enemy, are involuntary because condition (b) is not satisfied: benefitting my enemy is neither done for its own sake nor for the sake of something else. For this reason, Anscombe claims that 'voluntariness is relative to [a] description of action' (Anscombe & Morgenbesser, 1963, p. 399). However, such relativity to a description must be distinguished from the relativity to a description that is required for intentional action. Anscombe allows that children and animals can act voluntarily even if they lack the linguistic skills required to act intentionally.[12] Hence, *description* in cases of voluntary action must be understood so broadly that agents who lack certain skills are still capable of having such a description in their minds when setting out to act.[13]

Thus, to summarise: Anscombe's account distinguishes between intentional action, voluntary action, and action as such. Action is intentional when the question 'Why?' is given application. It is voluntary 'rather than' intentional when it is under the control of the agent and wanted but not performed for a specific reason or *intended* in the relevant way, for example, in cases of fiddling. It is voluntary 'though not' intentional when it brings about foreseen but unintended side-effects. Finally, action can be involuntary and unintentional: if someone mistakenly benefits his enemy, he acts neither intentionally nor voluntarily (under that description), but he acts nonetheless.[14]

Following this view, *Anscombian Models* had an ambivalent position on

(1) **Intention without Voluntariness:** One can act intentionally without acting voluntarily.

Kenny clearly rejected (1) *Intention without Voluntariness*, claiming that 'intentional actions appear to be a subclass of voluntary conscious actions' (1975, p. 53). And most of Anscombe's remarks support Kenny, for example, most notably when she says that 'every intentional action is also voluntary' (2000, §49). In these passages, Anscombe and Kenny imply that if a person's movements satisfy the requirements for intentional action, they will thereby also satisfy the requirements for voluntary action.

However, it is noteworthy that Anscombe, unlike Kenny, also made room for the opposite view, that is, that one can act intentionally without acting voluntarily. Towards the end of *Intention*, Anscombe says:

> *From another point of view*, however, such things [i.e. certain acts] can be called involuntary, if one regrets them very much, but feels 'compelled' to persist in the intentional actions in spite of that.
>
> (2000, §49, emphasis added)

And in a lecture titled *Sin*, Anscombe claimed that

> *'voluntary' is being used in a specially broad way* when we say that .... If someone does something under threat from another man, say of pain or death or eviction, ... it was forced on him. 'I did it quite voluntarily' implies that I acted without such compulsion.
>
> (2008, p. 178, emphasis added)

Thus, these passages suggest that Anscombe thinks voluntariness can be understood in two different ways. In one 'specially broad way', a person *can* act intentionally without acting voluntarily, for example, when he acts very reluctantly or under compulsion. And in another way, one *cannot* act intentionally without also acting voluntarily. As the latter sense finds greater support in Anscombe's work and is also supported by Kenny, I will assume that *Anscombian Models* adopt the view that one cannot act intentionally without acting voluntarily, that is, they reject (1) Intention without Voluntariness. On the other hand, *Anscombian Models* clearly accept (2) Voluntariness without Intention: One can act voluntarily without acting intentionally.

From Anscombe's perspective, it is not the *inclusive* 'rather than' contrast but her *exclusive* 'though not' contrast that matters here, as only the latter contrast states that one can act voluntarily *without* acting intentionally: Anscombe thinks that someone acts voluntarily *without* acting intentionally when he brings about an unintended but foreseen consequence.[15] Kenny, on the other hand, proposed a wider class of voluntary, though not intentional, action. Kenny calls 'actions which one does not do on purpose' (1975, p. 53) voluntary and not intentional and mentions as examples 'wincing in pain, fidgeting, sneezing, laughing, using an irritable tone of voice, mentally brooding over an injury' (p. 53), that is, cases that seem to come under Anscombe's inclusive 'rather than' contrast, as opposed to her exclusive 'though not' contrast. But despite this difference, both Anscombe and Kenny accept (2): one can act voluntarily without acting intentionally.

Finally, Anscombe led her inquiry of voluntariness beyond the category of agency and referred to passivity:

> Things may be voluntary which are not one's doing at all, but which happen to one's delight, so that one consents and does not protest or take steps against them: as when someone on the bank pushes a punt out into the river so that one is carried out, and one is pleased.
> (2000, §49)

In this example, it is not about 'one's doing at all', that is, activity or agency, but rather about being acted upon by others, that is, passivity. Hence, Anscombe shows that voluntariness is not restricted to agency but also applies to passivity. Moreover, in her ethical writings, Anscombe also allows for *states of affairs* to be voluntary, for example, she suggests that being in ignorance can be voluntary.[16]

Thus, *Anscombian* and *Ethical Models* both accept that (i) voluntary action is *not* action caused by a distinctive mental event; (ii) one can act voluntarily without acting intentionally; (iii) ignorance can cancel voluntariness. *Anscombian* and *Ethical Models* diverge as only *Anscombian Models* (i*) hold that one cannot act intentionally without acting voluntarily, (ii*) apply voluntariness to passivity and states, not just to agency, and (iii*) focus on voluntariness independent of any ethical context.

2.2 The Debate on Consent

I claimed that today's questions about the voluntariness of consent have grown from twentieth-century philosophy of action. I will now explain this claim in greater detail. Like twentieth-century philosophy of action, the debate on consent rejects theories that postulate volitions. Voluntary consent is never seen as consent caused by a volition. Like *Ethical Models*, the debate on consent considers voluntariness to be of general relevance to an ethical question, which – for the debate on consent – is the question as to when consent is valid and thereby makes an act permissible that would otherwise be impermissible.[17] Like *Ethical Models*, the debate on consent adopts a negative causal proposal: consent is considered voluntary unless it is caused by certain influences, for example, coercion. Like *Ethical Models*, the debate on consent accepts

(1) **Intention without Voluntariness:** One can act intentionally without acting voluntarily.

People in the debate on consent unanimously accept (1) because they think that consent will be given intentionally, but not voluntarily, if obtained by means of coercion.

Finally, like *Ethical Models*, the debate on consent is divided over the question of whether the voluntariness of one person's action depends on the *morality* of another person's action. In fact, almost exactly the same positions are defended again. Like Feinberg, Nelson et al. claim that 'whether an external influence is morally legitimate is conceptually and morally distinct from whether the action taken in response to that influence is voluntary or involuntary' (2011, p. 13) and thereby denies that the voluntariness of one person's behaviour depends on the morality of another person's behaviour. Moreover, like Feinberg, Nelson et al. focus on control and degrees of voluntariness when he says:

> There are degrees of control and noncontrol, and, in this respect, degrees of voluntariness as a function of the continuum from total control to total noncontrol. Each point on the continuum can be conceived as corresponding to a different degree of voluntariness, ranging from lowest to highest.
>
> (2011, p. 11)

Finally, like Feinberg, Nelson et al. also claim that deciding on the voluntariness of an act in a specific context requires setting 'threshold lines' (2011, p. 11) on an otherwise morally neutral scale of control.[18]

On the other side of the debate, Appelbaum et al. adopt Nozick's approach by claiming that consent is involuntary if and only if it is given under the influence of another person and 'the person exerting the influence does not have the *right* to act in this way' (Appelbaum et al., 2009,

p. 33, emphasis added). Thus, on Appelbaum et al.'s view, as on Nozick's view, the voluntariness of one person's behaviour depends on the morality of another person's behaviour. It is striking that these parallels between Feinberg and Nelson et al., and between Appelbaum et al. and Nozick, have not been acknowledged in the debate on consent.

However, unlike *Ethical Models* and *Anscombian Models*, the debate on consent is divided over:

(2) **Voluntariness without Intention:** One can act voluntarily without acting intentionally.

Appelbaum et al. and Wertheimer implicitly accept (2). Although they do not discuss (2), their accounts of voluntariness are consistent with the view that one can act voluntarily without acting intentionally.[19] However, on Appelbaum et al.'s and Wertheimer's view, intentional action is a requirement for an act to qualify as *consent* in the first place. Thus, any token of consent and *a fortiori* any instance of *voluntary* consent will be intentional anyway.

On the other hand, Nelson et al. reject (2) by claiming that the 'two conditions of voluntariness ... [are] noncontrol *and intentional action*' (2011, p. 11, emphasis added). Nelson et al. defend the condition of non-control, that is, the absence of controlling influences, to ensure that a person's consent is, negatively speaking, not interfered with, and he introduces the condition of intentional action to ensure that a person is, positively speaking, '*in control* [which] is likewise essential [to voluntariness]' (2011, p. 10, original emphasis). Thus, on Nelson et al.'s account, intentional action is a requirement for the *voluntariness* of consent, whereas on Appelbaum et al.'s and Wertheimer's view, intentional action is a requirement for an act to qualify as consent in the first place, independent of whether such consent will then also be voluntary.

Furthermore, unlike *Ethical Models* and *Anscombian Models*, the debate on consent is divided over whether ignorance cancels voluntariness. Whereas twentieth-century philosophy of action widely accepted that some types of ignorance cancel voluntariness, most people in the debate on consent rejected this view and claimed that only force, but not ignorance, negates the voluntariness of consent.

To be clear, they accept that ignorance can invalidate consent, but assume that it does so by preventing requirements relating to *intention* or *information* from being met, as opposed to the requirement that consent be *voluntary*. This is certainly true of Appelbaum et al. and Wertheimer as they clearly separated the requirements of information and intention from the requirement of voluntariness. Nelson et al., however, seem to adopt a different view after introducing intentional action as a condition of *voluntary* consent. On Nelson et al.'s account, if ignorance means that a person no longer consents intentionally, that is, that he no longer acts under the description of 'consenting',[20] his consent will therefore cease to be *voluntary*. Thus, for Nelson et al., certain types of ignorance may prevent the requirement of intention from being met and thereby *also* render consent involuntary.

These historical connections between the debate on consent and twentieth-century philosophy of action reveal the broad ramifications of investigating the voluntariness of consent. Accordingly, this book is not only a contribution to practical ethics but also to a modern understanding of voluntariness more generally and part of the attempt to explain voluntariness independently of theories that postulate volitions.

Furthermore, these historical connections raise the following important questions for the debate on consent:

- Does voluntary consent still require the presence of some mental states, for example, willingness, or at least the absence of some other mental states, for example, reluctance?
- Is *acting intentionally* a requirement for the *voluntariness* of consent, or is it a requirement for consenting in the first place, independent of whether such consent is then also voluntary?
- Do force *and* ignorance negate the voluntariness of consent?
- How do influences like coercion *cause* and thereby invalidate consent?
- Does the voluntariness of a person's consent depend on the morality of another person's influence? If so, how exactly?
- What types of influences can negate voluntariness, for example, threats, offers, manipulation, psychological influences, circumstantial influences, and so on?

Finally, these historical connections also provide important resources. The criticisms against Feinberg and Nozick also apply to Nelson et al. and Appelbaum et al. and can therefore be used to test and refine the positions in the debate on consent. For instance, Feinberg's view was criticised for arbitrarily basing a binary verdict (voluntary versus involuntary) on a scalar property (degrees of control) (Alexander, 2008; Shafer-Landau, 2005, pp. 171–172, 190–191), for being unable to account for the ethical context of voluntariness without making moral distinctions between different influences on a person's decision-making (Wertheimer, 2012), for conflating voluntariness with rational choice (Arneson, 1980, pp. 484, 487), for misconceiving the relation between voluntariness and autonomy (Olsaretti, 2004, chs. 4–6), and for his particular take on autonomy as a so-called exercise concept (O'Neill, 2002, chs. 2 and 4). On the other hand, Nozick has been criticised for making his view on voluntariness redundant and circular, as well as for falsely suggesting that an influence needs to be illegitimate in order to negate voluntariness (Bader, 2016, 2018; Cohen, 1995, p. 60; Kristjánsson, 2007, p. 72; Miller, 1983, p. 72; Olsaretti, 2004, p. 125; 2016; Ryan, 1977; Shnayderman, 2013, pp. 729–730; Wertheimer, 1987, pp. 307–310).[21] Moreover, since the debate on consent closely follows *Ethical Models* rather than *Anscombian*

Models, the latter provide a contrasting account against which the debate on consent can be evaluated. Moreover, *Anscombian Models* also offer further insights, for example, their take on how voluntariness applies not only to agency but also to passivity and states of affairs.

Working Definitions of Consent, Validity, and Voluntariness

Having explained the historical context of the debate on voluntary (medical) consent, I will now define the main terms of my inquiry in this book. More precisely, I will adopt the following working definitions: *Consent* is a communicative rather than a purely mental act. When consent is *valid*, it has its characteristic transformative effect, that is, the effect, roughly, that an act that was impermissible becomes permissible. Finally, *voluntariness* is a necessary condition for the validity of consent and requires the absence of controlling influences of potentially various kinds.

Consent

When a person consents, he permits another person to perform a certain kind of act. Being an act of *giving permission*, consent is *transformative* and, in medical settings, it is also *revocable*. People can withdraw their consent at any time. In addition, being an act of giving permission *to another person*, consent is always directed towards a recipient. In most cases, the recipient is a particular individual, for example, a particular physician. In other cases, it may be a group of people, for example, the members of a clinical team. Who exactly and how many people receive consent will depend on the consenter's decision, but the permission granted will be restricted to that person or that group of people.[22] Finally, giving permission for the *performance of a certain kind of act*, consent is always restricted to the kind of act specified by the consenter, for example, a medical procedure, sex, or transfer of property.

So far, this is common ground. Disagreement arises over what consent actually consists in. Three main views have emerged.

(1) According to a *subjectivist view*, consent is a mental act or state. The *expression* of consent is not part of consent itself and must not be confused with consent, just as the expression of belief is not belief itself and must not be confused with belief. As a result, subjectivist views claim that the expression of consent plays a purely evidential role. It informs others that consent has been given and, therefore, the content of the expression is truth-apt. It can correctly or falsely report on the presence of consent. Most of the subjectivist accounts focus on a mental *act*, that is, an intention, decision, or choice, rather than a mental *state*, that is, something that is merely felt or perceived in some way. However, opinions differ as to what the relevant mental act is. Consenting has been defined as 'specifically *intend*[*ing*]' (Hurd, 1996, p. 146, emphasis added) that

another person do something, '[mentally] *waiving* [one's] ... *right* that the conduct not occur' (Alexander, 2014, p. 107, original emphasis),[23] 'an internal choice ... – a decision that "this is okay with me"' (Ferzan, 2015, p. 398), or (heading more towards a mental *state*) a 'felt willingness to agree with – or to choose – what another person seeks or proposes' (Westen, 2016, p. 4).

Opposing the subjectivist view, other views define consent as a *communicative* act, that is, something people do publicly rather than just mentally. Two versions of this view need to be distinguished.

(2) On the one hand, there is a *hybrid view*. In this view, 'both a communication of consent *and* the existence of a certain mental state [respectively a mental act] are required in order for an agent to consent' (Healey, 2015, p. 354).[24] The hybrid view thereby adds something to the subjectivist view, namely the requirement of communication while still accepting that mental acts are part of consent and that communicating consent plays at least a partly evidential role.

(3) On the other hand, there is the *performative view*, according to which consent is exclusively a communicative act and not constituted by any mental acts or states whatsoever. Hence, communication does not *report* consent but *constitutes* it. The required communicative act may take various forms and does not have to be verbal. What counts as consent will depend on the context and could consist of a mere gesture, for example, nodding.

Opposing various characterisations, the performative view does not consider the intentions and beliefs of the person consenting altogether irrelevant.[25] But it has remained unclear how exactly proponents of the performative view account for them without incorporating at least some aspects of the subjectivist view.[26] It is here that I wish to go beyond reporting on existing accounts and specify the performative view by drawing two contrasts with the subjectivist and hybrid views.

Firstly, all subjectivist and hybrid views identify something like 'permitting' as the relevant mental act, whereas the performative view identifies 'intending to communicate permission'. In doing so, the performative view refrains from making any further demands on whether the person internally intends another person's conduct (Hurd), acquiesces to it (Westen), or mentally waives a particular right (Alexander). 'Intending to communicate permission' can be understood as a Gricean communicative intention.[27] Consent is given with the required communicative intention when a person (i) intends to make the recipient believe that he is permitted to perform a certain kind of act, (ii) intends the recipient to recognise her intention of giving him permission, and (iii) intends the recipient's recognition of her intention to provide him with reasons for believing that he is now permitted to perform a certain kind of act. Note that such a communicative intention does not imply that the person consenting wishes or desires the recipient to do the kind of act consent is given for. For instance, I may invite my colleague Daniel to a party (thereby consenting to him entering my house) even if I strongly prefer him not to be there. I may invite him only because I feel obligated to reciprocate an invitation, or because I want to avoid an awkward situation at work.[28] Moreover, I may consent to my friend taking my car to go on a holiday while strongly preferring that he does not do so and instead helps me with my gardening work.[29]

Secondly, the performative view takes a different stance on *why* a person's intentions are relevant. It holds that 'intending to communicate permission' is relevant because executing the communicative act of consent is something one can only do intentionally. In this respect, the communicative act of consent is similar to lying: one can only lie if one intends to do so, that is if one intends to deceive, rather than just inadvertently communicates something false.[30] But this does not mean that lying consists of *two* acts: a mental act and a communicative act. On the contrary, there is just *one* act, and the same holds for consent. In both cases, the respective intention is constitutive of the communicative act itself. The subjectivist and hybrid views diverge here and claim that there is a mental act *distinct* from the communicative act.

In the inquiry to follow, I will adopt – as a working definition – a performative view and consider consent to be a communicative act performed with the Gricean intention to communicate permission. However, I will do so *not because* it may ultimately be the correct view. In fact, I do not need to decide which of the three views is ultimately the correct one because an inquiry into voluntariness does not need to take a stance on the ontology of consent, that is, what consent ultimately consists in. Questions about the ontology of consent are independent from questions about the voluntariness of consent. A person can be pressured into performing the act of consent, whether it is a mental or communicative act, and the different ontological views all have to deal with questions about voluntariness. None of them imply any further assumption about voluntariness at this point, and my proposal on the voluntariness of consent will be compatible with all three views.

Validity

Earlier I claimed that when consent is *valid*, it has its characteristic transformative effect of making a previously impermissible act permissible. Now I wish to expand on this statement and claim that when consent is valid it 'changes the normative landscape so that an act that would have been impermissible *for some reason* is no longer impermissible *for that reason*' (Walker, 2018, p. 131, emphasis added). For example, prior to a competent person's valid consent, performing surgery on her would be impermissible *because* it would violate her right to bodily integrity. Subsequent to her consent, however, surgery is no longer impermissible *for that reason*. Her consent permits the surgeon to perform the operation.

The permission that consent creates is only a 'narrow' (or 'pro tanto') permission as opposed to a 'wide' (or 'all-things-considered') permission. Consent ensures that an act no longer wrongs the person consenting in a particular way (i.e. by violating the right to bodily integrity). However, this does not imply that the act has thereby become permissible all things considered. If a patient validly consents to a kidney transplant, the surgeon's performance of it will be narrowly permissible, which means that it will not wrong this patient. But the operation could still be all-things-considered impermissible if, for instance, the patient bribed the surgeon to manipulate the waiting list to allocate the kidney to him instead of to someone else.

On this basis, my inquiry will be concerned with the *moral* as opposed to the *legal* validity of consent. *Morally* understood, consent is valid if it makes an act *morally* permissible, which would otherwise be *morally* impermissible. In this way, consent regulates the extent to which people interacting with the consenter act immorally and, in the absence of an excuse or justification, become liable to moral criticism. Legally understood, consent is valid if it makes an act *legally* permissible, which would otherwise be *legally* impermissible. In this way, consent regulates the extent to which people interacting with the consenter act illegally and, in the absence of justification, become liable to legal action (as available in tort or criminal law).[31] Legal and moral validity are different and can diverge from each other because the law, unlike morality, is 'a blunt and expensive instrument' (Wertheimer, 2003, p. 5) and finds itself under constraints that morality is free from, for example, the criminal law's constraint to focus on the most serious wrongdoings only. As my concern will be the moral validity of consent, I will take into account the legal literature only to the extent that the considerations therein also apply to moral validity.

In addition, I will consider validity to be a binary notion. Consent is either valid or invalid. This is because validity determines permission and permission is itself a binary concept: one can be permitted or not permitted to do something, but not half-permitted. Hence, in order to maintain the link between validity and permission, the former must be considered a binary concept too. This view is widely accepted. But it also poses a challenge. Many factors determining the validity of consent may be scalar (e.g. whether consent is valid may depend on *the extent to which* a person's decision to consent was controlled by others[32]). Therefore, any account of consent must explain how to arrive at a binary verdict if such a verdict is based on scalar properties.

Finally, I will interpret '*valid*' as the *normative* property of consent, that is, the property that determines when consent has its transformative effect. I contrast this normative property of consent with the *constitutive* properties of consent, that is, the properties that determine whether there is a token of consent in the first place, independent of whether it is also transformative. Hence, according to my terminology, the phrase 'valid consent' is not pleonastic, nor is the phrase 'invalid consent' contradictory.[33]

Voluntariness

Voluntariness partly determines the validity of consent: it is a necessary condition for valid consent and, together with competence and information, provides sufficient conditions.

I will assume that the condition of voluntariness requires the absence of controlling influences on a person's decision-making. I will interpret 'influence' widely as anything that incentivises giving consent, respectively disincentivises refusing consent, for example, by changing the eligibility or availability of a person's option, or by directly interfering with a person's deliberation so that the motivation to consent is increased. Such influences include threats, offers, forms of manipulation, certain ways in which medical information is presented or made available, oppressive circumstances, and psychological states that exert pressure on a person's decision-making. An influence is controlling and therefore negates the voluntariness of consent if and only if it compels or forces a person to consent in a way yet to be specified. This view of voluntariness requires some explanation.

Firstly, it takes the voluntariness of consent to be the default. Unless a person's decision-making is controlled or pressured in some way, his consent will be voluntary. Considering voluntariness as the default aligns with the negative causal view of *Ethical Models* in twentieth-century philosophy of action.

Secondly, this view acknowledges that mental capacities are relevant to both competence and voluntariness. Mental capacities are relevant to competence because competence is *defined* by the possession of such capacities: the possession of certain capacities simply *is* what competence consists in. By contrast, mental capacities are relevant to voluntariness because questions about the voluntariness of a person's acts usually *presuppose* that this person possessed these capacities, that is, that he had the ability of being guided by reasons. Accordingly, I will stipulate that a person consents *voluntarily* if, in addition to being competent, he satisfies the requirements of voluntariness (i.e. the absence of controlling influences) and consents *involuntarily* if, despite being competent, he fails to satisfy these requirements. On the other hand, a person consents *non-voluntarily* if, independent of whether he satisfies the requirements of voluntariness, he lacks the basic mental capacities that define competence. This conclusion is consistent with the view that competence and voluntariness are still distinct conditions of valid consent: competence is defined by the possession of mental capacities, and voluntariness is defined by the absence of controlling influences. So understood, competence is more fundamental than voluntariness: competence determines whether a person is able to give consent in the first place, whereas voluntariness determines whether consent, once it is given by a competent person, generates a permission.[34]

Thirdly, I will reject Nelson et al.'s view, according to which intentional action is a condition of the *voluntariness* of consent. As one can only consent intentionally if one is to consent at all, the requirement of intentional action is already satisfied once there is a *token of consent*. Therefore, introducing intentional action again as a requirement of *voluntary* consent is superfluous. Moreover, Nelson et al.'s condition of intentional action also seems too narrow when applied to voluntariness more generally: if voluntariness requires intentional *action*, it is inconsistent with Anscombe's important insight that voluntariness applies not only to agency but also to passivity.

Finally, the voluntariness of consent, as I understand it, does not require the absence of ignorance. I thereby follow the majority view of voluntariness in the debate on consent, but depart from the view which was prevalent in the twentieth century. But to be clear: I accept that ignorance can invalidate consent, but I will assume that it does so by preventing the requirements relating to *intention* or *information* from being met, as opposed to the requirement that consent be *voluntary*.

Some types of ignorance prevent the requirement relating to intention from being met, that is, they undermine the intention constitutive of consent. For instance, suppose a person signs a consent form believing he is merely acknowledging receipt of information. Such ignorance means there is no consent in the first place. To consent, a person needs to *intend* the act to be one of granting permission. Other types of ignorance prevent the requirement of information from being met. Suppose a patient is ignorant about important risks of a procedure. Although he still gave his consent, his consent was not informed and potentially invalid for this reason.

There is no universal formula for deciding whether ignorance of some aspect cancels the very act of consent or prevents the requirement of information from being met. It will depend on the context of the situation, the importance of certain aspects for a person's self-determination, and potentially also the asymmetry between the consenting parties. Usually, performing an act without consent is a more serious wrong than performing an act subsequent to uninformed consent, and the law uses the distinction between different types of ignorance to account for these different wrongs (cf. Herring, 2016, pp. 156–158).

In this book, I will not attempt to analyse types of ignorance and rely on the assumption that the requirements of *intention* and *information* already provide comprehensive protection against ignorance. Therefore, there is no need for the requirement of voluntariness to include the absence of ignorance.

Hence, when investigating the voluntariness of consent, my central question will be which influences on a person's decision to consent are consistent with his consent being voluntary and which are not. In the remainder of this book, I will assume that the person giving consent is competent, fully informed, and acts with the required intentions. Hence, *if consent is invalidated or* (which I use interchangeably) *vitiated* in my examples, it will be due to the negation of voluntariness, and *if consent is valid* in my examples, it must also be voluntary.

2.3 Conclusion

This chapter aimed to render my inquiry historically informed and terminologically defined. The historical context showed that investigating the voluntariness of consent has broad ramifications, highlighted important questions for the further inquiry, and provided critical resources. The definitions of consent, validity, and voluntariness clarified important terminology and provided a clear focus amidst the multidisciplinary debates on consent. I will now proceed to outlining my own proposal on the voluntariness of consent, that is, providing a first exposition of it, before defending it with both a Top-Down and a Bottom-Up approach in Parts Two and Three.

Notes

1 There are still some challenges for how to interpret Locke here as he remained slightly ambiguous about the causal relata: one could interpret him as saying that the volition causes the act as a whole (e.g. the process of moving, raising one's arm), or only the result of the act (e.g. the state of motion, the rise of one's arm). Lowe opted for the latter interpretation on the grounds that otherwise a volition, being part of the act as a whole, would implausibly have to cause itself. Therefore, Lowe considers Locke to claim that an agent acts voluntarily if and only if he wills a certain act and such willing causes the result of the act. Applied to an example: 'An agent A raised his arm voluntarily if and only if A willed to raise his arm and A's willing to raise his arm caused A's arm to rise' (Lowe, 2002, p. 112). For the purpose of illustrating Locke's view as paradigmatic for theories postulating volitions, I do not need to take sides. I will rely on a general picture of such theories without discussing the many differences that exist between different accounts of them.

2 See Ryle (2009, ch. 3) and Wittgenstein (1958, pp. 151–152; 1981, §577; 1988, §726; 2013, §628). Arguably, also the works of James and Russell were particularly important in this regard. See James (1981, particularly ch. 26) and Russell (1995, particularly ch. 14). For a discussion, see Hyman (2015, chs. 1 and 4).

3 Admittedly, Ryle tied the concept of voluntariness closely to the ethical context of guilt. However, he also acknowledged that the use of the terms 'voluntary' and 'involuntary' is still intelligible when applied to acts like smiling or frowning.

4 It is only at the margins of the debate of the twentieth century that people reject (2) *Voluntariness without Intention*. Only Williams stated that 'an agent does X fully voluntarily if X-ing is an *intentional* aspect of an action he does which has no inherent or deliberative defect' (1990, p. 4, emphasis added) and thereby rejected the view that one can act intentionally without acting voluntarily. Williams highlights the methodological advantages of such an understanding of voluntary action: he argues that focusing on the class

of (in)voluntary acts so understood facilitates a more fine-grained evaluation of responsibility for intentional acts. Williams focuses on a particular aspect pertinent to responsibility, that is, the state of mind with which intentional actions are done, and claims that doing so 'helps to serve the purposes of justice' (1993, p. 67).

5 See Ryle (2009) and Feinberg (1986). An exception seems to be Nozick (1974).

6 See Aristotle (2019: Nicomachean Ethics, III).

7 Apart from Anscombe, the second most prominent proponent is Anthony Kenny.

8 See also Kenny (1975).

9 See also Anscombe (2000, §7) and Kenny (1975, p. 53).

10 See Anscombe (2000, §17): 'The question is not refused application because the answer to it says that there is *no* reason, any more than the question how much money I have in my pocket is refused application by the answer "None".'

11 I thank Erasmus Mayr for making me aware of this potential tension in Anscombe's account.

12 See Anscombe (1979, p. 221; 2000, §7).

13 At this point, I leave aside the difficult exegetical question of how Anscombe distinguishes between types of ignorance cancelling voluntary action and those types of ignorance cancelling intentional action. Doing so would also require taking into account Anscombe's ethical work where she claims that ignorance does not negate the voluntariness of an act if the state of being ignorant is itself voluntary, which is the case if the person could have known and should have known. See Anscombe (2008).

14 It is worth highlighting that Anscombe's main competitor, Donald Davidson, is not relevant in this respect. Davidson thought that all action is intentional: 'A man is the agent of an act if what he does can be described under an aspect that makes it intentional' (2001, p. 46). In addition, Davidson mentions voluntary action only very few times and seems to equate it with intentional action, most clearly in Davidson (2001, pp. 25, 28 [together with note 10], 230, 247). Hence, even though Davidson also rejects theories postulating volitions, he does not distinguish between voluntary action, intentional action, and action as such.

15 Gordon (1966), like *Anscombian Models*, did not make ethical considerations key to her discussion of voluntariness. However, unlike *Anscombian Models*, she rejected (2) and claimed that an analysis of ordinary language shows that voluntary action implies intentional action.

16 See Anscombe (2008, p. 189).

17 See, for instance, Faden, Beauchamp, and King (1986, pp. 256–226, 337–381), Nelson and Merz (2002), Appelbaum, Lidz, and Klitzman (2009), Nelson et al. (2011), Wertheimer (2012), Beauchamp and Childress (2013, pp. 137–140).

18 Unlike Feinberg, however, Nelson does not include a requirement of information in the concept of voluntariness.

19 Appelbaum et al. and Wertheimer did not introduce intentional action as a requirement of voluntariness. See Appelbaum et al. (2009) and Wertheimer (2012).

20 Nelson et al. later emphasise that 'the *action* must be … intentional' (2011, p. 14, emphasis added). I will interpret him to claim that, in order for

consent to be voluntary, the act *itself* must be intentional (under the description of consenting) rather than the act being the *product* of another intentional act.

21 Some of these references target Nozick's view on freedom, but their criticisms also apply to Nozick's account of voluntariness.

22 The law clearly acknowledges the recipient as an integral part of consent, not only in medical contexts but also in contract law and the criminal law concerning sexual relations. See *Grabowski v Quigley* [1996] and *Taylor v Albert Einstein Medical Center* [2000] (medical consent), *Boulton v Jones* [1857] (contract law), and *R v Elbekkay* [1995] (criminal law on sexual relations).

23 See also Alexander (1996).

24 See also Sherwin (1996).

25 Hurd, for instance, characterises such a view as holding that 'a victim's mental state is *irrelevant* to assessing whether she has consented to a defendant's conduct' (1996, p. 136, emphasis added). Similar statements can be found in Kazan (1998, p. 37), Alexander (2014, pp. 103–104), and Ferzan (2015, p. 412).

26 See, for instance, Archard (1998, pp. 4–5), Wertheimer (2003, pp. 150–151), and Kleinig (2010, p. 11).

27 I here draw on Grice's account of what he called non-natural meaning. See Grice (1957). For a useful discussion of Gricean communicative intentions, see Recanati (1986).

28 Alexander (2014, p. 108) mentions a similar example.

29 Tadros (2016, p. 209) mentions a similar example.

30 This is the majority position in the literature on deception and should therefore serve the purpose of an example here, even if it has not gone unchallenged that one can only lie intentionally.

31 See Herring (2016, pp. 156–158).

32 See Nelson et al., (2011).

33 This use of terms may differ from the legal terminology in the area of sexual relations where consent is often seen as *valid* by definition. I separate constitutive from normative properties in order to focus specifically on the normative realm where voluntariness becomes important.

34 This relation between competence and voluntariness in the context of consent strongly resembles the relation between competence and voluntariness in the context of responsibility. Regarding responsibility, the lack of competence provides a person with an *exemption*, which denies responsibility and holds that there is nothing for a person to answer for. By contrast, the lack of voluntariness, for example, due to coercion, provides a person with an *excuse*, which admits responsibility, that is, that a person is obliged to answer for his conduct but claims that it would be inappropriate to blame or punish him, for example, because he acted under coercion. Thus, as Duff explains, the 'difference between an *excusable* agent and a seriously disordered [i.e. *exempted*] agent is analogous to that between someone who makes an understandable mistake in playing a game and someone who is not playing the game at all' (2009, p. 287, emphasis added). I agree with Duff's account and generalise it to include the context of consent as well. In my view, competence determines whether a person is fit to 'play the game', that is, whether he is fit to be responsible *or* fit to give consent in the first place, whereas voluntariness

determines what happens *in* the game, that is, whether a competent person is worthy of praise or blame for their conduct, *or* whether a competent person's consent generates a permission.

References

Alexander, L. (1996). The moral magic of consent (II). *Legal Theory, 2*, 165–174.

Alexander, L. (2008). Scalar properties, binary judgments. *Journal of Applied Philosophy, 25*(2), 85–104.

Alexander, L. (2014). The ontology of consent. *Analytic Philosophy, 55*(1), 102–113.

Anscombe, G. (1979). Under a description. *Noûs*, 13(2), 219–233.

Anscombe, G. (1981). *The collected philosophical papers of G.E.M. Anscombe.* Minneapolis: University of Minnesota Press.

Anscombe, G. (2000). *Intention* (2nd ed.). Cambridge, MA: Harvard University Press.

Anscombe, G. (2008). Sin. In M. Geach & L. Gormally (Eds.), *Faith in a hard ground: Essays on religion, philosophy and ethics* (pp. 139–188). Exeter, UK; Charlottesville, VA: Imprint Academic.

Anscombe, G., & Morgenbesser, S. (1963). The two kinds of error in action. *Journal of Philosophy, 60*(14), 393–401.

Appelbaum, P. S., Lidz, C. W., & Klitzman, R. (2009). Voluntariness of consent to research: A conceptual model. *Hastings Center Report, 39*(1), 30–39.

Archard, D. (1998). *Sexual consent.* Boulder, CO; Oxford: Westview Press.

Aristotle. (2019). *Nicomachean ethics* (3rd ed.). Indianapolis: Hackett Publishing.

Arneson, R. J. (1980). Mill versus paternalism. *Ethics, 90*(4), 470–489.

Bader, R. (2016). Moralized conceptions of liberty. In D. Schmidtz & C. Pavel (Eds.), *The Oxford handbook of freedom* (pp. 59–72). Oxford: Oxford University Press.

Bader, R. (2018). Moralizing liberty. *Oxford Studies in Political Philosophy, 4*, 141–166.

Beauchamp, T. L., & Childress, J. F. (2013). *Principles of biomedical ethics.* New York: Oxford University Press.

Cohen, G. A. (1995). *Self-ownership, freedom, and equality.* Cambridge: Cambridge University Press.

Davidson, D. (2001). *Essays on actions and events.* Oxford: Clarendon Press; New York: Oxford University Press.

Duff, A. (2009). *Answering for crime: Responsibility and liability in the criminal law.* Oxford: Hart.

Faden, R. R., Beauchamp, T. L., & King, N. M. P. (1986). *A history and theory of informed consent.* New York: Oxford University Press.

Feinberg, J. (1986). *The moral limits of the criminal law. Volume 3: Harm to self.* New York: Oxford University Press.

Ferzan, K. K. (2015). Consent, culpability, and the law of rape. *Ohio State Journal of Criminal Law, 13*, 397–439.

Gordon, L. M. (1966). The range of application of 'voluntary', 'not voluntary' and 'involuntary'. *Analysis, 26*(5), 149–152.

Grice, H. P. (1957). Meaning. *Philosophical Review, 66*(3), 377–388.

Healey, R. (2015). The ontology of consent: A reply to Alexander. *Analytic Philosophy, 56*(4), 354–363.

Herring, J. (2016). *Medical law and ethics* (6th ed.). Oxford: Oxford University Press.
Hurd, H. M. (1996). The moral magic of consent. *Legal Theory, 2*(2), 121–146. doi:10.1017/s1352325200000434.
Hyman, J. (2015). *Action, knowledge, and will* (1st ed.). Oxford: Oxford University Press.
James, W. (1981). *The works of William James. The principles of psychology. Volume 1* (F. Burkhardt, F. Bowers, & I. Skrupskelis, Eds.). Cambridge, MA; London: Harvard University Press.
Kazan, P. (1998). Sexual assault and the problem of consent. In S. French, T. Wanda, & M. Purdy (Eds.), *Violence against women. Philosophical perspectives* (pp. 27–42). Ithaca, NY: Cornell University Press.
Kenny, A. (1975). *Will, freedom and power*. Oxford: Blackwell.
Kleinig, J. (2010). The nature of consent. In F. Miller & A. Wertheimer (Eds.), *The ethics of consent: Theory and practice* (pp. 3–21). New York; Oxford: Oxford University Press.
Kristjánsson, K. (2007). *Social freedom: The responsibility view*. Cambridge: Cambridge University Press.
Locke, J. (2008). *An essay concerning human understanding*. Oxford: Oxford University Press.
Lowe, E. J. (2002). *Routledge philosophy guidebook to Locke on human understanding*. London: Routledge.
Miller, D. (1983). Constraints on freedom. *Ethics, 94*(1), 66–86.
Nelson, R. M., Beauchamp, T., Miller, V. A., Reynolds, W., Ittenbach, R. F., & Luce, M. F. (2011). The concept of voluntary consent. *American Journal of Bioethics, 11*(8), 6–16.
Nelson, R. M., & Merz, J. F. (2002). Voluntariness of consent for research: An empirical and conceptual review. *Medical Care, 40*(9), V69–80.
Nozick, R. (1974). *Anarchy, state and utopia*. New York: Basic Books.
O'Neill, O. (2002). *Autonomy and trust in bioethics*. Cambridge: Cambridge University Press.
Olsaretti, S. (2004). *Liberty, desert and the market: A philosophical study*. Cambridge: Cambridge University Press.
Olsaretti, S. (2016). Voluntariness, coercion, self-ownership. In D. Schmidtz & C. Pavel (Eds.), *The Oxford handbook of freedom* (pp. 439–455). Oxford: Oxford University Press.
Recanati, F. (1986). On defining communicative intentions. *Mind and Language, 1*(3), 213–242.
Russell, B. (1995). *The analysis of mind*. London: Routledge.
Ryan, C. C. (1977). Yours, mine, and ours: Property rights and individual liberty. *Ethics, 87*(2), 126–141.
Ryle, G. (2009). *The concept of mind* (60th anniv. ed.). Abingdon: Routledge.
Shafer-Landau, R. (2005). Liberalism and paternalism. *Legal Theory, 11*, 169–191.
Sherwin, E. (1996). Infelicitous sex. *Legal Theory, 2*(3), 209–231.
Shnayderman, R. (2013). Social freedom, moral responsibility, actions and omissions. *Philosophical Quarterly, 63*(253), 716–739.
Tadros, V. (2016). *Wrongs and crimes*. Oxford: Oxford University Press.
Walker, T. (2018). Consent and autonomy. In P. Schaber & A. Müller (Eds.), *The Routledge handbook of the ethics of consent* (pp. 131–139). Abingdon, Oxon; New York, NY: Routledge.

Wertheimer, A. (1987). *Coercion*. Princeton: Princeton University Press.
Wertheimer, A. (2003). *Consent to sexual relations*. Cambridge: Cambridge University Press.
Wertheimer, A. (2012). Voluntary consent: Why a value-neutral concept won't work. *Journal of Medicine and Philosophy, 37*(3), 226–254.
Westen, P. (2016). *The logic of consent: The diversity and deceptiveness of consent as a defense to criminal conduct*. London: Routledge.
Williams, B. (1990). Voluntary acts and responsible agents. *Oxford Journal of Legal Studies, 10*(1), 1–10.
Williams, B. (1993). *Shame and necessity*. Berkeley: University of California Press.
Wittgenstein, L. (1958). *Preliminary studies for the 'Philosophical Investigations' generally known as the Blue and Brown Books*. Oxford: Basil Blackwell.
Wittgenstein, L. (1981). *Zettel* (G. E. M. Anscombe & G. Wright, Eds., 2nd ed.). Oxford: Basil Blackwell.
Wittgenstein, L. (1988). *Remarks on the 'Philosophy of Psychology'* (G. E. M. Anscombe & G. Wright Eds.). Oxford: Basil Blackwell.
Wittgenstein, L. (2013). *Philosophische Untersuchungen* (S. Schulte, Ed.). Berlin: Suhrkamp.

Legal Cases

- *Boulton v Jones* [1857] 2 Hurlstone & Norman 564, 157 ER 232.
- *Grabowski v Quigley* [1996] 684 A.2d 610 (Pa. Super).
- *R v Elbekkay* [1995] Crim LR 163 CA (Crim Div).
- *Taylor v Albert Einstein Medical Center* [2000] 754 A.2d 650 (Pa.).

3 Interpersonal Consenter–Consentee Justification (ICCJ)

Introduction

My proposal in this book is *Interpersonal Consenter–Consentee Justification* (ICCJ), the view that consent is voluntary unless it is motivated by an influence that cannot be interpersonally justified.

The word 'unless' indicates that voluntariness is the *default*: consent is voluntary *unless* something undermines it. Thus, ICCJ does not require any specific act of will, or volition, for consent to be voluntary. It only requires the absence of certain yet-to-be-specified influences on the consent-giver's decision-making. My view thereby rejects theories of volition and follows a key assumption from twentieth-century philosophy of action.

The novelty of ICCJ arises from its emphasis on *interpersonal justification*, familiar from contractualism in normative ethics and now introduced to the debate on consent. Interpersonal justification is agent-relative: the consent-receiver (the consentee) must be able to justify, not merely in general terms, but specifically *to the consent-giver* (the consenter) how he obtained consent, taking into account the claims that the consent-giver can make on him. Moreover, in my view, interpersonal justification requires that the consent-receiver justify not only the influences that he himself *exerted* on the consent-giver for the purpose of soliciting the latter's consent, but also that he *tolerated* other influences while obtaining consent, for example, influences from third parties. However, interpersonal justification is always hypothetical and need not actually be communicated. What is crucial is that such a justification could, in principle, be given.

3.1 The Three Distinctive Views of ICCJ

So understood, ICCJ advances three distinctive views. First, it presents a distinctive view on how influences, such as coercion or manipulation, *cause* and thereby *invalidate* consent. According to ICCJ, an influence such as coercion causes and thereby invalidates consent (if it does) when it induces a certain type of motivation, and regardless of

DOI: 10.4324/9781003301417-4

whether it does so directly or through deviant causal chains. ICCJ *neither* requires, as some views do, that consent counterfactually depend on the influence *nor*, as other views do, that the actual influence 'directly explain' the consent. I will elaborate on and defend this aspect of ICCJ in Chapter 4.

Second, ICCJ presents a distinctive view on *which* influences invalidate consent. ICCJ holds that only morally illegitimate or, more precisely, 'interpersonally unjustifiable' influences invalidate consent. In so doing, ICCJ rejects views that consider voluntariness to be a value-neutral 'psychological' concept indicative of the inner states of a person's mind (e.g. willingness or reluctance) as well as views that consider voluntariness to be a 'circumstantial' concept indicative of a person's set of options. Rather, ICCJ explains the voluntariness of consent as an 'interpersonal' concept focusing on the interaction between the person giving consent and the person receiving it and requiring the absence of illegitimate control by the consent-receiver. This focus on interpersonal justification also sets ICCJ apart from other so-called moralised views on voluntariness, that is, views that also hold that assessing the voluntariness of consent requires some moral judgement about the influences on the consent-giver. I will elaborate on and defend this aspect of ICCJ in Chapter 5.

Third, ICCJ restricts *whose* influences invalidate consent. ICCJ holds that it is ultimately only the consent-receiver's influences, or his conduct more generally, that can invalidate consent, even in cases where the influences are exerted by third parties. For consent to be valid, ICCJ requires that the consent-receiver be able to justify not only the influences that he himself exerted on the consent-giver for the purpose of soliciting the latter's consent, but also that he tolerated influences from others while obtaining consent. In one respect, this makes ICCJ less demanding than other views because third-party influences do not automatically invalidate consent. In another respect, this makes ICCJ more demanding than other views because the consent-receiver faces greater requirements to obtain valid consent. I will elaborate on and defend this most controversial aspect of ICCJ in Chapter 6.

But before I go on to support these three main features and thereby build up my Top-Down defence of ICCJ, I need to say more about the principles underlying interpersonal justification. So, what determines whether something is interpersonally justifiable?

3.2 The Principles of ICCJ

Generally, *interpersonal justification* focuses on what people can demand from each other as part of their general moral relationship. Interpersonal *consenter–consentee* justification focuses more specifically on what people can demand from each other *as consent-giver and consent-receiver*. With this more specific relationship, the relevant norms of interpersonal justification in my proposed view will be restricted too, namely to what is significant for the validity of consent, as opposed to what is only significant in other areas where the two parties may also interact.

At this point, ICCJ makes a first axiomatic assumption, namely that consent protects autonomy. In other words, a person's consent should be an expression of her autonomy and self-determination, and the conditions of valid consent, including voluntariness, ought to explain under which circumstances consent is, in fact, a proper expression of autonomy. Thus, the first principle of interpersonal *consenter–consentee* justification will concern autonomy. Fortunately, interpersonal justification not only links to autonomy but also provides a novel take on it.

The Obligation to Respect Autonomy

Interpersonal justification features a *second*-personal perspective. To give an interpersonal justification requires, in the context of consent, an answer to the question 'How can *you* (*qua* consent-receiver) obtain consent from *me* (*qua* consent-giver) in this way?' This question is second-personal in the sense that it (i) explicitly relates consent-receiver and consent-giver *to each other*, (ii) assumes the consent-giver's authority to demand justification *from the consent-receiver*, and (iii) emphasises that the consent-receiver is *accountable to the consent-giver.*[1] In contrast, neither a first-personal perspective (i.e. 'How could *I* obtain consent in this way?') nor a third-personal perspective (i.e. 'How could *she* obtain consent in this way?') implies these three aspects.

This emphasis on a second-personal perspective can provide a new take on autonomy. It allows for a categorisation of the numerous conceptions of autonomy in the published literature into two main approaches.

On the one hand, autonomy has been understood as 'a state of realizing a set of higher-order capacities of rational thought and agency, whereby [on some accounts] practical options are reflectively endorsed and plans of action formulated or brought to execution (with or without the assistance of others)' (Lillehammer, 2012, p. 197). Unlike ICCJ, autonomy so understood guides practical reasoning from a *first-personal perspective*. It provides an answer to the question 'How am *I* to act in order to satisfy the demands of autonomy and be a good ruler over myself?'[2] Requirements of autonomy are satisfied when people actually exercise their relevant capacities. The most prominent version of this approach has roots in Mill's philosophy and emphasises individuality and independence.[3] Millian versions of autonomy ramified into three main accounts, varying according to whether they focus on autonomous *action*, the autonomous *person*, or an autonomous *life*.

Faden, Beauchamp, and King focus on autonomous *acts* and *choices*. Acts and choices are autonomous if they are intentional, come with understanding, and are free from influences that impede the exercise of certain capacities. Such choices can be made by either an autonomous or a non-autonomous person. Moreover, having the capacity to make autonomous choices does not guarantee that one will make autonomous choices in every situation (Faden, Beauchamp, & King, 1986, Part III).

According to G. Dworkin, autonomy is a 'characteristic of *persons*', not of choices (1988, p. 108, emphasis added). Although there are different ways of explaining autonomy as a characteristic of persons, the most prominent account, also found in Dworkin, refers to the idea of a multi-layered structure of the human mind. According to Dworkin, autonomy is 'a second-order capacity to reflect critically upon one's first-order preferences and desires, and the ability either to identify with these or to change them in light of higher-order preferences and values' (p. 108).

Young widens the perspective to an entire *life*. According to Young, 'an autonomous, or self-determining, person chooses or devises a plan for her life' (2009, p. 520). Like Dworkin, Young also appeals to the idea of bringing into accordance one's first-order decisions with one's second-order aims and values. A person is self-determining when 'making decisions about her life that accord with her own aims and values' (p. 531).

Finally, even though so-called relational accounts of autonomy criticised what they considered an inappropriate focus on individuality in Millian accounts, they also fall into the approach of autonomy as an exercise concept featuring a first-personal perspective (albeit one that may relativise the singular 'I' to the plural 'We').[4]

On the other hand, autonomy has been understood as a more Kantian than Millian concept. O'Neill and Manson, who defend a Kantian proposal, explain that

> Kant used the term autonomy to refer not to a characteristic of individuals, but to the formal properties of principles of action that can serve for all, and in particular to the combination of law-like form and universal scope.
>
> (2007, p. 17)

Following Kant, O'Neill and Manson reject all the previous Millian accounts according to which autonomy is an attribute of acts, persons, their lives, or about individuality and independence. In contrast, O'Neill claims, now in her single-authored work, that autonomy 'is a matter of acting on certain sorts of principles, and specifically principles of *obligation*' (2002, p. 84, emphasis added) and that it focuses on 'a distinctive constraint or requirement, a test that shows which *principles of action could be chosen by all*' (p. 84, emphasis added).

Giving primacy to obligations, O'Neill adheres to the three aspects constitutive of the second-personal perspective explained above. Principles of obligations (i) relate the person who is under an obligation to at least one other person to whom the obligation is owed, (ii) imply that the person to whom the obligation is owed can demand its fulfilment, and (iii) allow the person to whom the obligation is owed to hold the obliged person accountable.

By referring to principles that 'could be chosen by all' (2002, p. 84), O'Neill reinforces this second-personal perspective since such principles will have to be explained in terms of the demands that free and rational agents can make on each other's conduct (see also Darwall, 2006, p. 35).

Hence, autonomy so understood, like ICCJ, guides practical reasoning from a *second-personal perspective*. It provides an answer to the question 'How am I to treat *you* so as to respond appropriately to your moral status and the claims you can validly make on me?' Requirements of autonomy are satisfied if a person's entitlement to control his situation is respected. As O'Neill explains: 'Kantian autonomy is manifested in a life in which duties are met, in which there is *respect for others* and their rights' (2002, p. 83, emphasis added). Accordingly, respect for a consent-giver's autonomy requires freedom from wrongful interference and his having the potential to exercise, as opposed to actually exercising, the capacities for self-governance.[5]

Hence, (Kantian) *autonomy qua respect* and ICCJ converge on the second-personal approach to practical reasoning, whereas (Millian) *autonomy qua exercising autonomous capacities* and ICCJ diverge. Therefore, only autonomy *qua* respect can be understood as extending the idea of interpersonal justification to the concept of autonomy. For this reason, ICCJ will rely on autonomy in terms of respecting the consent-giver as opposed to the consent-giver realising norms of self-governance. This will be a key feature of ICCJ, not only in its application to medical consent but also in other contexts of consent. Thus, the first principle of ICCJ is the consent-receiver's obligation to respect the consent-giver's autonomy in this second-personal sense of respect.

The Obligation to Act Beneficently

As previously stated, interpersonal *consenter–consentee* justification focuses on what people can demand from each other *as consent-giver and consent-receiver*. In the previous section, I outlined more specifically that a principle of respect for autonomy, understood from a second-personal perspective, is key in this respect. Yet, interpersonal *consenter–consentee* justification is not limited to autonomy and can also accommodate further considerations.

At this point, I will make a second axiomatic assumption, namely that consent protects well-being. Ideally, a person's consent should promote well-being, at least insofar as this is possible within the constraints of respecting autonomy. Consent allows people to authorise actions they think best cohere with their values and preferences, and these can thereby advance their well-being too. The concern about well-being is especially prominent in the context of *medical* consent and the relation between patient and physician. Physicians are under an obligation to act beneficently, that is, to protect and promote their patient's well-being. The obligation to act beneficently is necessary to account for the particular vulnerability of the patient, the asymmetry between patient and physician, and the importance of bodily and mental integrity.

For these two reasons, that is, the axiomatic assumption that consent protects well-being and the fact that beneficence is a central norm of the patient–physician relationship, ICCJ will adopt as a second principle, at least in its application to medical consent, that medical professionals ought to protect and promote their patient's well-being. To explain beneficence as part of ICCJ more clearly, I will now first elaborate on what I take the patient's well-being to consist of and, secondly, on how 'protecting and promoting' it is to be understood. From now until the end of this chapter, I will narrow my focus more specifically to the topic of *medical* consent.

I suggest that ICCJ's principles of beneficence should focus on four different elements of well-being, all of which connect to consent also. (1) There is health, that is, the proper functioning of body parts and psyche. It is an integral part of a person's well-being and therefore a paramount good (Pellegrino & Thomasma, 1988, ch. 6; Schroeder, 2015). Consent is a tool to authorise medical procedures which, ideally speaking, protect, promote, or at least do not (significantly) harm a person's health. (2) There is the good of overseeing one's own life and decisions (Crisp, 1997, pp. 61–62; Cullity, 2007, p. 24; Dworkin, 1988, p. 112; Groll, 2015 pp. 506–508). Consent provides the setting for a person to make decisions for himself. (3) There is the good of aligning medical procedures with one's overall values and preferences, which can contribute to a person's well-being. Consent enables people to choose the procedures that fit best with their values and preferences. (4) There is the relationship with medical personnel that can contribute to a person's well-being. Good rapport reduces the distance or asymmetry between patient and physician and can have immediate positive effects on a person's well-being. Consent is a means of interaction between patient and physician and thereby a means to build a potentially valuable relationship.

'Protecting' and 'promoting' these elements of well-being includes the principle of Nonmaleficence, according to which the physician must not harm the patient and diminish these elements of his well-being. Nonmaleficence is a negative obligation of non-interference. However, protecting and promoting the patient's well-being also includes beneficence in the narrow sense, which – understood as a positive obligation – requires actively promoting a person's well-being and removing what could diminish it. Hence, I will use the term Beneficence in a wide sense to include both Nonmaleficence (i.e. Do no harm) and beneficence in the narrow sense (i.e. Do good).[6]

Furthermore, protecting and promoting well-being are part of obligations of bene-*ficence* as opposed to bene-*volence*. Bene-*ficence* is a matter of outcome: an act is beneficent if it actually protects and promotes well-being, irrespective of the agent's intention. Bene-*volence*, by contrast, is a matter of intention: an act is benevolent if the agent *intends* to protect and promote well-being, irrespective of the outcome. Ideally, physicians would act beneficently, as well as benevolently, and benevolence is often the agent's guide to beneficence. However, physicians may sometimes act beneficently but not benevolently (e.g. when a physician contributes to a patient's well-being because of self-interest) and vice versa (e.g. when a physician intends to promote a patient's well-being but fails to do so). ICCJ will focus on bene-*ficence* and thereby make the actual impact on a patient's situation, rather than the physician's intention, central to its approach.

Finally, other moral norms and the boundaries of the medical context restrict the scope of a physician's obligation to act beneficently. With regard to other norms, a physician is not under an obligation to benefit a patient if doing so involves treating other patients unjustly, for example, by giving all the available resources to one patient, or if he thereby violates other important norms, such as norms of confidentiality, for example, by providing information about other patients. Moreover, a physician is not under an obligation to benefit a person in ways unrelated to the medical context: for example, a physician does not have to drive her patients back home and pick them up in the morning to save them from a stressful journey on public transport.

Combining Autonomy and Beneficence

So far, I presented two fundamental principles of ICCJ, that is, the obligation to respect the consent-giver's autonomy and, in the medical context, the obligation to act beneficently. I elaborated on these obligations with an eye to ICCJ's second-personal perspective: I opted for a second-personal approach to autonomy and included aspects of well-being that had an interpersonal dimension, that is, (2) being respected by others as the person in charge of his situation and (4) the valuable rapport with medical personnel.

However, these principles have remained rather general, and therefore, I need to clarify how they can inform specific judgements about the voluntariness of consent. To do so, I will now derive three further and more specific principles from my previous statements about autonomy and beneficence. In particular, I want to show how my considerations concerning autonomy and beneficence can be synthesised in three more specific ways and provide more concrete guidance regarding the voluntariness of medical consent.

Assisted Decision-Making

The first more specific principle is *Assisted Decision-Making*, which obliges the physician (i) not to control his patient's decision-making and (ii) to provide help when the patient has to make his decision under pressure.

(i) The physician controls a patient's decision-making when he compromises the latter's ability or opportunity to make a free decision, for example, when he threatens to harm a patient if he does not consent, renders non-consent costly in some significant way, prevents the patient from taking part in some aspects of the decision-making, or weakens a patient's emotional or cognitive capacities for decision-making.[7] Controlling a patient's decision-making becomes more severe when it influences the patient in directions that differ greatly from his otherwise existing preference, or when the patient lacks feasible means to protect himself against an influence or its consequences, for example, to protect himself against the threatened removal of his medical care.

The physician does *not* control a patient's decision-making when he affects the decision-making in other ways. Over and above providing medical information, the physician may actively help the patient to clarify views and options, make recommendations, and offer further help when possible and feasible. How much and which assistance is appropriate depends on what a person consents to and the wider circumstances. More serious medical procedures may require greater assistance than less serious procedures would. Moreover, in some cases, assistance may require joint deliberation, whereas in others, for example, emergency cases with little time for a decision, assistance should take the form of a straightforward recommendation.

Assisted Decision-Making resembles what is sometimes called *shared decision-making*. Like the latter, *Assisted Decision-Making* allows for the physician to engage in shared deliberation with his patients. Unlike the latter, however, *Assisted Decision-Making* makes it explicit that, in certain cases, assisting a patient may require something other than shared deliberation.

Furthermore, *Assisted Decision-Making* differs from narrow models of shared decision-making as it does not amount to a mere division of labour where physicians only provide technical information and patients contribute to the conversation with their values (Entwistle, 2016; Joffe, 2010; Sandman & Munthe, 2009; Stark & Fins, 2013). Physicians may assist their patients more actively and help them to reach a final decision with regard to their overall values too. Moreover, *Assisted Decision-Making* differs from more demanding models of shared decision-making as it does not require the final decision to be mutually agreed upon (Stiggelbout et al., 2012; Tilburt, 2011; Whitney, McGuire, & McCullough, 2004). The patient retains the final decision-making authority. Finally, *Assisted Decision-Making* is not, unlike some versions of shared decision-making, an alternative to valid consent but rather a device to specify the requirements of valid consent.

(ii) On the other hand, *Assisted Decision-Making* obliges the physician to provide help when the patient has to make his decision under pressure, as in cases of third-party pressure. I wish to specify these obligations in three ways, based on core aspects of ICCJ. Firstly, ICCJ is based on a second-personal approach to autonomy and respect, which I take to require the respect of the consenter as the final decision-maker. Thus, if the patient does not want the physician to intervene in cases of third-party pressure, the physician is not under an obligation to do so. Thus, just like in (i), the patient retains the final decision-making authority. Leaving the final decision-making authority with the patient enables *Assisted Decision-Making* to distinguish between the voluntariness of a decision and its reasonableness or rationality. If the patient has the final say, it may be possible that his decision remains unreasonable or ill-judged in some way. Yet, the patient ought to be respected in his decision-making and, other things being equal, can still consent voluntarily.[8]

Secondly, physicians have positive obligations of help towards their patients, given their special fiduciary relationship with patients. Thus, if a patient asks for help and the physician can help the patient escape third-party coercion without any cost to himself, the physician is obliged to provide such help, for example, by offering an alternative option or influencing the coercing third party.

Finally, the point up to which physicians are obliged to help, that is, the burden they are obliged to bear for the sake of the patient, is confined by the role a physician occupies. ICCJ situates the physician and patient to each other *qua* their roles as 'physician' and 'patient'. Hence, the claims the patient can make on the physician's help are restricted to these roles. For instance, physicians are not obliged to help if doing so would significantly disadvantage other patients to whom they also owe duties of care. Moreover, physicians are not obliged to bear a burden that harms them as a private person and goes beyond the obligations of beneficence they have *qua* physician.

On the basis of these three points, *Assisted Decision-Making* then holds that the physician's obligation to help in particular cases depends on the extent to which a patient is under an illegitimate constraint or how severe the third-party coercion is (i.e. the severity of the influence), in particular how harmful or intrusive the options are that the patient has to choose between the extent to which the physician can provide effective help (i.e. the possibility of help) and, finally, how costly it is for the physician to help the patient (i.e. the feasibility of help). The case for an obligation to help is strengthened when coercion is high and help is possible and feasible. It is weakened if coercion is low or help is either not possible or not feasible.

So understood, *Assisted Decision-Making* promotes respect for patient *autonomy* by granting the patient the final decision-making authority as well as by assisting the patient to exercise his decisional capacities. *Assisted Decision-Making* promotes *beneficence* because (i) the physician's assistance reportedly increases the patient's adherence to the procedure chosen and can thereby promote his health; (ii) it can make it more likely that the patient's decision aligns with his overall values, (iii) it respects the patient as being in charge of his situation, (iv) it develops valuable rapport between the patient and the physician.

Equal Moral Standing

The second more specific principle is *Equal Moral Standing* and obliges the physician to respect a patient's entitlement to plan, revise, and pursue a conception of the good.

This principle is important because people base their medical decision not only on purely medical considerations but also on aspects related to their values and preferences more generally. For instance, a pianist may accept greater side-effects of a particular treatment option to avoid other procedures that could paralyse his hands; someone may reject certain blood transfusions to avoid violating a religious commitment; and a father may undergo strong chemotherapy to live until his daughter's next birthday.

I call this principle *Equal 'Moral' Standing* because, in all these cases, people exercise what Rawls called a *moral power*: the capacity to plan, revise, and pursue a conception of the good (Rawls, 2005). I also term it *'Equal' Moral Standing* because it obliges physicians to acknowledge that patients, despite being in an asymmetrical relationship to physicians in other respects, are still on a par with them regarding their entitlement to pursue a conception of the good.

People can valuably pursue a conception of the good in various circumstances. For example, (1) they do so even when they eventually consent to something with great reluctance, for example, when someone consents to exposure therapy in order to overcome some phobia; (2) when they promote other-regarding interests, that is, interests concerning other people's fate and preferences, for example, when a mother takes into account the welfare of her child; (3) when there are only very few alternatives to choose from. In fact, once the situation has become dire, it may become particularly important for a person to be able to select what aligns best with his values and preferences.

These aspects have important implications. If *Equal Moral Standing* ought to inform judgements about voluntariness, then voluntariness may not require the absence of reluctance (from 1), an influence may not be more problematic simply because it induces a person to do what benefits someone else (from 2), and lacking acceptable alternatives may not automatically negate the voluntariness of a person's consent either (from 3).

Equal Moral Standing will be called into question when a person is treated paternalistically. Quong, discussing paternalism in general, claimed that a paternalistic act is always 'motivated by a *negative judgment*' (2011, p. 80, original emphasis) about the other person's ability to make the right decision or behave reasonably by herself. The relevant abilities here are 'practical reasoning, willpower, and emotion management' (p. 81). '*Physical abilities* and *informational deficits* are ... excluded categories' (p. 82, original emphasis). Such a negative judgement amounts to 'denying that another person or group has the necessary capacity, in a given context, to ... plan, revise, and rationally pursue their own conception of the good' (p. 101, original emphasis) and, therefore, the 'paternalizer fails to accord the paternalizee *equal* status' (p. 101; Shiffrin, 2000).

However, not every paternalistic influence violates *Equal Moral Standing*. An influence violates *Equal Moral Standing* only if it is sufficiently severe, which depends on how much it restricts rather than expands a person's options, the extent to which it is guided by independent standards and ends rather than a person's own ones, the extent to which it steers a person into a particular option rather than enabling him to make a better decision on his own, and the extent to which the circumstances cannot justify considering a person's judgement temporarily inferior (e.g. pain in emergency cases may justify such a judgement). A physician's attempts to convince his patient that a certain option is best for him, that is, what Savulescu (1995) called 'rational non-interventional paternalism', are not paternalistic so as to violate *Equal Moral Standing*.

Equal Moral Standing promotes respect for *autonomy* as it respects a person's entitlement to pursue his own conception of the good. *Equal Moral Standing* promotes *beneficence* as it acknowledges that people are often the best judges of their own good, and exercising this capacity itself promotes well-being (Dworkin, 1988, p. 112).

Equal Moral Standing differs from *Assisted Decision-Making* in three main respects. Firstly, *Equal Moral Standing* does not require the physician to provide assistance when a patient is pressured by others, but only focuses on the restriction of influences that the physician himself exerts. Secondly, *Equal Moral Standing* is specifically concerned with influences that aim to *benefit* a patient rather than influences in general. It thereby enables ICCJ to separate *beneficent* influences, that is, influences that aim to benefit the consenter but could be morally wrong due to being paternalistic, from *adversarial* influences, that is, influences that do *not* aim to benefit the consenter at all and could be morally wrong due to steering someone in a direction contrary to his interests. This distinction is relevant as the former have greater prospects of being interpersonally justifiable, given that only they aim to promote the interests of the person *to whom* an influence needs to be *justifiable*. Thus, ICCJ can potentially treat beneficent influences more leniently than adversarial influences. And thirdly, *Equal Moral Standing*, unlike *Shared Decision-Making*, explains why certain psychological states, for example, great reluctance, will at least sometimes fail to invalidate consent: they fail to do so when a person pursues his conception of the good as being an integral part of his autonomy.

Trusted Partner

Finally, *Trusted Partner* is the third more specific principle and obliges the physician to honour his patient's trust, that is, the patient's reliance that the physician will satisfy certain norms when the patient cannot control or monitor him. Honouring a patient's trust requires adherence to two central norms. The first norm, as I argued elsewhere, is:

> the *proviso of hypothetical transparency*. Even though a trusting person refrains from 'the precise spelling out of terms' (Greenspan 2003, 161) which the trusted person may operate on, trust always comes with the proviso that the trusted party's relevant actions as well as 'the motives of the trusted party have to be able to be made transparent to the one who extends trust' (Ibid.). This proviso is respected only if full transparency did not lead to the trusting person being justified in feeling resentment or insulted. As Greenspan claimed, 'appropriate trust is trust that would survive a certain kind of knowledge on the part of the person who extends trust' (Ibid.).
>
> (Kiener, 2018, pp. 193–194)

The norm of transparency will be particularly important in cases of manipulation because some manipulative influences are completely hidden from the patient and such non-transparency is precisely what makes them problematic.

The second central norm of trust is what I call *loyalty in power*, which requires that the physician, independent of aspects concerning transparency, never abuses his position of power. This norm applies to the *professional* power that he has *qua physician*, for example, the power to use confidential information in different ways, or the power to control a patient's access to medical care. The norm also applies to the *factual* power that a physician has over patients due to their asymmetrical relation in terms of medical knowledge and state of health. For instance, a physician would abuse his factual power by shaming an already psychologically vulnerable patient. *Loyalty in power* is an important norm because patients need to be certain that their physicians are trustworthy when acting from their much stronger positions.

The principle *Trusted Partner* is violated when either of these two norms is breached, which is what happens when the physician uses non-transparency or his superior position of power to dominate rather than support a patient's decision-making. The more the physician relies on non-transparency or power to dominate the patient's decision-making, the more serious the violation of *Trusted Partner.* Moreover, a violation becomes more serious when the patient is in a particularly weak position.

Trusted Partner promotes respect for *autonomy* because trust has strong instrumental value for autonomy. It facilitates cooperation with medical personnel as an important option for pursuing one's conception of the good (Castelfranchi & Falcone, 2010, ch. 7; McLeod, 2015). If a patient could not trust his physician, the complexity of medical matters would make it impossible for those without medical training to make decisions. Moreover, trust has also intrinsic value as honouring the trust of another person is part of what it means to respect that person (O'Neill, 2002, pp. 15–27; 2012). *Trusted Partner* promotes *beneficence* as trust fosters cooperation conducive to the patient's well-being, promotes the patient's adherence to medical procedures, promotes valuable rapport, and produces immediate positive side-effects for health outcomes.

Trusted Partner differs from *Assisted Decision-Making* and *Equal Moral Standing* in two ways. Firstly, *Trusted Partner* introduces the abuse of non-transparency and positions of power as additional considerations that can make an influence particularly wrongful. Secondly, *Trusted Partner*, unlike *Assisted Decision-Making* and *Equal Moral Standing*, specifically links to the asymmetry between patient and physician, the patient's vulnerability, and the patient's lack of control over many aspects of his medical situation.

Thus, to conclude: ICCJ bases interpersonal justification on the principles of *Assisted Decision-Making*, *Equal Moral Standing*, and *Trusted Partner*, as derived from a physician's obligation to respect autonomy and act beneficently. Accordingly, consent is voluntary if and only if the physician's conduct in obtaining consent is in accordance with *all* of these principles. A violation of *any* of them is enough to negate the voluntariness of consent.

3.3 Health Care and Clinical Research

So far, I have explained ICCJ with reference to the context of medical treatment and healthcare, focusing on physicians and patients. But what about clinical research, which is not about healthcare and which concerns the relationship between investigators and participants in a clinical trial, rather than the relationship between physician and patients?

Treatment and clinical research are indeed different. Treatment offers personalised care, whereas clinical research aims to produce generalisable knowledge. Yet, when it comes to consent, ICCJ holds that the principles fundamental to the consenter–consentee relationship are roughly the same in both contexts.

To explain ICCJ's view, let me begin with the principle of beneficence, where the contexts of treatment and research seem to differ most clearly from each other. Admittedly, investigators do not have the same obligations of beneficence as physicians and healthcare providers. Unlike physicians, investigators test new medicines and therapies and may subject people to procedures that are not designed to benefit them at all. However, investigators still remain under certain obligations of beneficence.

Conducting clinical research is a privilege accorded to investigators, firstly, by the social consensus that some clinical research ought to be permitted for the sake of scientific progress and, secondly, by those individuals who serve as participants (Pellegrino, 1992, p. 362). This privilege is accorded on the understanding that exposing participants to risks of harm for the benefit of future patients is inherently problematic and must therefore be kept to a minimum. It comes with the restriction that procedures exceeding a certain threshold of harm or risk must not be performed under any circumstances, and this restriction is an obligation of beneficence: investigators are obliged to protect their participants' health within the scope of clinical research.

Moreover, if it is in the investigator's power to prevent harm or promote well-being without sacrificing scientific objectives of considerable importance (or incurring considerable costs), she remains under a moral obligation to treat individuals beneficently. Only by acting beneficently in such situations can investigators do justice to the aforementioned proviso and appropriately respect those individuals who give up or consider giving up legitimate moral claims to safety for the benefit of others.

Finally, other aspects of beneficence, as explained by ICCJ, hold equally for treatment and research. These include the investigator's obligation to help a person to reach a decision that takes into account that person's well-being, the obligation to respect a person as being in charge of his life and decisions, the obligation to help a person to reach a decision that aligns with his values and preferences, and the obligation to promote a valuable relationship to participants.

Thus, aside from the lowered requirement concerning the protection of a person's health, investigators are still under obligations of beneficence.

Furthermore, the obligation to respect autonomy holds equally in the context of treatment and research. Just like physicians, investigators need to respect a person's right to decide which medical procedures to undergo, if any. And given that clinical trials are not designed to benefit those who participate, the importance of respecting a person's decision whether to enrol seems particularly important.

Thus, the more specific principles of ICCJ also apply to the context of clinical research. *Assisted Decision-Making* also obliges investigators not to control their participants' decision-making and instead provide help when people have to make their decision under pressure.

Equal Moral Standing obliges investigators to respect their participants' entitlement to plan, revise, and pursue a conception of the good. However, in the context of clinical research, *Equal Moral Standing* may apply only indirectly. An investigator will not try to persuade people to undergo procedures that benefit them, and therefore, *Equal Moral Standing* will not apply to the investigator's influences. However, *Equal Moral Standing* obliges an investigator to tolerate other influences when they are consistent with the person pursuing his conception of the good.

Finally, *Trusted Partner* obliges investigators to honour their participants' trust. In fact, trust may become particularly important in the context of research where participants' interests potentially conflict with scientific interests. Here, it is vital that participants can trust that investigators will not abuse their position of power and always protect participants' interests as required in clinical research.

Hence, save for a slight modification of beneficence, ICCJ's principles apply equally to the context of research and treatment. But to be clear, ICCJ does not challenge the view that research and treatment may be governed by different norms in many other respects. ICCJ will always remain neutral with regard to the central aspects of an alleged difference between research and treatment, such as the permissibility of placebos, the randomised allocation of procedures, the need to stop clinical trials early in certain cases, the obligation to provide post-trial access to medication, the obligation to inform subjects about incidental findings, the duty to provide ancillary care, the permissibility of medication wash-out periods, and so on (Resnik, 2009). It is noteworthy, however, that also these differences between research and treatment have remained contentious (Emanuel, Wendler, & Grady, 2000; Miller & Brody, 2001; Miller & Rosenstein, 2003).[9] ICCJ only focuses on the requirements of informed consent and, in this regard, claims that the norms and principles are roughly the same in research and treatment. With this scope in mind, such a claim is hardly novel and is indeed widely accepted. Even those who argue most vehemently for a distinction between research and treatment accept very similar norms when it comes to informed consent, either implicitly[10] or explicitly, like Nelson-Marten:

> Common feature of informed consent in clinical practice [i.e. treatment] and clinical research is that its ethical foundation is respect for human dignity and individual autonomy. Furthermore, the essential nature of informed consent does not materially differ between the two areas.
>
> (Nelson-Marten & Rich, 1999, p. 81)[11]

Finally, this view still allows ICCJ to acknowledge that informed consent may have developed differently in the contexts of research and treatment,[12] that it may face different challenges in each context,[13] and that it may have different means of enforcement.[14]

3.4 Conclusion

This chapter explained the key proposal in this book, ICCJ. I outlined ICCJ's three distinctive features and the principles it is based on. I aimed to show how the idea of interpersonal justification, together with the twentieth-century rejection of theories of volition and the two axiomatic assumptions about autonomy and well-being, allows us to build a novel account of voluntary consent. I thereby gave an exposition of, rather than already substantive arguments for, the key aspects of ICCJ. Providing substantive arguments will be my focus in the following chapters. The Top-Down defence of ICCJ in Part Two will primarily support the three distinctive views explained in section 3.1, whereas the Bottom-Up defence in Part Three will primarily defend ICCJ's more specific principles outlined in section 3.2. (In what follows, I will continue to assume that the protagonists in all my examples are competent and informed, so that when their consent is invalid, it will always be so because it is involuntary.)

Notes

1 See Darwall (2006) on a second-personal approach to morality and practical reasoning.

2 Here, the first-personal perspective relates to the patient's point of view.

3 To clarify: Mill himself did not talk about autonomy but rather about individuality and liberty. Nevertheless, the views on autonomy described in this section resemble some of Mill's statements. For a discussion, see O'Neill (2002, chs. 2 and 4).

4 According to accounts of relational autonomy, a person's identity is necessarily *relational*, namely, socially embedded and interdependent. Therefore, autonomy designates not the fostering of individuality or independence, but rather the promotion of a person's flourishing within the context of versatile relations based on the 'values of love, loyalty, friendship, and care' (Herring, 2020, p. 213). For a good overview of accounts of relational autonomy, see Mackenzie and Stoljar (2000), Donchin (2001), Herring (2014, ch. 3), and Laufer-Ukeles (2011).

5 For more detailed discussion on how Kantian moral philosophy connects to a second-personal approach to morality, see Darwall (2006, especially ch. 9 and pages 35, 118, and 242).

6 This is a terminological choice that is shared by some but not others, for example, Beauchamp and Childress (2013). However, nothing substantial depends on whether one uses Beneficence in a wide or narrow sense.

7 Shaming may weaken emotional capacities as it intimidates a person and reduces his feeling of self-worth. Forms of distraction, as will be discussed in Chapter 7, may weaken cognitive capacities.

8 Note that ICCJ thereby sidesteps another criticism that was levelled against views like Feinberg's, that is, the criticism of conflating voluntariness with rational choice, which I mentioned in Chapter 2.

9 However, whether one should draw a sharp distinction between treatment and research has remained contentious too. Some argue that norms of treatment apply equally to settings of research (Miller & Weijer, 2007), while others hold that neither the complete unification of treatment and research nor its complete separation is defensible, thereby supporting a contextual approach (Resnik, 2009), a partial entrustment model (Richardson & Belsky, 2004), or a capacity-based approach (Bright & Nelson, 2012).

10 See Emanuel et al. (2000); Grady (2012); Morreim (2005).

11 See also Berg, Appelbaum, Lidz, and Parker (2001, p. 279); Boddington (2012, p. 178).

12 Whereas informed consent in the context of treatment developed as an answer to medical paternalism and was initially defended in courts, informed consent in clinical research developed as an answer to abuse and was initially presented in international documents such as the Nuremberg Code. https://history.nih.gov/research/downloads/nuremberg.pdf
13 Whereas some challenges arise only in clinical research (e.g. therapeutic misconception and payments for undergoing a procedure), others arise mainly in the context of treatment (e.g. paternalism).
14 Whereas courts review informed consent in the context of treatment *retrospectively*, ethics committees also review informed consent in clinical research *prospectively*.

References

Beauchamp, T. L., & Childress, J. F. (2013). *Principles of biomedical ethics*. New York: Oxford University Press.

Berg, J. W., Appelbaum P. S., Lidz, C. W., & Parker, L. S. (2001). *Informed consent: Legal theory and clinical* practice. Oxford; New York: Oxford University Press.

Boddington, P. (2012). *Ethical challenges in genomics research: A guide to understanding ethics in context*. Berlin: Springer.

Bright, P. L., & Nelson, R. M. (2012). A capacity-based approach for addressing ancillary care needs: Implications for research in resource limited settings. *Journal of Medical Ethics, 38*(11), 672–676.

Castelfranchi, C., & Falcone, R. (2010). *Trust theory: A socio-cognitive and computational model*. Hoboken, NJ: Wiley.

Crisp, R. (1997). *Routledge philosophy guidebook to Mill on utilitarianism*. London: Routledge.

Cullity, G. (2007). Beneficence. In R. Ashcroft, A. Dawson, H. Draper, & J. McMillan (Eds.), *Principles of health care ethics* (pp. 19–26). Chichester, West Sussex: John Wiley and Sons.

Darwall, S. (2006). *The second-person standpoint: Morality, respect, and accountability*. Cambridge, MA: Harvard University Press.

Donchin, A. (2001). Understanding autonomy relationally: Toward a reconfiguration of bioethical principles. *Journal of Medicine and Philosophy, 26*(4), 365–386.

Dworkin, G. (1988). *The theory and practice of autonomy*. Cambridge: Cambridge University Press.

Emanuel, E. J., Wendler, D., & Grady, C. (2000). What makes clinical research ethical? *JAMA, 283*(20), 2701–2711.

Entwistle, V., & Watt, I. (2016). Broad versus narrow shared decision making. In G. Elwyn, A. Edwards, & R. Thompson (Eds.), *Shared decision making in health care: Achieving evidence-based patient choice* (pp. 7–12). Oxford: Oxford University Press.

Faden, R. R., Beauchamp, T. L., & King, N. M. P. (1986). *A history and theory of informed consent*. New York: Oxford University Press.

Grady, C. (2012). Ethical principles in clinical research. In J. Gallin & F. Ognibene (Eds.), *Principles and practice of clinical research* (pp. 19–30). Amsterdam; Boston: Elsevier.

Groll, D. (2015). Medicine and well-being. In G. Fletcher (Ed.), *The Routledge handbook of philosophy of well-being* (pp. 504–516). London; New York: Routledge.

Herring, J. (2014). *Relational autonomy and family law.* Cham, Germany: Springer.

Herring, J. (2020). *Medical law and ethics* (8th ed.). Oxford: Oxford University Press.

Joffe, S., & Truog, R. (2010). Consent to medical care: The importance of fiduciary context. In F. Miller & A. Wertheimer (Eds.), *The ethics of consent: Theory and practice* (pp. 347–373). New York; Oxford: Oxford University Press.

Kiener, M. (2018). Truth-telling and respect for autonomy. *AJOB Neuroscience, 9*(3), 193–194. doi:10.1080/21507740.2018.1496169.

Laufer-Ukeles, P. (2011). Reproductive choices and informed consent: Fetal interests, women's identity, and relational autonomy. *American Journal of Law & Medicine, 37*(4), 567–623.

Lillehammer, H. (2012). Autonomy, value, and the first person. In L. Radoilska (Ed.), *Autonomy and mental disorder* (pp. 192–213). Oxford: Oxford University Press.

Mackenzie, C., & Stoljar, N. (2000). *Relational autonomy: Feminist perspectives on autonomy, agency, and the social self.* New York: Oxford University Press.

Manson, N. C., & O'Neill, O. (2007). *Rethinking informed consent in bioethics.* Cambridge: Cambridge University Press.

McLeod, C. (2015). Trust. In *The Stanford encyclopedia of philosophy.* Retrieved from https://plato.stanford.edu

Miller, F. G., & Brody, H. (2001). The internal morality of medicine: An evolutionary perspective. *Journal of Medicine and Philosophy, 26*(6), 581–599.

Miller, F. G., & Rosenstein, D. L. (2003). The therapeutic orientation to clinical trials. *New England Journal of Medicine,* 348, 1383–1386.

Miller, P. B., & Weijer, C. (2007). Equipoise and the duty of care in clinical research: A philosophical response to our critics. *Journal of Medicine and Philosophy, 32*(2), 117–133.

Morreim, E. H. (2005). The clinical investigator as fiduciary: Discarding a misguided idea. *Journal of Law, Medicine & Ethics, 33*(3), 586–598.

Nelson-Marten, P., & Rich, B. A. (1999). A historical perspective of informed consent in clinical practice and research. *Seminars in Oncology Nursing, 15*(2), 81–88. doi:10.1016/S0749-2081(99)80065-5.

O'Neill, O. (2002). *Autonomy and trust in bioethics.* Cambridge: Cambridge University Press.

O'Neil, C. (2012). Lying, trust, and gratitude. *Philosophy & Public Affairs, 40*(4), 301–333.

Pellegrino, E. D. (1992). Beneficence, scientific autonomy, and self-interest: Ethical dilemmas in clinical research. *Cambridge Quarterly of Healthcare Ethics, 1*(4), 361–369. doi:10.1017/S0963180100006551.

Pellegrino, E. D., & Thomasma, D. C. (1988). *For the patient's good: The restoration of beneficence in health care.* New York: Oxford University Press.

Quong, J. (2011). *Liberalism without perfection.* Oxford: Oxford University Press.

Rawls, J. (2005). *Political liberalism* (expanded ed.). New York: Columbia University Press.

Resnik, D. B. (2009). The clinical investigator-subject relationship: A contextual approach. *Philosophy, Ethics, and Humanities in Medicine,* 4(1), 1–15.

Richardson, H. S., & Belsky, L. (2004). The ancillary-care responsibilities of medical researchers: An ethical framework for thinking about the clinical care that researchers owe their subjects. *Hastings Center Report, 34*(1), 25–33.

Sandman, L., & Munthe, C. (2009). Shared decision-making and patient autonomy. *Theoretical Medicine and Bioethics, 30*(4), 289–310.

Savulescu, J. (1995). Rational non-interventional paternalism: Why doctors ought to make judgments of what is best for their patients. *Journal of Medical Ethics, 21*(6), 327–331.

Schroeder, S. (2015). Health, disability, and well-being. In G. Fletcher (Ed.), *The Routledge handbook of philosophy of well-being* (pp. 221–232). London; New York: Routledge.

Shiffrin, S. V. (2000). Paternalism, unconscionability doctrine, and accommodation. *Philosophy & Public Affairs, 29*(3), 205–250.

Stark, M., & Fins, J. J. (2013). What's not being shared in shared decision-making? *Hastings Center Report, 43*(4), 13–16.

Stiggelbout, A. M., Van der Weijden, T., De Wit, M. P., Frosch, D., Légaré, F., Montori, V. M., ... Elwyn, G. (2012). Shared decision making: Really putting patients at the centre of healthcare. *BMJ, 344*, 1–6.

Tilburt, J. (2011). Shared decision making after MacIntyre. *Journal of Medicine and Philosophy, 36*(2), 148–169.

Whitney, S. N., McGuire, A. L., & McCullough, L. B. (2004). A typology of shared decision making, informed consent, and simple consent. *Annals of Internal Medicine, 140*(1), 54–59.

Young, R. (2009). Informed consent and patient autonomy. In P. Singer & H. Kuhse (Eds.), *A companion to bioethics* (pp. 530–540). Chichester, UK; Malden, MA: Wiley-Blackwell.

International Document (Not Legally Binding But Very Widely Accepted)

The Nuremberg Code (1947).
https://history.nih.gov/research/downloads/nuremberg.pdf (3).

Part 2

The Theory of Voluntary Consent

4 Voluntariness and Causation

Introduction

Suppose Alfred threatens to hit Berta unless she consents to his driving her car. Coercive threats like Alfred's are paradigmatic consent-invalidating influences. But whether Alfred does, in fact, invalidate Berta's consent does not just depend on him; it also depends on Berta's reaction.

Suppose Berta just laughs and wrongly believes that Alfred is joking. Later, Berta hands over the keys only because, prior to the threat, she had already decided to allow him to drive her car anyway. In this situation, Berta may have acted in accordance with Alfred's demand. However, since Alfred's threat did not affect Berta's decision-making at all, it did not invalidate her consent. But if this is true, when exactly does a coercive threat, or a seriously illegitimate influence more generally, affect a person's decision-making in the way that invalidates her consent? Appelbaum et al. answer as follows:

> To invalidate a decision [i.e. consent], an influence must be *causally* linked to the subject's choice. If a person exerts illegitimate external pressure on a subject to consent to research participation when the person was inclined to participate *anyway* and intended to accept the offer, the voluntariness of the subject's decision [and the validity of consent] is not negated. Applying such pressure may be reprehensible, but since it is not *causally* related to the decision, it does not render the decision involuntary [or invalidate consent].
>
> (2009, pp. 33–34, emphasis added)[1]

This answer has two components. Firstly, Appelbaum et al. invoke the concept of *causation* to explain when an influence invalidates consent. On their view, an influence invalidates consent only if it is *causally* linked to consent, that is, if there is a causal link between the influence and a person's motivating reasons for consenting. Secondly, Appelbaum et al. explain the required *causal link* in terms of *counterfactual dependence*. They claim that there is *no* causal link if the person had consented 'anyway' (2009, p. 34), that is, in absence of the influence. Formulated

DOI: 10.4324/9781003301417-6

positively, there *is* a causal link if the person had *not* consented in the absence of the influence. Thus, causation is explained in terms of counterfactual dependence.

Applied to my example, Appelbaum et al.'s view states that Berta's consent remains valid because Alfred's threat did not 'cause' her consent. After all, Berta's consent did not counterfactually depend on it.

Appelbaum et al. thereby adopt the *negative causal view*, which was also key to accounts of voluntariness in twentieth-century philosophy of action: an action, including consent, is voluntary *unless* caused by certain influences, for example, coercion or manipulation. Thus, voluntariness requires (negatively speaking) the absence of certain causes rather than (positively speaking, as theories of volitions argued) the presence of certain causes.

But from there, Appelbaum et al. then offer a particular interpretation of what it means for an influence to cause and thereby invalidate consent, namely an interpretation of causation in terms of counterfactual dependence. And this emphasis on counterfactual dependence is indeed representative for many other views in the literature on consent (Archard, 2018, p. 180; Dougherty, 2013; Herring, 2002, 2005; Horder, 1999, p. 107; Lazenby & Gabriel, 2018; Williams, 2007). On these views too, an influence invalidates consent only if it *causes* consent, which requires that consent *counterfactually depend* on the influence.

In this chapter, I will accept the *negative causal view*, that is, that consent is voluntary unless caused by certain influences, but I reject the counterfactual approach presented by Appelbaum et al. and others. I will show that my proposal in this book, ICCJ, provides a better answer to the question of how influences such as coercion cause, and thereby invalidate, consent, and in so doing, I will defend the first distinctive view of ICCJ, mentioned at the beginning of Chapter 3. This is the view that an influence, such as coercion, causes and thereby invalidates consent (if it does) when it induces a certain type of motivation, and regardless of whether it does so directly or through deviant causal chains. So understood, ICCJ *neither* requires, as Appelbaum et al. do, that consent counterfactually depend on the influence *nor*, as some further views do, that the influence 'directly explain' the consent. I will label ICCJ's account in this respect the *Bad-Reasons-View* and explain its implication in the second part of this chapter, following a rejection of counterfactual approaches in the first.

But before I proceed, one clarification is needed: to restrict my focus on *how* influences *cause* and invalidate consent, as opposed to *which* exact influences do so (which will be my focus in Chapter 5), I will – for now – discuss only paradigmatic consent-invalidating influences, such as coercive threats. With this restricted focus on paradigmatic consent-invalidating influences, Appelbaum et al.'s counterfactual view can be understood as stating a necessary *and* sufficient condition: a paradigmatic consent-invalidating influence from the consent-receiver invalidates consent *if and only if* consent counterfactually depends on the influence.

4.1 Rejecting Counterfactual Models

It is striking how closely Appelbaum et al. and others follow the view defended by David Lewis in the debate on causation in metaphysics. Lewis, aiming to explain the concept of causation as such and without any reference to consent, claimed:

> We think of a cause as something that makes a difference, and the difference it makes must be a difference from what would have happened without it. Had it been absent, its effects – some of them, at least, and usually all – would have been absent as well.
>
> (1973, p. 557)

Hence, on Lewis' view, just as on Appelbaum et al.'s, an event C cannot be the cause of another event E if E would have occurred *anyway* without C. They all understand causation in terms of counterfactual dependence. This parallel between Appelbaum et al. and Lewis is an important asset for the debate on consent because the debate around Lewis' view contains a rich discussion of counterfactual dependence highlighting challenges for any counterfactual view (including Appelbaum et al.'s) as well as various tools designed to address them. In what follows, I shall utilise the more general literature on causation and counterfactuals to disprove the counterfactual view in the context of consent.

Consider the following two cases, which I adapted from the discussion of Lewis' account, and which show why Appelbaum et al.'s counterfactual view cannot be correct:

Preemption: Berta considers enrolling in a clinical trial. As she trusts investigator Wayne, Berta eventually decides to participate. But Wayne does not know this and thinks Berta will never consent freely. Being afraid of insufficient recruitment, Wayne threatens Berta with removing all her medical care if she does not enrol. After Wayne's threat, Berta loses all the trust in Wayne and her previous motivation for enrolment, and she consents to participation merely out of fear of losing her medical care.[2]

Anonymous Blackmail: Berta urgently needs medical treatment to overcome some disease but is unwilling to consent to it. Her physician Wayne really cares about Berta's health and, seeing no other option, he sends Berta an anonymous blackmailing letter threatening to report Berta's drug crimes to the police if she does not consent. Berta thinks the letter is a bad joke from one of her

> friends, but the letter still prompts her to search for the name of her disease again online. She finds a video of another ill woman who became infertile as a result of having the disease. Being frightened that this may happen to her too, Berta now consents, but only for reasons concerning her own health.[3]

Preemption shows that simple counterfactual dependence is not *necessary* for an influence to invalidate consent. In *Preemption*, Berta would have consented anyway. Hence, according to the counterfactual view, Wayne's threat did not cause and invalidate Berta's consent. However, Wayne's threat *did* cause and also invalidate Berta's consent because, as a matter of fact, Wayne forced Berta to consent and Berta consented only out of fear.

Anonymous Blackmail shows that counterfactual dependence is not *sufficient* for an influence to invalidate consent. In *Anonymous Blackmail*, Berta would not have consented had Wayne not threatened her. It was Wayne's threat that initiated Berta's second deliberation about the treatment, which eventually led to her decision to consent. Hence, the counterfactual view yields the result that Wayne's threat caused and invalidated Berta's consent. It may seem correct that Wayne's threat *caused* Berta's consent in some way (and I will return to this point later), at least if *Anonymous Blackmail* can be seen as an unproblematic case of transitive causation.[4] But it is incorrect that Wayne's threat therefore also *invalidated* Berta's consent. After all, Berta's decision to consent was not motivated by the desire to escape what Wayne threatened to do, but only by considerations of her own health.

Hence, *Preemption* and *Anonymous Blackmail* show that the counterfactual view, at least as presented by Appelbaum et al., fails. But this might not be the final word. To deflect such criticism, one could resort to two strategies, as also explored in the metaphysical literature on causation.

Strategy 1: Ancestral Dependence

Lewis initially tried to save his counterfactual view against cases like *Preemption* by redefining causation as 'the ancestral of dependence' (2004, p. 79). He claimed that 'event C causes event E if and only if there is a *chain of dependencies* running from C to E' (p. 93, emphasis added). Hence, Lewis not only talks about the cause C and the effect E but also about intermediary steps leading from C to E.

Thus, let us assume a standard case of preemption: there are two potential causes, c1 and c2, both of which would be sufficient to cause event e on their own. However, c1 preempts c2 and causes event e through an intermediate event d. As a result, c2 does not cause e.[5] Focusing on such a case, Lewis says:

> As far as causal dependence goes, there is no difference: e depends neither on c1 nor on c2. If either one had not occurred, the other would

> have sufficed to cause e. So the difference must be that, thanks to c1, there is no causal chain from c2 to e; whereas there is a causal chain of two or more steps from c1 to e. Assume for simplicity that two steps are enough. Then e depends causally on some intermediate event d, and d in turn depends on c1. Causal dependence is here intransitive: c1 causes e via d even though e would still have occurred without c1.
>
> (1973, p. 567)

Applied to my example of *Preemption*, Wayne's threat is c1, Berta's counterfactual willingness to consent is c2, Berta's fear of Wayne carrying out his threat is the intermediate step d, and Berta's consent is e. At first, it seems plausible that Berta's consent (e) depends on Berta's fear (d), which in turn depends on Wayne's threat (c1) and not on Berta's willingness to consent (c2). Thus, there is a causal chain between c1 and e but not between c2 and e. However, there is an obvious objection to this line of reasoning, and Lewis anticipates it:

> It remains only to deal with the objection that e does not depend causally on d, because if d had been absent then cl would have been absent and c2, no longer preempted, would have caused e. We may reply by denying the claim that if d had been absent then c1 would have been absent. That is the very same sort of spurious reverse dependence of cause on effect that we have just rejected in simpler cases. I rather claim that if d had been absent, c1 would somehow have failed to cause d. But c1 would still have been there to interfere with c2, so e would not have occurred.
>
> (1973, p. 567)

Lewis does not give an example of the instance of causation he has in mind. But what he says here is not true in *Preemption*. It is not true that 'if d had been absent, c1 would somehow have failed to cause d. But c1 would still have been there to interfere with c2, so e would not have occurred' (p. 567). Admittedly, c1 (Wayne's threat) could have been there without causing d (Berta's fear), for example, because Berta might not have been afraid of the threat or might have falsely thought Wayne was only joking. However, even if c1 (Wayne's threat) does no longer lead to d (Berta's fear), it is still an open question whether c1 (Wayne's threat) interferes with c2 (Berta's willingness to consent): subsequent to the threat, Berta may lose the confidence in Wayne and withhold consent, in which case c1 would have interfered with c2; or alternatively, Berta may consider this incident ridiculous or unimportant and consent to the medical procedures only for reasons related to her health. Hence, there is no guarantee that c1 (Wayne's threat) always interferes with c2 (Berta's willingness to consent). Therefore, e (Berta's consent) does not counterfactually depend on d (Berta's fear), and there seems to be no other candidate for an intermediate step d that could fare any better.

Hence, employing 'the ancestral of dependence' (Lewis, 2004, p. 79) cannot deflect the criticism illustrated by *Preemption*. It still fails to highlight what is actually relevant in *Preemption*, namely that Berta consented out of fear.

Strategy 2: Co-variation

So far, I have relied on Appelbaum et al.'s version of counterfactual dependence and focused on a *whether–upon–whether* dependence: *whether* E occurs depends upon *whether* C occurs. But this is certainly not the only option.

Why not think about different alterations of E? An alteration of E would be any event that shares with E its essential features but differs from it in its contingent ones, for example, the time at which it occurs, or the manner in which it occurs. Accordingly, we could then formulate a *whether/when/how–upon–whether* dependence: *whether* or *when* or *how* E occurs depends upon *whether* C occurs. And once we differentiate between alterations of E, we can do the same with C. Accordingly, we will arrive at a *whether/when/how–upon–whether/when/how* dependence: *whether* or *when* or *how* E occurs depends upon *whether* or *when* or *how* C occurs.

In fact, Lewis chose this strategy to deal with yet another set of preemption cases. He framed his account of counterfactual dependence in terms of *causal connections* and *influences* and summarised his preferred counterfactual as follows:

> Where C and E are distinct actual events, let us say that C *influences* E iff there is a substantial range C_1; C_2; ... of different not-too-distant alterations of C (including the actual alteration of C) and there is a range E_1;E_2; ... of alterations of E, at least some of which differ, such that if C_1 had occurred, E_1 would have occurred, and if C_2 had occurred, E_2 would have occurred, and so on. Thus we have a pattern of counterfactual dependence of whether, when, and how on whether, when, and how.
>
> (2004, p. 91)

On this basis, Lewis developed a test for causal connections. If cause and effect relate to each other as outlined, alterations of the cause lead to alterations in its effect. Therefore, 'seeing what else "wiggles" when you "wiggle" one or another event tells you which ones are causally connected to which' (p. 91). Thus, in order to find out whether X is a cause of Y, one alters X while holding everything else fixed and one looks at whether anything is happening in Y. This modification of Lewis' account renders what used to be a simple counterfactual *dependence* of C and E into a counterfactual *co-variation* of C and E.

This account of counterfactual co-variation can now handle my example of *Preemption*. Admittedly, *whether* Berta consents does still not depend on *whether* Wayne threatens her. But *how (or why)* she consents, that is, from fear and with particular motives, depends on *how* Wayne threatened her. Had Wayne not threatened her, Berta would not have consented from fear and with the intention of avoiding the loss of her medical care. Had Wayne threatened Berta differently, for example, with violence instead of removing medical care, Berta's intention to consent would have changed accordingly.

Thus, changes in Wayne's threat, while holding everything else fixed, effect changes in the reasons for which Berta consents. By contrast, changing Berta's initial willingness to consent (e.g. assuming she is *not* willing to consent before being threatened, or assuming she is willing to consent on different grounds), while holding everything else fixed, does not change Berta's reasons for consenting: she would still consent because of Wayne's threat.

Hence, there is counterfactual co-variation between Wayne's threat and Berta's consent, but not between Berta's willingness and Berta's consent. Therefore, Wayne's threat causes and thereby invalidates Berta's consent in *Preemption*. The account of counterfactual co-variation arrives at the right result.

However, there are two problems. Firstly, counterfactual co-variation still falsely suggests that Wayne invalidates Berta's consent in *Anonymous Blackmail*. After all, there is still a *whether–upon–whether* dependence: had Wayne not threatened Berta, she would not have consented; and the view on counterfactual co-variation still accepts that, once there is such a dependence between an influence and consent, the influence invalidates consent.

Secondly, there are other cases in which co-variation is unable to capture a causal link in the first place. Consider the following example:

> **Controlled Letter:** Investigator Charlotte writes a letter to Harry threatening to report him to the police for his drug crimes if Harry does not participate in her clinical trial. Unbeknownst to Charlotte, her colleague George watches her and thinks that Charlotte is doing exactly the right thing. In fact, if Charlotte had not written the letter, slightly deviated from writing this particular letter, or written it at a different time, George would have intervened and written it himself. Harry receives Charlotte's letter without George's interference and consents to enrolment to avoid prosecution.[6]

In *Controlled Letter*, let us assume there is no counterfactual co-variation between Charlotte's action and Harry's consent: no matter what Charlotte does, Harry will still receive the same letter at the same time. This is because George would intervene and send the letter himself if Charlotte writes it only slightly differently or at another time. However, there is great counterfactual co-variation between George's action and

Harry's consent: if George destroys Charlotte's letter or writes another one, Harry will receive no letter at all or a very different one. Yet, in the actual case, it is Charlotte's action and not George's that causes and invalidates Harry's consent. Therefore, an influence can cause and invalidate consent even if there is no co-variation (e.g. Charlotte's letter), and it can fail to cause and invalidate consent even if there is great co-variation (e.g. George's behaviour).

Lewis was aware of such examples. He would call Charlotte's letter a *preempting cause* and George's behaviour a *preempted backup*. But he cannot offer a convincing reply to defend his view of counterfactual co-variation. Lewis could only require *preempted backups* to be removed from an example before the test of counterfactual co-variation is applied. However, not only would this be an ad hoc reply, it is sometimes also unclear what should count as a preempted backup, or even whether there is a preempted backup at all. Most importantly, however, cases like *Controlled Letter* highlight that causation requires something that counterfactual dependence will sometimes be unable to capture, that is, an *actual link* between cause and effect, or between an influence and consent. Therefore, counterfactual dependence, that is, the second component in Appelbaum et al.'s view on consent and influences, needs to be abandoned.

In the next section, I will show that also Appelbaum et al.'s first component, that is, a *causal connection* between an influence and the motivating reasons for consenting, requires substantial modification because not every causal connection will ensure that a seriously illegitimate influence invalidates consent.

4.2 My Proposal: The *Bad-Reasons-View*

In *Anonymous Blackmail*, Wayne threatens Berta and unintentionally initiates her second deliberation, which eventually leads to her consent. I claimed that counterfactual models falsely imply that Wayne invalidates Berta's consent. Yet, if we understand these models as explanations of *causation*, they correctly imply that Wayne's threat *causes* Berta's consent. After all, Wayne's threat makes Berta research her illness, which in turn led to her consent. Thus, if causation is transitive, Wayne's threat caused Berta's consent.[7]

However, if this is correct, *Anonymous Blackmail* shows that not every causal connection between a coercive threat and a person's reasons for consenting is enough to invalidate consent. Thus, we need to think afresh and identify the more specific causal connection which is necessary to invalidate consent. In this section, I will defend an alternative view as implied by my proposal, ICCJ. Earlier, I explained that, according to ICCJ, an influence such as coercion causes and thereby invalidates consent (if it does), roughly, when it induces a certain type of motivation and regardless of whether it does so directly or through deviant causal chains. Now, I want to specific this view further. With regard to coercive threats, that is, paradigmatic consent-invalidating influences, ICCJ's position can be expressed in the following view, in which my formulation inducing a 'certain type of motivation' is explained in terms of inducing 'bad reasons':

> **Bad-Reasons-View:** A coercive threat invalidates consent if and only if it makes a person consent for a bad reason. A reason is bad if either (a) it is the reason linked to the coercer's threat, that is, consenting to avoid the threatened harm, or (b) it is a reason that corresponds to a perceived threat which, if it were the coercer's actual threat, would qualify as a consent-invalidating influence.[8]

To support the *Bad-Reasons-View*, I will firstly explain its components in greater detail (i), then defend it on the basis that it delivers the correct result in a variety of different cases (ii), and finally distinguish it from other prominent views (iii).

(i) The Bad-Reasons-View *Explained*

The *Bad-Reasons-View* requires that a threat *make* a person consent. 'Make', like 'affect' a person's decision-making, is causal terminology. Therefore, like counterfactual models, the *Bad-Reasons-View* still requires a causal connection between the threat and a person's motivating reasons for consenting. However, unlike counterfactual models, the *Bad-Reasons-View* requires a causal connection between the threat and *bad* reasons, as opposed to *any* reasons that make a person eventually consent. As stated above, a reason can be bad in two ways, and I shall now elaborate on each of these ways in turn.

Condition (a)

According to condition (a), a reason is 'bad' if it is the reason linked to the coercer's threat. In such a situation, a person consents precisely *because of the actual threat*, as in paradigmatic examples of coercion and in my example of *Preemption*, in which Berta consented because she wanted to avoid the harm Wayne threatened her with.

However, to satisfy condition (a), it does not matter whether the reason for consenting has been induced in a straightforward way, or whether there was some deviant causal chain.[9] By way of illustration, consider the following case:

> **Laughter:** Investigator Wayne threatens Berta with violence unless she participates in his trial. Berta thinks this is a joke and, after coming home, laughs out loud. Berta's friend Michael hears her laughing, asks about her amusement, and eventually tells Berta

that she really needs to take the threat seriously. Berta believes Michael, takes Wayne's threat to be sincere, and consents to participate in order to avoid serious harm.

In *Laughter*, Wayne intentionally exerts an influence on Berta and makes her consent for the very reason linked to Wayne's threat. Yet, the process that led to Berta's consent unfolded in a way that Wayne did not intend, anticipate, or control. Wayne did not intend his threat to become effective only after Berta laughed out loud and talked to her friend Michael. For this reason, there was a deviant causal chain linking Wayne's threat to Berta's consent. Nevertheless, condition (a) is satisfied: Wayne's threat induced in Berta the reason for consenting that is linked to his threat, and therefore, the reason is 'bad'.

In addition, to satisfy condition (a), it does not matter whether, through some even greater deviance, the person consenting lacks justification for her beliefs. The following case illustrates such a scenario:

Misread Story: Investigator Wayne threatens Berta with violence unless she participates in his trial. Berta thinks this is a joke and, being quite amused, researches to find out more about Wayne. Berta finds a website where someone different, but with the same name, is reported to have committed violent assaults. Berta mistakes this other person for Wayne, consequently believes Wayne's threat to be sincere, and consents to participate in order to avoid serious harm.

In *Misread Story*, like in *Laughter*, there is a deviant causal chain: at first, Wayne's threat only causes amusement in Berta and leads to consent only after such amusement prompts Berta to conduct inaccurate online research. Moreover, in *Misread Story*, like in *Laughter*, Berta eventually consents for the reason linked to Wayne's threat. However, unlike in *Laughter*, the deviant causal chain now comes with some epistemic flaw on Berta's part: she makes a mistake in her online research and, merely due to epistemic luck, ends up having the correct belief about Wayne threatening her. To use Turri's terminology, Berta may have *propositional* justification for believing in Wayne's threat because the threat is in fact real, but she lacks *doxastic* justification because the evidence she bases her belief on does not warrant holding that belief (Turri, 2010). Nevertheless, condition (a) is satisfied: there is a causal link between Wayne's threat and Berta's motivating reasons, and Berta consents for the very reason that is linked to Wayne's threat. Therefore, Berta's reason is bad and her consent invalid.

To summarise: condition (a) requires that there is a causal connection between the threat and a person's motivating reasons, and that the motivating reason is the one linked to the coercer's threat, but nothing more.

Condition (b)

According to condition (b), a reason is 'bad' if it corresponds to a perceived threat which, if it were the coercer's actual threat, would qualify as a consent-invalidating influence. Condition (b) thereby captures cases in which someone issues a coercive threat, succeeds in making the victim of coercion consent, but – again through some deviant causal chain – the motivating reason of the person consenting differs from the one linked to the coercer's actual threat. The following example illustrates such a scenario:

> **Pain:** Wayne threatens to put Berta through agonising pain unless she participates in his clinical trial. Berta does not think Wayne would do this but consents because she believes that otherwise Wayne would remove her medical care.

In *Pain*, there is a causal connection between Wayne's threat and Berta's motivating reason for consent: Wayne made Berta consent. However, Berta's reason for consenting is not the one linked to Wayne's threat. It is a reason that corresponds to another perceived threat, different from the actual threat. Berta falsely beliefs (for whatever reason) that she will lose her medical care if she does not consent, although Wayne did not issue that threat. However, let us assume that this perceived threat would invalidate consent if it were also the actual threat: if a person is threatened to have her medical care removed unless she participates in a clinical trial, her consent to such participation (when given because of this threat) is invalid. Therefore, in *Pain*, condition (b) holds: Berta's reason corresponds to another perceived threat which, if it were the actual threat, would qualify as a consent-invalidating influence. Thus, Wayne's threat, although it induces a different reason, still invalidates Berta's consent.

It is worth emphasising that, according to condition (b) just as it was according to condition (a), it does not matter whether Berta has doxastic justification for holding certain beliefs. Even if Berta not only believes what is false but also lacks any warrant for holding this belief,[10] Wayne's actual threat still invalidates Berta's consent, as long as it retains the causal connection to Berta's consent and induces the bad reason in Berta.

Moreover, note that condition (b) treats *Pain* very differently from my earlier example *Anonymous Blackmail*. In *Anonymous Blackmail*, Berta also consented for a reason different from the one linked to Wayne's threat, that is, Berta consented to promote her own health after being threatened with the removal of her medical care. Unlike in *Pain*, however, Berta's reason for consenting in *Anonymous Blackmail* did not correspond to any other perceived threat from Wayne which, if it were the actual threat, would also invalidate consent. Therefore, my *Bad-Reasons-View* considers consent valid in *Anonymous Blackmail* but invalid in *Pain*.

(ii) The Bad-Reasons-View *Defended*

After explaining the individual components of the *Bad-Reasons-View*, I will now defend this view by arguing that it delivers the correct results in all the examples given so far. I will start with the examples in the first half of this chapter.

In my opening example, Berta consents to Alfred taking her car. Although Berta is threatened by Alfred, this threat does not affect Berta's decision at all and therefore does not invalidate her consent. The *Bad-Reasons-View* correctly implies that Berta's consent is valid because Alfred did not *make* Berta consent.

The next case was *Preemption* in which Wayne, not knowing about Berta's willingness to participate in his trial, threatens to remove her medical care unless she consents. Wayne's threat thereby preempts Berta's counterfactual willingness to participate. In this case, I argued that Wayne seriously infringed Berta's autonomy and thereby invalidated her consent. The *Bad-Reasons-View* yields this correct result because condition (a) is satisfied: Wayne makes Berta consent by inducing the very reason that is linked to his threat.

The next example was *Anonymous Blackmail*, in which Berta receives an anonymous letter threatening to report her drug crimes to the police unless she consents to some medical treatment. Berta thinks the letter is a bad joke from one of her friends, but it still initiates another causal chain culminating in Berta's consent. I claimed that Berta's consent is valid because deciding to undergo medical treatment necessary to promote one's own health is a valuable expression of autonomy. The fact that Berta's deliberation about what is important to her has been triggered by an illegitimate threat in some deviant way does not diminish the value of Berta's consent.

The *Bad-Reasons-View* correctly aligns with this result. Although there is a causal connection between the threat and Berta's consent, neither condition (a) nor condition (b) is satisfied. Berta's reason for consenting is neither the one linked to Wayne's threat nor corresponds to a perceived threat which, if it were the actual threat, would invalidate consent.

Finally, the last case in my discussion of counterfactual models was *Controlled Letter*. Here, investigator Charlotte writes a letter to Harry threatening to report him to the police for his drug crimes unless Harry participates in her clinical trial. Harry believes the threat and consents only to avoid the threatened harm. I claimed that, despite the lack of counterfactual dependence, Charlotte seriously infringes Harry's autonomy and thereby invalidates his consent.

The *Bad-Reasons-View* again provides the correct result and holds that Harry's consent is invalid. Charlotte's threat *made* Harry consent and, as stated in condition (a), induced in Harry the very reason to consent that is linked to her threat.

Hence, so far, the *Bad-Reasons-View* is superior to counterfactual models. It delivers the correct result in all the cases in which the latter failed. However, it now remains to be seen whether the results of the *Bad-Reasons-View* are also correct in the cases of *Laughter*, *Misread Story*, and *Pain*, which I referred to in the previous section to explain the details of the *Bad-Reasons-View*. These latter cases are more controversial, and to avoid relying on intuitions only, I will now introduce additional theoretical considerations about the double function of consent to support my judgements about these cases.

On the one hand, consent protects autonomy. By deciding whether or not to consent, a person controls how others can legitimately interact with her, and the conditions for valid consent must ensure that such control is an expression of this person's autonomy. On the other hand, consent regulates responsibility. By acting on the basis of someone else's consent, a person avoids breaching consent-sensitive obligations and potentially becoming liable to moral criticism and legal redress. Thus, the conditions for valid consent must ensure that a recipient's responsibility for wrongdoing is appropriately accounted for too.

This double focus on the autonomy of the person giving consent and the responsibility of the person receiving consent constitutes the Janus face of consent. Any satisfactory account of (in)valid consent must do justice to both faces and show how consent can fulfil its double function. As a result, consent is most clearly *invalid* when a threat infringes a person's autonomy *and* the recipient of consent can also be held responsible for such an infringement.

In the following discussion, I will show that we find such clear cases of invalidity in *Laughter*, *Misread Story*, and *Pain*: not only was Berta's autonomy seriously infringed (first face), but it was also appropriate to hold Wayne responsible for invalidating consent (second face). Therefore, the *Bad-Reasons-View* is justified in considering consent invalid in these cases.

In *Laughter*, investigator Wayne threatens Berta with violence unless she participates in his trial. Berta laughed out loud and believed in the threat only after her friend Michael, who came to speak to Berta after hearing her laugh, explained that Wayne's threat was real.

Applying the Janus-faced rationale suggests, as the *Bad-Reasons-View* claims, that consent is invalid in *Laughter*. Given that Berta consents to avoid being seriously wronged by Wayne, her autonomy has been infringed. On the other hand, given that Wayne deliberately issued a violent threat, he can be held responsible for doing so, and if he proceeds, performing medical procedures on Berta will amount to assault. The deviant causal chain simply delayed the effect that Wayne's threat would have had anyway, and the threat thereby still constrains Berta's autonomy in the same way as initially intended. Thus, mere deviance does not prevent an influence from invalidating consent, and the *Bad-Reasons-View* correctly captures this fact.

My next example was *Misread Story*, in which Berta consents for the reason Wayne intended to induce, but only after some inaccurate online research, which deprived Berta of doxastic justification for believing in the threat.

Applying the Janus-faced rationale suggests, as the *Bad-Reasons-View* seconds, that consent is invalid. Again, Berta consents to avoid being seriously wronged by Wayne, and therefore, her autonomy has been infringed. The fact that she lacks doxastic justification does not mitigate this infringement. She is still in need of protection, just as she was in *Laughter*. From the perspective of Wayne, on the other hand, the differences between *Misread Story* and *Laughter* do not diminish his responsibility either. He deliberately issued a violent threat, which made Berta consent merely out of fear, and he should be held responsible for doing so. Thus, the deviance in *Misread Story* does not prevent Wayne's threat from invalidating consent, even though Berta lacks doxastic justification for her belief that there is a threat.

Finally, there was the example of *Pain*, in which Wayne threatens to put Berta in agonising pain unless she participates in his trial. Berta does not think Wayne will do this, but consents only because she thinks Wayne will otherwise remove her medical care.

Applying the Janus-faced rationale again suggests, as the *Bad-Reasons-View* holds, that consent is invalid. Starting with Berta's autonomy, there is an objective and a perceived constraint on Berta's autonomy. The objective constraint is the one that Wayne actually imposes and intends to use to receive Berta's consent. The perceived constraint is the one that Berta *believes* Wayne imposes and intends to use to receive her consent. But the difference between the objective and perceived constraints does not render Berta's consent a valuable expression of her autonomy. Neither the real facts nor Berta's perception can describe her decision as one free from coercive pressure. This aspect distinguishes *Pain* from *Anonymous Blackmail*, in which there was no perceived constraint: Berta believed herself to be free to consent and consented only to promote her health. Thus, the perspective on Berta's autonomy suggests that a change of reasons does not prevent a threat from invalidating consent if the induced motivating reason for consenting corresponds to another perceived threat which, if it were the actual threat, would also invalidate consent.

But what about the second face of consent, that is, Wayne's responsibility? Surely people should only be held responsible for things that can be attributed to them. If the chain leading to Berta's consent becomes too deviant and induces reasons significantly different from those Wayne had in mind, eliciting consent in that way may no longer be attributable to Wayne and, thus, he is not responsible for it.

I agree that Wayne might not be able to be held responsible for inducing certain beliefs. However, the question at stake is more specific: can he be held responsible for *invalidating consent*? Answering negatively would imply that the deviant causal chain and Berta's false and potentially unjustified beliefs exempt Wayne from responsibility, that is, the responsibility that he would have had if all worked out in the way he had planned. But this seems wrong. Wayne should be held responsible for imposing such an illegitimate constraint on Berta, and his conduct disqualified him as someone receiving Berta's permission. Thus, even though we may hesitate to hold Wayne responsible for inducing Berta's beliefs, we can still hold Wayne responsible for invalidating her consent. As a result, *Pain* is another case of invalid consent, and the *Bad-Reasons-View* delivers the correct result.

Note that this position of the *Bad-Reasons-View* aligns with an important part of criminal law, in which people are also held responsible for deviant acts. By way of illustration, the law holds that a person P is responsible for murdering V2 even if P intended to kill V1 and only accidentally ended up killing V2 through some deviant causal chain. But if people can be held responsible even when the *outcome* is different, that is, killing V2 instead of V1, they must also be held responsible when the intended outcome remains the same, that is, forcing Berta into consenting, and only *the way in which the intended outcome is brought about* is different (Bohlander, 2010; Horder, 2012).

Thus, I conclude that the *Bad-Reasons-View*, unlike counterfactual models, delivers the correct result in all the examples discussed.

(iii) The Bad-Reasons-View *Distinguished*

Finally, I will explain how the *Bad-Reasons-View* differs from another prominent view. So far, I have shown how it differs from counterfactual models and yields different results in a variety of cases. But the *Bad-Reasons-View* also differs from those accounts which reject counterfactual reasoning too. Most importantly, it differs from the view presented by Victor Tadros, who claimed:

> When we assess the effectiveness of a threat, then, we should identify its actual role in explaining Y's decision .... If Y's decision is a *direct response* to X's threat, X's threat is effective.
>
> (2016, p. 226, emphasis added)

On Tadros' view, a threat invalidates consent only if consent is 'a direct response' to it. By 'response', Tadros refers to a person's motivating reasons for consent as induced by the threat. Tadros claims, and I agree, that the validity of consent does not depend on counterfactual dependence but on a person's motivating reasons.

But Tadros also requires that a person's response be 'direct'. Tadros does not fully explain what exactly he means by 'direct' or 'indirect'. To evaluate this requirement nevertheless, I will make the following stipulation: a person's response to a threat is *weakly indirect* when, as in *Misread Story*, there is a deviant causal chain from the threat to consent but the person still consents for the very reason linked to the coercer's threat; and a person's response is *strongly indirect* when, as in *Pain*, there is not only a deviant causal chain but the threatened person also consents for a reason other than the one linked to coercer's threat.

On my *Bad-Reasons-View*, threats invalidate consent in both of these cases. By contrast, on Tadros' view, it seems that threats fail to invalidate consent at least if a person's response is strongly indirect. However, as I argued earlier, this is a false result. Threats can invalidate consent even when a person's response is not only weakly indirect, like in *Misread Story*, but also strongly indirect, like in *Pain*.

Thus, my view differs from Tadros' account by excluding a requirement that a person's response to a threat be 'direct'. What matters, according to the *Bad-Reasons-View*, is only that there is a causal connection between the threat and a person's motivating reasons, and that these reasons are 'bad', as specified in conditions (a) and (b).

However, I still think the notion of a 'direct response' remains important. For consent to be invalid, it needs to be a direct response, not to the threat as it was actually posed (as Tadros seems to suggests) but to the consenter's *perception* of the threat. This was true in all my examples of deviant causal chains. For instance, in *Pain*, Berta's belief that Wayne will remove her medical care if she refuses to consent directly explains her motivation for consent. Thus, whereas Tadros holds that the *relata* of the necessary 'direct response' are consent and the actual threat, I hold that the *relata* are consent and the perceived threat. So understood, my view can account for the cases with deviant causal chains while still allowing the notion of a 'direct response' to play an important role.

But once we focus on how a person subjectively perceives a threat, a more radical view becomes available, as defended by Tom Dougherty. Dougherty argues that consent is invalid if 'the consent-giver believes or has a credence that they would suffer a penalty for refusing consent, this penalty is illegitimate [from an objective perspective], and this belief or credence causes them to consent' (2021a, p. 1). On this view, it is *not* relevant how the consent-giver came to believe in a threat, whether the consent-receiver did anything to cause or encourage such a belief, or whether there is any real threat in the first place.

In so arguing, Dougherty implicitly distinguishes between two different causal connections: (i) that between the subjectively perceived threat and consent, and (ii) that between the objectively issued threat (or the consent-receiver's conduct more generally) and consent. Dougherty accepts (i) when he claims that, for consent to be invalid, it is required that a person's 'belief or credence [in a threat] *causes* them to consent' (2021a, p. 1). Yet, Dougherty denies (ii) when he says that 'there are cases in which consent is invalidated even though the consent-giver's doxastic attitudes do not arise from the consent-receiver wronging them' (p. 11).

Dougherty and I agree in outline but disagree in detail. We agree that there needs to be *some* causal link in (i), but we may disagree about which *exact* link is needed. Dougherty (2013) defended a counterfactual account of causing consent, which I reject in favour or Tadros' 'direct response'-view with regard to the causal *relata* in (i). This is important because even a counterfactual account with the causal *relata* in (i) would be vulnerable to counterexamples like *Preemption*.[11]

Moreover, I agree with Dougherty that the causal link in (ii) is not needed for consent to be invalid, yet we disagree on what else is needed for consent to be invalid. To see this, consider the following example that Dougherty uses to illustrate his view:

> [***False Fear***] Suppose that Leo emails their new roommate Ally asking to use their bread-making machine while they are away on their meditation retreat. Ally emails back, 'I'm off to the retreat now, and I can't be contacted until it is over. I'm not generally inclined to let people use my stuff. However, in the last apartment that I lived in, I refused a request like this, and I got bullied as a result. Since I don't want to go through all that again, I am letting you borrow the breadmaker.' This comes as a surprise to Leo, who has been exemplary in their behavior towards Ally and has done nothing to cause Ally to fear bullying. Since Leo can no longer communicate with Ally, Leo is now causally disconnected from Ally's doxastic attitudes. Therefore, Leo has not wronged Ally either by causing Ally to have this belief or by omitting to correct this belief. Yet Leo lacks Ally's valid consent.
>
> (2021a, p. 11)

For consent to be invalid, Dougherty's view requires not just (as quoted before) that 'the consent-giver believes or has a credence that they would suffer a penalty for refusing consent, this penalty is illegitimate [from an objective perspective], and this belief or credence causes them to consent' (p. 1) but also (as Dougherty claims in an earlier paper) that the consent-receiver's conduct not be an 'extension' of the consent-giver's agency (p. 11). An extension of the consent-giver's agency means that 'if [the consent-giver] were directly able to control [consent-receiver's] behavior with their own [*correctly informed*] choices, then [the consent-giver] would choose that [consent-receiver act on the consent]' (p. 11). Thus, even on Dougherty's view, the validity of consent ultimately still depends on something connected to the consent-receiver, that is, whether the consent-receiver's conduct is an extension of the consent-giver's agency. In *False Fear*, Ally believes that she would suffer a penalty, that the penalty is illegitimate, that this belief causes her to consent, and that Leo's use of the breadmaker would not be an extension of Ally's agency. Thus, Ally's consent is invalid.

I agree with Dougherty that consent (like Ally's) can be invalid even if the consent-receiver did not cause consent-giver's fear or issue any threat at all. I also agree that the validity of consent ultimately depends on something related to the consent-receiver's conduct. Yet, I disagree with

Dougherty that the significance of the consent-receiver's conduct can be explained in terms of an 'extension of the consenter's agency', but this disagreement lies beyond the scope of the current chapter. The disagreement does not concern the question, central to this chapter, how the consent-receiver's illegitimate threat causes and invalidates consent, where the consent-receiver's illegitimate threat is already taken as granted. Rather, it concerns the different question as to how, if at all, the consent-receiver needs to be involved in wronging the consent-receiver for consent to be invalid. This latter question will be my main focus in Chapter 6, and I will therefore return to Dougherty's view in this part of the book. At this point, I only wish to highlight where my and Dougherty's views coincide and where they diverge.

4.3 Conclusion

When does a coercive threat invalidate consent? In this chapter, I firstly discussed Appelbaum et al.'s counterfactual view, according to which a coercive threat invalidates consent when it *causes* consent, where causation is understood to require *counterfactual dependence*. Drawing on the more general literature on causation and counterfactuals, I argued that counterfactual views, simple or more sophisticated, yield wrong results in a range of cases and the question at hand requires focusing on more than just causation.

I then proposed my own view, that is, the *Bad-Reasons-View*, according to which a coercive threat invalidates consent when it makes a person to consent for a *bad* reason. I explained that a reason is bad either if (a) it is the reason linked to the coercer's threat, that is, consenting to avoid the threatened harm, or (b) it is a reason that corresponds to a perceived threat which, if it were the actual threat, would qualify as a consent-invalidating influence.

The *Bad-Reasons-View* stands out as a distinctive account by focusing on a person's motivating reasons for consenting, rather than mere causation and counterfactuals, as well as by allowing threats to invalidate consent even if there was a deviant causal chain and the person consents for a reason other than the one linked to the coercer's threat. I supported the *Bad-Reasons-View* on the grounds that it yields, better than any other view, the correct results in a wide variety of cases, and that it aligns with what I called the Janus face of consent. For this reason, the *Bad-Reasons-View* contributes to an adequate understanding of the voluntariness of consent, of the protection of a person's autonomy, and of the value of consent more generally.

Throughout my arguments, I discussed coercive threats only, that is, the paradigmatic consent-invalidating influence. Doing so allowed me to restrict my focus to the question of *how* an influence causes and invalidates consent, and I postpone to the next chapter the different question as to *which* influences invalidate consent. However, the view I developed in this chapter can, in principle, apply to all types of influences. It can apply to offers where the 'reasons' for consenting are no longer to avoid harm but to attain some good. Thus, *if* offers were to invalidate consent (which remains to be seen), my view would hold that a certain consent-invalidating type of offer causes and invalidates consent when it induces in the consenter a 'bad' reason too, where a 'bad' reason is either the one liked to the actual offer or the one liked to another perceived offer, when this perceived offer also qualifies as consent-invalidating.

Moreover, my view can also apply to cases where an influence no longer provides a person with *any reason* for consenting at all, but rather changes the motivation in some other way. For instance, in cases of nudging, a person's psychological mechanisms are targeted in a way that makes certain behaviour more likely, but do not give a person a *reason* to act in a particular way. In these cases, my account would hold that an influence causes and (other conditions being met) invalidates consent when it either triggers the 'psychological mechanism' linked to the influence under consideration or triggers another mechanism that corresponds to a perceived influence which, if it were the actual influence, would qualify as a consent-invalidating influence. Let me call such mechanisms broadly 'motivations' for consenting and contrast them with 'reasons', which I understand to be a subset of motivations. Accordingly, in such cases of manipulation, my view would be more appropriately called the *Bad-Motivations-View* rather than, as in cases of threats or offers, the *Bad-Reasons-View*.

These views taken together – the *Bad-Reasons-View* and the more general *Bad-Motivations-View* – constitute a key component of my proposal, ICCJ. These views provide ICCJ's answer to the question as to how influences such as coercion or manipulation cause and thereby invalidate consent. These views provide the correct elaboration of the first distinctive view of ICCJ, outlined in Chapter 3, that is, the view that an influence causes and thereby invalidates consent (if it does) when it induces a certain type of motivation (e.g. a bad reason or motivation) and regardless of whether it does so directly or through deviant causal chains. But note again that this account only explains the type of causation relevant to consent and still stays neutral on the separate question as to *which* types of influence invalidate consent. Addressing this further question will be my task in the next chapter.

Notes

1 See also Nelson et al. (2011), who follow Appelbaum et al.'s view in this respect.

2 Cases like *Preemption* have been discussed in Lewis (1973), Coady (2004), Collins (2004), and Hall (2004). In such cases, it is always about two causes, c1 and c2, which could cause an event e on their own. But as it stands, c1 causes e and thereby prevents c2 from causing e.

3 *Anonymous Blackmail* is similar to those cases in the metaphysical literature that question whether causation is transitive. See Lewis (2004), Hall (2004), Paul (2004), Maslen (2004), and Hitchcock (2007).

4 If the transitivity of causation is correct, then the following claim is true: if A causes B, and B causes C, then A causes C. Applied to the cases at hand: Wayne's blackmailing letter causes Berta's online search, which in turn causes Berta's consent. Transitivity has been challenged in various ways, but at least a somewhat restricted version of transitivity remains common ground in the literature on causation. See Lewis (2004), Hall (2004), Paul (2004), Maslen (2004), and Hitchcock (2007).

5 To clarify: I am using capitalised and non-capitalised letters (e.g. c and C, e and E) interchangeably to align with Lewis' own usage in the respective quotations. There is no difference between the capitalised C and the non-capitalised c.

6 Schaffer presented an analogous critique of Lewis' account and also claimed that causation does not require co-variation. However, Schaffer's critique focused on physical causation and he concluded that causation required a physical link, that is, what he calls *effluence*. See Schaffer (2001). Cases like *Controlled Letter* also resemble Harry Frankfurt's example of the counterfactual intervener in the context of moral responsibility and alternate possibilities. See Frankfurt (1969).

7 As outlined in note 4, the transitivity of causation is sometimes called into question. Yet, it is universally accepted that causation is at least sometimes transitive, and *Anonymous Blackmail* seems to be a good example of a situation where it is.

8 Note that I use the term 'bad' in a more technical and restricted sense than ordinary language.

9 These cases of deviant causal chains are often called non-basic and are contrasted with basic deviant causal chains. They are called non-basic because a person still acts intentionally under some description. In cases of basic deviance, a person fails to act intentionally under any description, as illustrated by Davidson's famous case of the climber: 'A climber might want to rid himself of the weight and danger of holding another man on a rope, and he might know that by loosening his hold on the rope he could rid himself of the weight and danger. This belief and want might so unnerve him as to cause him to loosen his hold, and yet it might be the case that he never chose to loosen his hold, nor did he do it intentionally' (2001, p. 79). For further discussion of different cases of deviant causal chains in the philosophy of action, see Keil (2007), Mayr (2011), and Stout (2010). It is worth emphasising that the interest in deviant causal chains in the philosophy of action and my interest here are very different. Whereas the philosophy of action exclusively focuses on the person initiating the deviant causal chain and whether he can be seen as acting intentionally, my sole concern is whether the person affected by a deviant causal chain still consents validly.

10 I here allude to the possibility that people may sometimes be justified in holding a false belief, for example, when, from their perspective, adopting the belief is best supported by the evidence.

11 At this point, however, the extent of my disagreement with Dougherty is unclear. This is because, recently, Dougherty cast doubt on some counterfactuals in the context of questions about the *scope* of consent, that is,

questions about the range of things that a token of consent permits (2021b, p. 46), but without explaining the role that counterfactuals still play in his view about the *validity* of consent, that is, questions about the morally transformative effect of consent more generally.

References

Appelbaum, P. S., Lidz, C. W., & Klitzman, R. (2009). Voluntariness of consent to research: A conceptual model. *Hastings Center Report, 39*(1), 30–39.

Archard, D. (2018). Sexual consent. In P. Schaber & A. Müller (Eds.), *The Routledge handbook of the ethics of consent* (pp. 174–184). Abingdon, Oxon; New York, NY: Routledge.

Bohlander, M. (2010). Transferred malice and transferred defenses: A critique of the traditional doctrine and arguments for a change in paradigm. *New Criminal Law Review: An International and Interdisciplinary Journal, 13*(3), 555–624. doi:10.1525/nclr.2010.13.3.555.

Coady, D. (2004). Preempting preemption. In J. D. Collins & E. J. Hall (Eds.), *In causation and counterfactuals* (pp. 325–339). Cambridge, MA: MIT Press.

Collins, J. D. (2004). Preempting prevention. In J. D. Collins & E. J. Hall (Eds.), *Causation and counterfactuals* (pp. 107–117). Cambridge, MA: MIT Press.

Davidson, D. (2001). *Essays on actions and events.* Oxford: Oxford University Press.

Dougherty, T. (2013). Sex, lies, and consent. *Ethics, 123*(4), 717–744.

Dougherty, T. (2019). Why does duress undermine consent? Noûs *55*(2), 317–333. doi:10.1111/nous.12313.

Dougherty, T. (2021a). Coerced consent with an unknown future. *Philosophy and Phenomenological Research, 103*(2), 441–461.

Dougherty, T. (2021b). *The scope of consent.* Oxford: Oxford University Press.

Frankfurt, H. G. (1969). Alternate possibilities and moral responsibility. *Journal of Philosophy, 66*(23), 829–839. doi:10.2307/2023833.

Hall, N. (2004). Two concepts of causation. In J. D. Collins & E. J. Hall (Eds.), *Causation and counterfactuals* (pp. 225–276). Cambridge, MA: MIT Press.

Herring, J. (2002). Does yes mean yes: The criminal law and mistaken consent to sexual activity. *Singapore Law Review, 22*, 182–201.

Herring, J. (2005). Mistaken sex. *Criminal Law Review*, 511–524.

Hitchcock, C. (2007). Prevention, preemption, and the principle of sufficient reason. *Philosophical Review, 116*(4), 495–532.

Horder, J. (1999). Consent, threats and deception in criminal law. *King's Law Journal, 10*(1), 104–108.

Horder, J. (2012). *Homicide and the politics of law reform.* Oxford: Oxford University Press.

Keil, G. (2007). What do deviant causal chains deviate from? In C. L. S. Nannini (Ed.), *Intentionality, deliberation and autonomy: The action-theoretic basis of practical philosophy* (pp. 69–90). Aldershot, England; Burlington, VT: Ashgate.

Lazenby, H., & Gabriel, I. (2018). Permissible secrets. *Philosophical Quarterly, 68*(271), 265–285.

Lewis, D. (1973). Causation. *Journal of Philosophy, 70*(17), 556–567.

Lewis, D. (2004). Causation as influence. In J. D. Collins & E. J. Hall (Eds.), *Causation and counterfactuals* (pp. 75–106). Cambridge, MA: MIT Press.
Maslen, C. (2004). Causes, contrasts, and the nontransitivity of causation. In J. D. Collins & E. J. Hall (Eds.), *Causation and counterfactuals* (pp. 341–357). Cambridge, MA: MIT Press.
Mayr, E. (2011). *Understanding human agency*. Oxford: Oxford University Press.
Nelson, R. M., Beauchamp, T., Miller, V. A., Reynolds, W., Ittenbach, R. F., & Luce, M. F. (2011). The concept of voluntary consent. *American Journal of Bioethics, 11*(8), 6–16.
Paul, L. A. (2004). Aspect causation. In J. D. Collins & E. J. Hall (Eds.), *Causation and counterfactuals* (pp. 205–224). Cambridge, MA: MIT Press.
Schaffer, J. (2001). Causation, influence, and effluence. *Analysis, 61*(1), 11–19.
Stout, R. (2010). Deviant causal chains. In C. S. T. O'Connor (Ed.), *A companion to the philosophy of action* (pp. 159–165). Malden, MA: Wiley-Blackwell.
Tadros, V. (2016). *Wrongs and crimes*. Oxford: Oxford University Press.
Turri, J. (2010). On the relationship between propositional and doxastic justification. *Philosophy and Phenomenological Research, 80*(2), 312–326.
Williams, R. A. (2007). Deception, mistake and vitiation of the victim's consent. *Law Quarterly Review, 124*, 132.

5 Voluntariness and Morality

Introduction

A central question in twentieth-century philosophy of action was whether the *voluntariness* of A's action could depend on the *morality* of B's influence on it. For instance, when Berta influences Alfred's decision as to how to act (and also appropriately causes the action), does it make any difference to the voluntariness of Alfred's subsequent action if Berta's influence on him was in some sense morally impermissible? Robert Nozick thought so and claimed that only *rights-exceeding* influences could negate voluntariness (Nozick, 1974), whereas Joel Feinberg rejected any such view and held that the legitimacy of an influence lacks any bearing on whether it negates voluntariness (Feinberg, 1986). Rather, what matters is how strongly, psychologically speaking, an influence impacts a person's decision-making.

It is intriguing to see that these exact views about voluntary *action* resurface in the debate concerning voluntary *consent*. Appelbaum et al. adopt Nozick's approach and claim that consent is involuntary if and only if it was elicited by an influence and 'the person exerting the influence d[id] not have the *right* to act in this way' (2009, p. 33). On the other hand, Nelson et al. adopt Feinberg's view and argue that 'whether an external influence is morally legitimate is conceptually and morally distinct from whether the action taken in response to that influence is voluntary or involuntary' (2011, p. 13). In Nelson et al.'s view, voluntariness is a value-neutral notion and influences negate voluntariness if and only if they reach a certain strength in terms of their psychological impact. Strong influences negate voluntary consent; weak influences do not.

In this chapter, I will claim that both views are false. I disagree with Nelson et al. on the grounds that the strength of an influence cannot determine whether it negates voluntariness and thereby invalidates consent. Rather, we have to take into account the moral legitimacy of an influence, and this will lead to a moralised rather than value-neutral account of voluntariness. But I also disagree with Appelbaum et al. on the grounds that the Nozickian focus on whether the influencing person *exceeds his rights* fails to capture the moral aspect relevant to

DOI: 10.4324/9781003301417-7

voluntariness. Instead, I explain and thereby support what I have identified as the second distinctive view of my proposal, ICCJ, mentioned at the beginning of Chapter 3, that is, the view that only 'interpersonally unjustifiable' influences invalidate consent. Thus, it is the notion of interpersonal justification that allows us to distinguish those influences that invalidate consent from those that do not.

To support ICCJ in this respect, I will use a method inspired by Peter Strawson, who, in *Analysis and Metaphysics*, distinguishes between *reductive* and *connective* conceptual analysis. Reductive conceptual analysis explains a concept by breaking it down into simpler parts, revealing its various fundamental components. Connective conceptual analysis, on the other hand, explains a concept by highlighting the connections it has with other concepts, thereby allowing us to gain new insights from understanding its conceptual relations (Strawson, 1992, ch. 2). It is this latter type, connective conceptual analysis, that I will use for my inquiry into the voluntariness of consent. I will analyse the connection between voluntary consent and the right to withdraw consent to disprove the psychological approach as presented by Nelson et al., and I will analyse the connection between consent and responsibility to argue for my preferred account of voluntariness, based on the notion of interpersonal justification as distinct from the view presented by Appelbaum et al.

5.1 Voluntariness and the Right to Withdraw Consent

The right to withdraw consent is key in medical ethics. It entitles people who have already consented to a medical procedure to withdraw such consent and thereby make it impermissible for the medical team to proceed any further. The medical team, for example, a physician or clinical investigator, will only ever receive a revocable permission but never an enforceable entitlement.

Explaining the right to withdraw consent further, the *WMA Medical Ethics Manual* claims that a person must be free to withdraw consent 'without any sort of reprisal'.[1] The Universal Declaration on Bioethics and Human Rights adds that a person must be free to withdraw 'without any disadvantage'.[2] And the *CIOMS Guide* holds that a person must be free to withdraw consent 'without penalty or loss of benefits to which he or she would otherwise be entitled'.[3]

Accordingly, the right to withdraw consent is violated if a person upholds his consent because he would otherwise face a penalty or reprisal for withdrawing it. By way of illustration, suppose Peter enrols in a clinical trial, but when he considers withdrawing, the investigators threaten him. They insist that he remain enrolled otherwise he will lose his medical care. The threat works and Peter stays enrolled. In this case, Peter's right to withdraw consent is violated.

But the violation of Peter's right to withdraw consent does not require that he also be very strongly affected by the threat of his investigators.

Although most people may be likely to be heavily influenced by threats of losing their medical care, we could suppose that Peter is different. Suppose Peter has various reasons for and against staying enrolled, and the investigators' threat is only one among many. As a result, the threat influences Peter only slightly. Yet, in the end, it tips the balance and makes Peter uphold his consent.

Even in this version of the case, Peter's right to withdraw consent is violated because he still decides to uphold consent in order to avoid the penalty he would otherwise face. The fact that the psychological impact of the threat was low and only affected a small part of his motivation is irrelevant. As the aforementioned guidance confirms, the right to withdraw consent requires freedom from '*any* sort of reprisal'[4] and *any* loss of 'benefits to which he or she would otherwise be entitled'.[5] Thus, the extent to which an influence psychologically affects a person's decision-making does not determine whether it violates his right to withdraw consent. As long as there is a morally significant penalty which affects *some* part of a person's motivation to uphold consent, this is sufficient for a violation.

Therefore, in the context of the right to withdraw consent, there is no requirement like the one Nelson et al. demand for voluntariness. An influence does not need to reach a certain strength, psychologically speaking, to violate the right to withdraw consent. Weak influences can amount to a violation too, but once this is clear, we should also reject a similar requirement for voluntariness, as I shall argue now.

When the investigators violate Peter's right to withdraw consent, they also undermine Peter's self-determination more generally. Self-determination, as relevant in medical ethics, means that 'every human being of adult years and sound mind has a right to determine what shall be done with his own body' (*Schloendorff v New York Hospital* [1914], 126). The investigators violate Peter's self-determination because, properly understood, it includes not only the right to *authorise* a new medical procedure, that is, give initial consent, but also 'the right to *stop* a [medical] procedure', that is, withdraw consent (*Ciarlariello v Schacter* [1993], 121) (Grubb, Laing, McHale, & Kennedy, 2010, pp. 449–452).

What is more, when the investigators undermine Peter's self-determination, they also – more specifically – invalidate his consent to continued participation in the trial. This is because self-determination is the very reason why we care about consent in the first place: consent is morally significant precisely because it is a tool for people's self-determination. Thus, if a token of consent fails to promote a person's self-determination in the relevant sense, consent loses its value and becomes invalid.

But let me be even more specific here. Consent can be invalid for three different reasons, namely incompetence, lack of information, and involuntariness; the first two reasons do not apply to Peter. Despite the investigators' threat, Peter may still be fully competent in that he possesses all mental capacities required for medical decision-making. Moreover, despite the investigators' threat, Peter may also still know everything about the trial he remains enrolled in. Thus, if Peter's consent is invalid, it can only be because it is involuntary. After all, the investigators' threat exerted pressure on Peter's decision-making, that is, it exerted exactly the type of influence which the requirement of voluntariness is supposed to preclude. Hence, in Peter's case, the violation of his right to consent invalidates his consent *because it negates its voluntariness*.

On this basis, I can now draw together the threads of my argument against Nelson et al.'s view. Peter's consent is involuntary even though the investigators' threat had only a low impact on him, that is, even though it was, psychologically speaking, a weak influence. Thus, the involuntariness of Peter's consent is independent of how strongly the threat affected him psychologically. Therefore, voluntariness cannot be a value-free psychological notion in the way Nelson et al. suggest. Whether a person's consent is voluntary, I therefore suggest, crucially depends on the morality of the influence on that person, that is, whether the influence amounts to the kind of reprisal or penalty that the right to withdraw consent aims to preclude. Hence, once we understand the relation between the right to withdraw consent and the requirement of voluntariness, we must reject Nelson et al.'s view. Such a value-neutral psychological approach to voluntariness is inconsistent with the right to withdraw consent.

Thus, my argument against Nelson et al. is essentially an argument in three steps. First, the extent to which an influence psychologically affects a person's decision-making does not determine whether it violates this person's right to withdraw consent; even weak influences can violate this right. Second, an influence on a person's decision-making that violates the right to withdraw consent also negates the voluntariness of continued consent. Hence, third, the extent to which an influence psychologically affects a person's decision-making does not determine whether it negates the voluntariness of consent either. Weak influences can negate voluntariness too, and therefore, Nelson et al.'s view is mistaken.

Moreover, we can extend this conclusion about the voluntariness of *continued* consent, which I have been focusing on so far, to *initial* consent. If certain influences invalidate a person's consent to the continuation of a procedure (by violating the right to withdraw consent), such influences will also invalidate consent if exerted at the time before initial consent has been given. For instance, a physician's threat to remove medical care seems to invalidate consent, irrespective of whether it is intended to obtain initial consent to a procedure, or whether it aims to prevent the patient from withdrawing initial consent. In both scenarios, the threat invalidates consent because it illegitimately threatens to penalise the patient if he withholds consent. Hence, the exclusive focus on the strength or psychological impact of influences is misplaced more generally.

Unlike Nelson et al.'s stance, my proposal of ICCJ can account for this conclusion. The influence on Peter in my example may have remained weak from a psychological perspective, but it is still interpersonally unjustifiable to him. Interpersonal justification concerns the claims that one person, for example, the consent-giver, can make on another person, for example, the consent-receiver, and people like Peter certainly have a claim against influences that violate their right to withdraw consent. Violating this right is a fundamental breach of the norms of the patient–physician relationship, and therefore, according to ICCJ, this invalidates consent.

Hence, ICCJ aligns with this important conclusion of my argument against Nelson et al. However, this conclusion can only be the first step in my support of ICCJ in this chapter because I have not yet provided direct and explicit support for the idea of interpersonal justification. Doing so will be my objective in the next section, where I turn to my second argument using a Strawsonian connective conceptual analysis. I will argue that, once we understand the relation between consent and responsibility, we can identify the notion of interpersonal justification as a key consideration for voluntary consent.

5.2 Consent and Responsibility

The debates concerning consent and responsibility have their own separate lives. Yet, it is nevertheless intriguing to see that they overlap significantly: consent and responsibility are considered to have the same three conditions, which I will term competence, information, and voluntariness.[6]

To give morally valid consent, and to be morally responsible (which I will understand as being a fitting target of praise or blame), a person must be competent, namely, possess the mental capacity to understand their specific situation and reason appropriately about it. Insanity precludes competence and thereby not only renders consent invalid but also rules out responsibility (Beauchamp & Childress, 2013, p. 115; Sinnott-Armstrong & Levy, 2011; Wertheimer, 2003, p. 217).

In addition, to give morally valid consent, and to be morally responsible, a person must be aware of what he is doing, namely, that he is actually *consenting to X* or, for instance, that his action *harms others*. Certain types of ignorance preclude both valid consent and moral responsibility. With consent, this often develops into an explicit requirement for information, especially in the medical context of *informed* consent (Beauchamp & Childress, 2013, pp. 125–137), whereas in the context of responsibility, it is often called the *epistemic condition* of responsibility (Robichaud & Wieland, 2017).

Finally, morally valid consent and moral responsibility require voluntariness, by which I mean the absence of certain types of pressure, most notably coercion. Regarding consent, I have already explained how central voluntariness is. Regarding responsibility, voluntariness is important because people who act under coercion lack a fair opportunity to comply with moral or legal norms and are therefore not (or are less so) a fitting target of blame and punishment (Hart, 2008), for example, someone who committed perjury because they were threatened to be 'cut up' (*R v Hudson and Taylor* 1971 2 QB 202) (cf. Dressler, 2011).

This overlap of conditions has not received sustained attention in the literature. Yet, two accounts deserve attention. H. L. A. Hart claims that there is an 'analogy' (2008, p. 29) between consent and responsibility, at least in the legal realm, when consent means civil transactions and responsibility means criminal liability. When Hart points to an 'analogy', he means to say that the connections are no coincidence: they exist because the conditions of both consent and responsibility purport to respect individuals as 'choosing being(s)' (p. 49), namely, they purport to make the legal consequences of an individual's action depend on whether that individual had a fair opportunity to act or not, as they did. But the term 'analogy' is also meant to highlight that there is no 'identity'. The conditions are likely to apply differently to consent and responsibility because, as Hart explains, what invalidates consent is 'qualified or limited by other principles' (p. 34) than those that excuse criminal wrongdoing. Unfortunately, Hart remains vague about these qualifying principles and does not provide much further guidance.

Heidi Hurd presents a bolder view. Hurd adopts a *moral* perspective, in contrast to Hart's solely legal one. She claims a connection between the conditions of *morally* valid consent and the conditions of *moral* responsibility (1996, p. 140). And, most importantly, Hurd not only presents an 'analogy' between the conditions of consent and responsibility but boldly asserts 'identity':

> The conditions under which prima facie consent is defeated *are identical to* the conditions under which defendants are properly excused from moral blame, and, to the extent that the law mirrors morality, from legal liability.
>
> (p. 122, emphasis added)[7]

I shall argue that Hurd's identity-view is wrong and that something close to Hart's analogy-view is correct. Once this is established, we will then be able to draw a further important conclusion about voluntary consent, namely that the notion of interpersonal justification is key to the assessment of voluntariness. To make my case, I will first outline two key differences between consent and responsibility (thereby rejecting Hurd's identity-view and favouring something closer to Hart's analogy-view). I will then argue that the best explanation for these differences leads us to the notion of interpersonal justification which, as a result, will become key to assessing voluntary consent as well.

Difference 1: The Effect of Culpability

When a person fails to meet a condition of responsibility, she can still be responsible for her conduct, as long as the failure to meet that condition was her own fault. The paradigmatic example is drink-driving: if a person freely intoxicates herself and then drives a car, she cannot defend herself by pointing out that she lacked capacity while driving, where capacity or competence is a central condition of responsibility. If she culpably intoxicated herself, the temporary lack of capacity does not absolve her from responsibility.[8]

By contrast, a similar reasoning does not apply in the context of consent. Even if it is a person's own fault that she fails to satisfy a certain condition, failing that condition may still be sufficient for consent to be invalid. Consider the following case:

> **Drunk sex:** Jane drinks a lot at a conference and meets Bill at a bar. Bill clearly sees that Jane is heavily intoxicated. Yet, Bill still obtains Jane's consent to sex and acts on it.

Jane is no longer competent to consent: she lacks the capacity to make a reasoned decision about whether to have sex with Bill. Her consent is therefore insufficiently autonomous, invalid, and does not create a permission for Bill to have sex with her. If Bill *did* have sex with Jane, he would wrong her and exploit her temporary weakness. The fact that Jane intoxicated herself does not make a difference in this regard.

A similar contrast also arises for the requirement of voluntariness. In the context of responsibility, coercion only excuses if one did not culpably put oneself in a situation where one would be (foreseeably) subject to it. If one joins a criminal gang and is subsequently coerced into committing wrongs, one cannot (at least not normally) rely on such coercion to excuse one's wrongdoing. By contrast, the same is not true for consent. Entering into a relationship with someone one knows to be abusive, or joining the clinical trial of an investigator whom one knows to have abusive tendencies, does not preserve the validity of one's coerced consent to sex or medical procedures, even when the coercion was foreseeable and one which, in some way, one culpably exposed oneself to.

Thus, whether a person culpably or non-culpably failed to meet a certain condition is often relevant for responsibility but not for consent.

Difference 2: The Effects of Rising Stakes

The conditions of consent and responsibility react differently when the stakes increase. Consider the requirement of information. The higher the stakes in a decision to consent, the more information a person may need to know to be able to give valid consent. In medicine especially, the most intrusive medical procedures require that a person know a lot, mostly about essential risks, benefits, and alternatives, whereas minor procedures, like a blood draw, may not even have an explicit informed consent procedure at all. By contrast, in the context of responsibility, when the stakes increase (which normally means that one's action could be especially harmful to others), people are usually under more stringent demands to inform themselves, and *fewer* mistakes would excuse them. In a high-stakes situation, ignorance may more readily translate into insufficient regard for others than it would in a low-stakes situation, and it would thereby preclude an excuse. In other words, when stakes rise, the normative effect of consent (i.e. permission) becomes more fragile and more mistakes undermine it, whereas the reverse is true for the normative effect of responsibility (i.e. blameworthiness), as it becomes more robust and fewer mistakes undermine it.

This situation also holds for the requirement of voluntariness. Suppose that I am threatened to be beaten unless I trample my neighbour's flowers. Such a threat might excuse (or even justify) my trampling the flowers. But if the same threat aims to make me kill my neighbour, and I subsequently do kill my neighbour, then the threat may no longer excuse my action, let alone justify it. In such a case, I would be morally expected to show greater fortitude. Hence, in the context of responsibility, rising stakes require greater fortitude, and fewer instances of pressure will excuse wrongdoing.

The reverse is true for consent: when stakes increase, some pressure may invalidate consent, even if the same token of pressure would not invalidate consent in a situation with lower stakes. By way of illustration, suppose a patient must decide between two treatment options, for example, major surgery and aggressive drug treatment. In this context, the physician is under an increased obligation to assist, or at least not to sabotage, the patient's decision-making. If the physician *does* sabotage the patient's decision-making, for example, by body-shaming him in order to obtain consent to the surgery, the physician seriously wrongs the patient. More precisely, the wrong caused by such body-shaming is also more serious in a high-stakes situation than it would have been in a low-stakes situation, for example, when the physician uses this tactic to make the patient consent to a new diet. This is because, in a high-stakes situation, manipulative conduct displays even greater disrespect for the patient's autonomy and well-being. However, when it becomes more seriously wrong to exert pressure, it is also more likely that such pressure will invalidate consent (Dougherty, 2019; Kiener, 2021; Millum, 2014; Wertheimer, 2012).

Thus, rising stakes have different effects on consent and responsibility. They tend to make the requirements of consent *more* demanding so that a person needs to satisfy *higher* standards to give valid consent, whereas the reverse is true for responsibility. Often, higher stakes make the requirement of responsibility *less* demanding so that a person needs to satisfy *lower* standards to be morally responsible.

So, how can it be that consent and responsibility share the very same three conditions, when these conditions also apply in significantly different ways?

Explaining the Conditions of Consent and Responsibility in Terms of Interpersonal Justification

Concerning the first difference, I argue that culpability plays a role in responsibility because, as members of a moral community, we can expect each other not to create circumstances that make it more likely that we wrong or harm others. Therefore, people have to bear the risk of blame and punishment when they intoxicate themselves, culpably fail to inform themselves, or put themselves in a position where others will foreseeably coerce them into wrongdoing. In so acting, a person shows insufficient regard for, or commitment to, the interests of others and thereby rules out an excuse for their behaviour.

By contrast, the same reasoning does not apply to consent. Even if a person intoxicates herself (*Drunk Sex*) or puts herself in a position where others will coerce her (the example of an abusive partner or investigator), another person cannot normally obtain valid consent from this person on the grounds that the consenter herself brought about her situation. This is because, in the role of a consent-receiver, people are obliged, at a minimum, not to take advantage of the consent-giver's weakness. I take this to be a norm fundamental to the consenter–consentee relationship. Although the norms of this relationship may vary across contexts, for example, the medical and sexual contexts, they shape what people owe each other and thereby also affect the conditions of valid consent.

Thus, to understand the differences between consent and responsibility with regard to the role of culpability in failing to meet a condition, we need to attend closely to the relevant relationships: in the context of responsibility, it is the relationship between members of a moral or legal community and what people can expect from each other *qua* such members; in the context of consent, it is the relationship between consenter and consentee and what people can expect from each other *qua* consenting parties.

The same rationale can help explain the difference concerning the effect of increasing stakes. When stakes increase in the context of responsibility, members of a moral or legal community can demand from each other that they do not fail too easily to abide by the norms of that community. In this way, the values of the moral or legal community will be sufficiently protected. Duff and Fletcher highlight this aspect clearly in the legal context. When Fletcher discusses duress, he claims that the relevant consideration is 'what we can fairly expect of each other in a civilized society' (1998, p. 83), where the term 'civilised society' purports to highlight the norms of this specific legal community. When Duff discusses duress, he claims that the relevant consideration is what 'kind and degree of courage we can properly demand of citizens' (2002, p. 64) when crucial values and interests are at stake, thereby also stressing the community of citizens as the decisive factor in determining whether an excuse is available.

A similar rationale explains why increased stakes affect consent differently, namely, why they may make requirements more demanding so that even *lower* pressure could invalidate consent. Consider the medical context again: for reasons previously outlined, when a patient has to make a very important decision, the physician's obligation not to sabotage the decision-making becomes more stringent. This obligation is a central norm in the patient–physician relationship and is especially important in the context of obtaining consent. So, the ultimate explanation of why the consent requirements change in the way they do when stakes increase has, once again, to do with the norms of the relationship between the consenter (patient) and consentee (physician). If the physician violates these norms in the process of obtaining consent, she disqualifies herself as someone receiving the patient's permission to proceed and therefore cannot obtain valid consent.

Thus, the two differences between consent and responsibility, that is, concerning the culpable failure to meet conditions and the effects of increasing stakes, can be explained in the same way. In both cases, interpersonal norms of what people can demand from each other (either as consenting parties or, more generally, as members of a moral or legal community) explain why the conditions of consent and responsibility diverge. But these interpersonal norms not only explain *di*-vergence, they can also acknowledge the *con*-vergence between consent and responsibility: responsibility and consent share the same three conditions because interpersonal norms, understood generally, are key to both areas. Thus, interpersonal norms allow us to account at once for the parallels and differences between consent and responsibility.

On this basis, I will now return to my proposal, ICCJ. Earlier, I explained ICCJ's focus on interpersonal justification in terms of what claims people can make on each other and what claims they can make on each other's conduct, where such claims are relative to relationships, such as the consenter–consentee relationship. Hence, the core idea behind ICCJ captures exactly what I have so far argued and explains both the parallels and differences between consent and responsibility. This conclusion confirms that the notion of interpersonal justification must be key to our understanding of the conditions of consent and, by extension, to understanding the condition of voluntariness as one central requirement of valid consent.

However, my inquiry cannot conclude here as it is necessary to determine whether my idea of interpersonal justification can withstand further scrutiny, especially in comparison with alternative proposals in the literature.

5.3 Varieties of Moralised Voluntariness

To say that interpersonal justification is key to assessing the voluntariness of consent leads to a moralised view of voluntariness because it implies that assessing voluntariness requires a genuine moral judgement. What is more, this view leads to a *distinct* moralised view because it focuses specifically on interpersonal justification, as opposed to other moral considerations, such as rights or illegitimate constraints more generally. In this section, I want to explain further what makes my proposed view on interpersonal justification distinctive. To do so, I will discuss other moralised views of voluntariness, expose their weaknesses, and show why my proposal is superior to them. I thereby aim to consolidate the support for ICCJ's second distinctive view, that is, that only interpersonally unjustifiable influences invalidate consent.

Wrongdoing versus Wronging

As mentioned earlier, Appelbaum et al. adopt Nozick's approach by arguing that an influence invalidates consent when 'the person exerting the influence does not have the *right* to act in this way' (2009, p. 33, emphasis added). This is also a moralised view of voluntariness because it holds that assessing the voluntariness of consent requires a genuine moral judgement, which in this case is a judgement about whether exerting an influence exceeds a right. Yet, Appelbaum et al.'s view cannot be correct because it neglects the distinction between wrongdoing and wronging. Consider the following example:

> **Professional Obligations:** Clinical investigator Charlotte is obliged to offer no financial compensation to the participants of her clinical trial. This is because doing so would interfere with the scientific validity of this specific research project and also obstruct equal distribution of participants among several research sites. Nevertheless, Charlotte offers Peter money for his participation, and Peter enrols for that reason.

By offering Peter money, Charlotte breaks a professional obligation and acts wrongly. However, if Peter enrols, Charlotte will not violate any of Peter's rights when subjecting him to medical procedures, no matter how morally or legally severe the breach of her obligation. (Let us assume for now that moderate financial compensation is not per se problematic.) Hence, Peter must have consented validly. Charlotte's illegitimate influence on Peter's decision-making, that is, the monetary offer, did not invalidate his consent. Why?

The reason is that Charlotte's influence did not *wrong Peter.* The wrongness of Charlotte's influence was exclusively due to a violation of a more general professional obligation. But if Peter was not wronged in how his consent was obtained, that is, if none of *Peter's rights* was violated, then such consent is not invalid either. Hence, a morally illegitimate influence invalidates consent only if it *wrongs* the consent-giver, as opposed to being a form of *wrongdoing* more generally.

Appelbaum et al.'s view cannot account for this conclusion because their focus on what the consent-receiver 'does not have the right' to do is blind to the distinction between wrongdoing and wronging. In cases of wrongdoing and wronging alike, 'the person exerting the influence does not have the right to act in this way' (Appelbaum et al., 2009, p. 33). By contrast, my focus on interpersonal justification, that is, agent-relative justification *to a person*, specifically accounts for this aspect of wronging, as both wronging and interpersonal justification are explicitly second-personal. In *Professional Obligation*, Charlotte may have acted wrongly, but she did not wrong Peter and can therefore interpersonally justify how she treated *him*.

Pressure-Related Wronging

Like my proposal, Owens also avoids the weakness in Appelbaum et al.'s view. Instead of focusing on the rights of the *consent-receiver*, and whether an influence *exceeds* them (as Appelbaum et al. do), Owens focuses on the rights of the *consent-giver* and whether an influence *violates* them. On this basis, Owens proposes the view that an influence invalidates consent '[when and] because it *wrongs* the [consenter]' (2007, p. 305, emphasis added), where wronging also means violating a right of the consenter. Owens's view has been very influential. For instance, Pallikkathayil specifies Owens's focus on 'wronging' in terms of impermissibly constraining the consenter's options. On Pallikkathayil's view, an influence invalidates consent when 'the [consenter] does not have access to the options she is entitled to' (2011, p. 17). Thus, Pallikkathayil says: 'Impermissibly constrained options make the exercise of normative discretionary powers [such as consent] impossible' (p. 18).

However, taken at face value, these views cannot be correct either, because one can wrong the consenter and impermissibly constrain the consenter's options without also invalidating consent. Consider the following case:

> **Discrimination:** Clinical investigator Daniel offers Peter free lunches for his participation in a clinical trial, and Peter subsequently consents to participation. But Daniel offered other participants both free lunches and additional financial compensation. Daniel offers Peter less because he is racist, and Peter is a person of colour.

Daniel treats Peter unjustly by giving him too little in comparison to what others receive and thereby seriously wrongs Peter: he violates Peter's right to equal respect and discriminates against him. Daniel also illegitimately constrains Peter's options by withholding the option of equal pay. Yet, Peter's consent can still be valid. Why?

The requirement of voluntariness protects against controlling influences. In other words, it protects against influences that wrong the consent-giver *due to* their controlling or pressure-creating nature. By contrast, it does *not* protect against interventions that wrong the consenter in other ways, for example, by discrimination, as in Peter's case. Such wrongs lie outside the specific scope of voluntariness and are covered by other principles and norms, for example, a principle of justice. And although such wrongs remain serious and must be accounted for, they do not concern the specific requirement of voluntariness. What is more, such wrongs do not affect other conditions of consent either, such as information and competence, that is, they do not make the consenter less informed or less competent. Therefore, they are not the type of wrong that could undermine the validity of consent.

Thus, 'wronging' and 'illegitimately constraining options' are still too broad to cover the specific wronging of the consenter that invalidates consent. To negate voluntariness and thereby invalidate consent, an influence needs to be wrongful specifically on the grounds of how it incentivises consent (or, respectively, disincentives the refusal of consent), rather than on the grounds of, say, how it discriminates against a person.

Hence, Owens's and Pallikkathayil's focus on 'wronging' and 'impermissible constraints of options' is still too general to identify which influences negate voluntary consent (and thereby invalidate consent). By contrast, my own proposal, ICCJ, fares better. First, ICCJ is based on the principles of autonomy and beneficence, but does not include a principle of justice. Therefore, if the wrong to the consent-giver is primarily due to a violation of justice, as is the case with discrimination, ICCJ's principles are not triggered and consent can remain valid. To exclude justice-related wrongs, I suggest the following rationale: justice-related wrongs concern the unequal treatment of different people and, therefore, any wrong – the explanation of which requires a comparison of how *different* people are treated, as opposed to an explanation of how *only the consent-giver* is treated – is a justice-related wrong and will therefore not invalidate consent.

In addition, however, ICCJ also contains another, more general component designed to narrow the focus on the relevant wrongs. Recall that, according to ICCJ, consent is voluntary unless motivated *by an influence* that cannot be interpersonally justified. So understood, interpersonal justification takes an 'influence' as its object. And, as I explained in Chapter 2, an influence is any intervention that incentivises the giving of consent or disincentivises the refusal of consent. Accordingly, to invalidate consent, an influence needs to be interpersonally unjustifiable *qua* influence, that is, it needs to be interpersonally justifiable on the grounds of how it incentivises the giving of consent or disincentivises its refusal.

Since this is not the case in *Discrimination*, ICCJ does not highlight such wrongs as consent-invalidating either, however severe they are in other respects.

Threats, Offers, and the Morality of Proposals

At this point, however, there may still be an alternative to my proposal, namely the view that the ultimate reason why consent is valid in all my examples so far is that these examples featured offers but not threats, and only threats invalidate consent. In fact, this is Alan Wertheimer's view. Wertheimer says that A's influence on B invalidates B's consent 'only if it is immoral *in a special way*, namely, that A proposes [i.e. threatens] to violate B's rights (or fails to fulfill an obligation to B) should B reject A's proposal' (2003, pp. 169–170, original emphasis). So understood, Wertheimer's view can deliver the correct verdict in all my examples. Yet, his view is mistaken for other reasons.

To begin with, Wertheimer's focus on 'proposing to violate the consenter's right' is inadequate because one can invalidate consent by threatening to violate not the consenter's rights but the rights of other people. Suppose a physician makes a threat to a patient that she will kill another person, or kill herself, unless the patient consents to participate in a trial. Threats of this type, sometimes termed 'moral coercion' (Bazargan-Forward, 2014), can invalidate consent too. But on Wertheimer's view, which focuses on whether 'A proposes to violate B's rights', this seems to be precluded.[9]

Second, Wertheimer's view fails to capture blackmailing as a consent-invalidating influence. In cases of blackmail, the blackmailer threatens to do what he has a right to do, maybe even a duty. In such cases, the moral wrongness does not lie in the threatened act but rather in its combination with what is asked in return for not doing it. Here is one of Wertheimer's own examples of blackmailing:

> **IRS.** A has information that B has significantly underreported her income to the IRS. He tells B that he will report her to the IRS unless she agrees to sexual relations.
>
> (2003, p. 182)

As Wertheimer says: 'It is not wrong for A to carry out his declared unilateral plan. Indeed, it might be his obligation to do so' (p. 182). So, A's proposed act would not violate B's rights and therefore, on Wertheimer's view, A's blackmailing proposal does not invalidate consent. Wertheimer says: 'We might want to regard A's behavior as criminal without regarding it as a sexual offense against B' (p. 182).

However, blackmailing can invalidate consent, and it certainly does in a medical context. Suppose a physician blackmails a patient to report the patient's crimes to the police unless he participates in his clinical trial. Reporting crime is what the physician has a right to do, or even a duty. Yet, it is still blackmailing as it exerts seriously illegitimate pressure and thereby invalidates consent, despite Wertheimer's account to the contrary.[10]

But Wertheimer himself was not firm in his rejection of blackmailing as a consent-invalidating influence. Consider the following example that Wertheimer also discusses:

> **Detention Home**: A, who has agreed to take B (nineteen years old) into his home, threatens to return her to the detention home unless she has sexual relations with him.
>
> (2003, p. 180)

For the sake of argument, Wertheimer assumes that 'A is under no obligation to keep B in his home' (p. 181). Thus, A's threat does *not* propose to violate B's rights as B does not have a right to stay, and therefore this is another case of blackmail. Yet, Wertheimer says that his view is 'likely to regard [B's] consent [to sex] as invalid' (p. 181) and further explains:

> Why might this be so? Because there are some contexts in which it is unacceptable for people to use their capacity to help another person in order to obtain sexual favors and some where it is acceptable (or less unacceptable), and that this is to be explained, at least in part, in terms of the social consequences of regarding such arrangements as morally or legally permissible.
>
> (p. 181)

I share Wertheimer's view: B's consent is invalid. But I cannot see how Wertheimer's account can deliver this result. After all, A did not propose to violate B's rights, which – for Wertheimer – is the only way for a threat to invalidate consent. Thus, Wertheimer's explanation of B's invalid consent seems ad hoc and at odds with the formulation of his view.

To account for cases of blackmail, we need to adopt a distinction that Wertheimer himself drew in his earlier work, namely between the *morality of proposals* and the *morality of actions*. The morality of proposals concerns the question of whether it is legitimate to exert a certain influence, such as issuing a blackmailing threat, whereas the morality of actions solely concerns the morality of the threatened act itself, taken separately (Wertheimer, 1987, p. 102). In cases of blackmail, these aspects come apart: the proposal is illegitimate, but the threatened act is legitimate, if considered separately. Thus, an adequate account needs to be sensitive to both the morality of proposals and the morality of actions, not just the latter. Wertheimer's view only accounts for the morality of actions.

Furthermore, there is another reason why Wertheimer's focus on 'proposing to violate rights' and the morality of actions is inadequate. This is because it cannot apply to manipulation because manipulation does not work by proposing to violate rights, unless a person complies with a demand. Rather, it directly sabotages a person's decision-making and, if severe enough, also potentially undermines consent. Thus, without focusing on the morality of proposals as well (as opposed to on actions alone, as Wertheimer does), an account of consent would have a blind spot with regard to manipulation.

But let me now come back to Wertheimer's more fundamental claim that only threats but not offers invalidate consent. I believe Wertheimer to be wrong here too. A closer look at blackmailing cases can show that at least some offers can invalidate medical consent after all. Consider the following variation of a blackmailing case:

> **Last-Minute Rescue:** The police started investigating Peter on alleged drug crimes. Roger, who had no prior contact with the police on this matter, offers to hide important evidence against Peter if Peter participates in his trial.

Roger proposes not to prevent the occurrence of harm to Peter that is already underway, unless Peter consents to participate in his clinical trial. On widespread definitions, Roger thereby makes a genuine offer: he proposes to make an option available which Peter would not otherwise have and is not entitled to have (i.e. not being prosecuted). On the canonical understanding of threats, Roger does not threaten Peter because he refrains from proposing to *make* Peter worse off if he declines. Roger would simply do nothing in that case. And doing nothing is what Roger has a right to do (and probably even a duty) (Kiener, 2019, 2020).

Yet, Roger's conduct attracts the kind of criticism that is normally directed at blackmailing. It has been argued that blackmail invalidates consent on the grounds that a person's 'power of considering whether he ought to do it or not [e.g. trial participation], whether it is prudent to do it or not, is altogether taken away from [him]' (*Williams v Bayley* [1866], 219) and because '(a) the defendant [e.g. the blackmailed person] has no reasonable grounds for making the demand and (b) the threat would not be considered by reasonable and honest people to be a proper means of reinforcing the demand' (*Al Nehayan v Kent* [2018], 188).

These arguments, which reflect not only the law but also moral debates, apply to *Last-Minute Rescue* too. Roger exerts control over Peter's decision-making which he is not entitled to have. Moreover, the harm that would await Peter when he declines participation is very severe, and Roger's unwarranted demand is clearly illegitimate. As a result, the 'power of considering whether he ought to do it or not [e.g. trial participation], whether it is prudent to do it or not, is [still] altogether taken away from [Peter]' (*Williams v Bayley* [1866], 219), and there are 'no reasonable grounds for making the demand' (*Al Nehayan v Kent* [2018], 188). For these reasons, we should consider Peter's consent involuntary and invalid, despite the fact that it may qualify as an offer rather than a threat on the widespread understanding of these terms.

So, to come full circle: although Wertheimer presents an elaborated and helpful proposal, his view still fails in important respects, for example, in its lack of sensitivity to moral coercion, blackmailing, the morality of actions, and the morality of proposals, and it does not allow for influences to invalidate consent when they qualify as offers rather than as threats. By contrast, my proposal, ICCJ, based on the notion of interpersonal justification, fares better. It covers cases of moral coercion and blackmail: neither can be justified *to* the person consenting. Moreover, interpersonal justification is sensitive to the morality of actions as well as to the morality of proposals. Threatening an illegitimate action (morality of actions) and impermissibly interfering with a person's decision-making (morality of proposals) can be equally interpersonally unjustifiable. And finally, interpersonal justification does not preclude influences that blur the lines between threats and offers, as in *Last-Minute Rescue*. Using a patient's liability to criminal prosecution as leverage to obtain consent severely conflicts with the norms of the patient–physician relationship and therefore invalidates consent. Thus, ICCJ's focus on interpersonal justification promises to build on the strength of Wertheimer's account without suffering from its shortcomings.

Voluntariness and the Lack of a Reasonable Choice

Finally, I will consider an alternative view to Wertheimer's which also focuses on threats, namely that of Sarah Conly. Conly argues that an influence invalidates consent when it makes it the case that 'the options from which ... [the consenter] had to choose were illegitimately narrow' (2004, p. 104) *and* 'the [consenter] has no reasonable choice between doing what the coercer wants and the bad option which the coercer has introduced' (p. 106). Thus, Conly focuses on threats, adopts a requirement of an illegitimate constraint of options (similar to Pallikkathayil's view), and adds the condition that not complying with a threat must be *unreasonable*.

Conly delivers the correct results in my cases of *Professional Obligation* and *Discrimination*, as none of these cases features a threat that leaves the consenter without a reasonable choice. Moreover, Conly's view could also avoid the core flaws in Wertheimer's account and be sensitive to cases of moral coercion and blackmail. Nevertheless, the distinctive feature in Conly's view, namely the requirement of a lack of a reasonable choice, is mistaken.

Suppose Peter is threatened with deprivation of his medical care unless he consents to participate in a risky clinical trial. Let us assume that both options, that is, the loss of medical care and participation in the trial, would be severely harmful for Peter. In fact, they are almost equal in their harmfulness, and so this makes Peter's choice extremely difficult.

However, from a prudential perspective, their near-identical levels of harmfulness make it equally reasonable to choose either of them. It just so happens that Peter slightly prefers keeping his medical care. Hence, in this case, Peter could have *reasonably* failed to comply with the threat. Yet, when he complies, his consent is still invalid and, therefore, Conly's view is mistaken.

To explain where the mistake in Conly's view happens, let me introduce some of Feinberg's metrics in analysing coercive threats. Feinberg introduced the notion of *(differential) coercive pressure* and explained it as follows: 'The greater the difference between the "cost" of the threat and the "cost" of the demand, the greater the coercive pressure' (1986, p. 202). When coercive pressure is great, that is, when the threatened harm is *much* worse than compliance, a person does, in fact, lack any reasonable choice. If threatened with 'Your money or your life', anything but giving away one's wallet is unreasonable. So, Conly's view describes such cases very well.

However, sometimes the distance between the threatened harm and compliance is limited, as in my example of Peter. In such cases, Feinberg would say, the differential coercive pressure is very small. Yet, further increased is what Feinberg calls the *coercive burden*: 'The total coercive burden ... is determined by *adding* the cost of the demand ... to the cost of the threat' (1986, p. 205, emphasis added). So understood, Peter is still under great coercion, given the two highly undesirable options he is forced to choose between. The fact that any decision would be reasonable does not change this. So, it is this metric of coercive burden that Conly's account fails to account for.

Thus, whether non-compliance remains reasonable or rational for a person does not determine whether an influence is coercive and thereby invalidates consent. Therefore, an adequate theory of consent needs to keep apart the reasonableness of a person's decision and the validity of their consent. To do so, an account has to be sensitive not only to 'coercive pressure' but also to 'coercive burdens'.

My proposal, ICCJ, accounts for this conclusion. Influences are interpersonally unjustifiable even when the differential coercive pressure is low. Imposing a high coercive burden is sufficient to undermine interpersonal justification. Thus, according to ICCJ, consent can be invalidated even if a person could reasonably refuse to comply with a threat.

Thus, the focus of interpersonal justification in assessing voluntary consent proves superior to a number of alternative moralised views in the literature.

5.4 Conclusion

My main objective in this chapter was to support the second distinctive view of my proposal, ICCJ, that is, the view that the notion of interpersonal justification allows us to distinguish those influences that invalidate consent from those that do not. My support for ICCJ proceeded in three steps. First, I argued against Nelson et al.'s view, according to which the psychological impact of an influence determines whether that influence negates the voluntariness of consent. I concluded that even weak influences can invalidate consent, and I showed that ICCJ's focus on interpersonal justification can account for this important aspect. Second, I compared the conditions of consent and responsibility and argued that the notion of interpersonal justification is key to understanding them. On these grounds, I then claimed that interpersonal justification must also be key to the assessment of which influences negate the voluntariness of consent. Finally, I discussed various alternative moralised views of voluntariness. I argued that ICCJ's focus on interpersonal justification can build on these views' merits without sharing their flaws. On this basis, I now conclude my support for the second distinctive view of my proposal, ICCJ: only 'interpersonally unjustifiable' influences, as defined by ICCJ, negate the voluntariness of consent.

Notes

1 *WMA Medical Ethics Manual*, 2005, page 106.
2 Universal Declaration on Bioethics and Human Rights, 2005, article 6.
3 *CIOMS Guide*, 2002, guideline 9.
4 *WMA Medical Ethics Manual*, 2005, page 106, emphasis added.
5 *CIOMS Guide*, 2002, guideline 9.
6 The case of children is particularly interesting with regard to the requirements of consent and responsibility because, legally speaking, requirements for consent and responsibility often diverge for children. I discuss related challenges in Kiener (Forthcoming).
7 Mandava and Millum adopted this view too, although without referring to Hurd. 'When is a threat controlling, such that it would invalidate consent? We suggest that it reaches this point when we would no longer consider the threatened person morally responsible for her actions [in the sense of deserving praise or blame]' (2013, p. 42).
8 Some scholars explain responsibility in terms of 'tracing', where responsibility for an action at t2, for example, drink-driving, is 'traced back' to the responsibility for an earlier action at t1, for example, voluntary intoxication (Fischer & Ravizza, 1998, pp. 49–51; Fischer & Tognazzini, 2009). Other scholars avoid the notion of tracing and focus on negligence or recklessness (King, 2014; Vargas, 2005). Since both sides agree that the drunk driver is responsible, despite the temporary suspension of capacity, I can remain neutral on this debate.
9 At one point, Wertheimer considers a case where a mother is threatened with the death of her child unless she consents to sex. I concede that such a threat might be considered as a proposal to violate the mother's rights insofar as her parental authority includes a right to her child. Hence, Wertheimer's view can correctly explain this mother's consent as invalid (2003, p. 180). Yet, Wertheimer's view becomes unable to account for other cases where there is no such close relation between the consenter and the person who might be harmed. But in these cases too, consent is still invalid.
10 For further discussion of blackmailing, see Kiener (2019).

References

Appelbaum, P. S., Lidz, C. W., & Klitzman, R. (2009). Voluntariness of consent to research: A conceptual model. *Hastings Center Report, 39*(1), 30–39.

Bazargan-Forward, S. (2014). Moral coercion. *Philosophers' Imprint, 14*(11), 1–18.

Beauchamp, T. L., & Childress, J. F. (2013). *Principles of biomedical ethics*. New York: Oxford University Press.

Conly, S. (2004). Seduction, rape, and coercion. *Ethics, 115*(1), 96–121.

Dougherty, T. (2019). Why does duress undermine consent? *Noûs, 55*(2), 317–333. doi:10.1111/nous.12313.

Dressler, J. (2011). Duress. In J. Deigh & D. Dolinko (Eds.), *The Oxford handbook of philosophy of criminal law* (pp. 269–298). Oxford: Oxford University Press.

Duff, A. (2002). Rule-violations and wrongdoings. In S. Shute & A. Simester (Eds.), *Criminal law theory: Doctrines of the general part* (pp. 47–74). Oxford: Oxford University Press.

Feinberg, J. (1986). *The moral limits of the criminal law. Volume 3: Harm to self*. New York: Oxford University Press.

Fischer, J. M., & Ravizza, M. (1998). *Responsibility and control: A theory of moral responsibility*. Cambridge: Cambridge University Press.

Fischer, J. M., & Tognazzini, N. A. (2009). The truth about tracing. *Noûs, 43*(3), 531–556.

Fletcher, G. P. (1998). *Basic concepts of criminal law*. New York: Oxford University Press.

Grubb, A., Laing, J. M., McHale, J. V., & Kennedy, I. (2010). *Principles of medical law* (3rd ed.). Oxford: Oxford University Press.

Hart, H. L. A. (2008). *Punishment and responsibility* (2nd ed.). Oxford: Oxford University Press.

Hurd, H. M. (1996). The moral magic of consent. *Legal Theory, 2*(2), 121–146. doi:10.1017/s1352325200000434.

Kiener, M. (2019). Consent, threats, and offers. *American Journal of Bioethics, 19*(9), 66–68.

Kiener, M. (2020). Coercion. In *Routledge encyclopedia of philosophy*. Routledge.

Kiener, M. (2021). When do nudges undermine voluntary consent? *Philosophical Studies*, 1–26.

Kiener, M. (Forthcoming). Consent and Responsibility. In I. Black, F. Forsberg, J. Herring, & A. Skelton (Eds.), *Consenting children: Autonomy, responsibility, and well-being*. Oxford: Oxford University Press.

King, M. (2014). Traction without tracing: A (partial) solution for control-based accounts of moral responsibility. *European Journal of Philosophy, 22*(3), 463–482.

Mandava, A., & Millum, J. (2013). Manipulation in the enrollment of research participants. *Hastings Center Report, 43*(2), 38–47.

Millum, J. (2014). Consent under pressure: The puzzle of third party coercion. *Ethical Theory and Moral Practice, 17*(1), 113–127.

Nelson, R. M., Beauchamp, T., Miller, V. A., Reynolds, W., Ittenbach, R. F., & Luce, M. F. (2011). The concept of voluntary consent. *American Journal of Bioethics, 11*(8), 6–16.

Nozick, R. (1974). *Anarchy, state and Utopia*. New York: Basic Books.

Owens, D. (2007). Duress, deception, and the validity of a promise. *Mind, 116*(462), 293–315. doi:10.1093/mind/fzm293.

Pallikkathayil, J. (2011). *The possibility of choice: Three accounts of the problem with coercion*: Philosophers' Imprint 11(16), 1–20.

Robichaud, P., & Wieland, J. W. (2017). *Responsibility: The epistemic condition* (1st ed.). Oxford: Oxford University Press.

Sinnott-Armstrong, W., & Levy, K. (2011). Insanity defenses. In J. Deigh & D. Dolinko (Eds.), *The Oxford handbook of philosophy of criminal law* (pp. 299–324). Oxford: Oxford University Press.

Strawson, P. F. (1992). *Analysis and metaphysics*. Oxford: Oxford University Press.

Vargas, M. (2005). The trouble with tracing. *Midwest Studies In Philosophy, 29*(1), 269–291. doi:10.1111/j.1475-4975.2005.00117.x.

Wertheimer, A. (1987). *Coercion*. Princeton: Princeton University Press.

Wertheimer, A. (2003). *Consent to sexual relations*. Cambridge: Cambridge University Press.

Wertheimer, A. (2012). Voluntary consent: Why a value-neutral concept won't work. *Journal of Medicine and Philosophy, 37*(3), 226–254.

Legal Cases

- *Al Nehayan v Kent* [2018] EWHC 333 (Comm).
- *Ciarlariello v Schacter* [1993] 2 SCR 119 (SCC).
- *R v Hudson and Taylor* 1971 2 QB 202.
- *Schloendorff v New York Hospital* [1914] 105 N.E. 92 (N.Y.).
- *Williams v Bayley* [1866] LR 1 HL 200.

International Documents (Not Legally Binding But Very Widely Accepted)

- The Universal Declaration on Bioethics and Human Rights (2005). http://unesdoc.unesco.org/images/0014/001428/142825e.pdf#page=80.
- *The WMA Medical Ethics Manual* (2005). www.whcaonline.org/uploads/publications/em_en.pdf.
- International Ethical Guidelines for Biomedical Research Involving Human Subjects (*CIOMS Guide*) (2002). www.cioms.ch/publications/layout_guide2002.pdf.

6 Voluntariness and Coercion

Introduction

I will now focus on the third distinctive view of ICCJ, which is ICCJ's most controversial feature, namely the view that the validity of consent ultimately depends on the consent-receiver's conduct, even when the influences on the consent-giver are exerted by third parties. Such a view, which I call a *Recipient-Focus-View*, seems least plausible when third-party influences are most severe, as in cases of coercion. I will therefore address these cases as the strongest possible challenge to my proposal, ICCJ. I will argue that there is a puzzle in cases of consent and third-party coercion and solving this puzzle requires exactly the view ICCJ proposes. So, after focusing on *how* influences cause and invalidate consent (Chapter 4) and *which* influences invalidate consent (Chapter 5), I will now turn to the question *whose* influences (or conduct) invalidate consent.[1]

6.1 A Puzzle about Consent and Third-Party Coercion

When we consent to a medical procedure, sex, or a tattoo, we permit people to act in ways that would otherwise be impermissible. But our consent is valid, that is, it creates a permission, only if we have not been coerced into giving it. Relying on this common-sense description of consent, one may extract the following two principles central to the ethics of consent:

> **Permissibility Principle:** The permissibility of certain acts (e.g. executing a tattoo) requires valid consent.
> **Coercion Principle:** Coercion invalidates consent.

The *Permissibility Principle* describes the function of consent: when we give valid consent to something, we make it permissible for certain people to act in ways that would otherwise be impermissible. So understood, however, the *Permissibility Principle* requires immediate qualification: permissibility can be given two interpretations. Performing a certain act is *narrowly* permissible if and only if the agent's conduct is

DOI: 10.4324/9781003301417-8

justified in relation to what is owed to a particular person and therefore does not wrong that person; by contrast, performing a certain act is *widely* permissible if and only if it is justified in light of all the morally relevant facts.

Acts can be permissible in one way but not the other. If a patient validly consents to a kidney transplant, the surgeon's performance of it will be narrowly permissible, which means that it will not wrong this patient. But the operation could still be all-things-considered impermissible if, for instance, the patient bribed the surgeon to manipulate the waiting list to allocate the kidney to him instead of to someone else.

Conversely, there may be cases where an act wrongs a person, that is, is narrowly impermissible, but is still justified all things considered, that is, is widely permissible. For instance, one might wrong a person by twisting their arm (narrow impermissibility) but may still be justified in doing so, all things considered, when twisting that arm is necessary to save many people's lives (wide permissibility) (Nagel, 1986, p. 176).

I am concerned with narrow permissibility only, as this is the kind of permissibility that people create when they give valid consent. This distinction between narrow and wide permissibility is indeed widespread in the ethical literature and the debate on consent, even though often expressed with different terminology (Dougherty, 2015, p. 232; Mayr, 2019, pp. 118–124; Schaber, 2018, p. 56; Tadros, 2016, p. 201; Thompson, 2004, pp. 333–335).

On the other hand, the *Coercion Principle* holds that coercion invalidates consent. More precisely, it holds that coercion *always* invalidates consent, irrespective of who exerts it; and for the purpose of this chapter, I will adopt the canonical understanding of coercion as the use of illegitimate, severe threats to make a person comply with a specific demand (cf. Kiener, 2020). In such cases, inflicting the threatened harm would also violate an important moral right, such as the right to bodily integrity.[2]

The *Coercion Principle* is also widely held (Appelbaum, Lidz, & Klitzman, 2009, p. 33; Feinberg, 1986, p. 196; Ferzan, 2018, pp. 1000–1001; Millum, 2014, p. 114; Nelson et al., 2011, p. 8). Millum, for instance, supports the *Coercion Principle* as follows: he argues that 'valid consent requires that the person who has the authority to make a decision make that decision herself' (2014, p. 118). If someone is under an illegitimate controlling influence, for example, coercion, she is 'not making the decision ... herself' (p. 118) and hence her consent is invalid, no matter who exerted the coercion. Finally, the *Coercion Principle* can be found in most European jurisdictions in civil and criminal law.

Unfortunately, the *Permissibility Principle* and the *Coercion Principle* cannot both be true without qualification. Inconsistency between the two principles arises once we consider a case of third-party coercion, that is, a case where a person is coerced into consenting not by the recipient of consent but by a third party. I will assume that someone is a 'third party' if and only if he is not the recipient of consent *and* does not collaborate with the recipient. The following case, taken from a paper by Joseph Millum, provides a good example of third-party coercion:

> **Tattoo:** 'Coercer threatens to beat up Victim unless she gets a tattoo from Recipient's tattoo parlor. Recipient has no particular interest in tattooing her, but he cannot otherwise prevent the threat from being carried out and, although she would otherwise not want a tattoo, the beating is clearly worse for Victim than the tattoo. When she explains the situation to Recipient, Victim confirms that she prefers that he tattoo her than take any other action' (2014, p. 118).

Coercer is a third party: he is not the person receiving Victim's consent and does not collaborate with Recipient. Yet, his threat clearly coerces Victim. Recipient is the person receiving consent and, let us assume, Recipient behaves flawlessly towards Victim. Recipient would offer anything he could to help Victim, but Recipient cannot help Victim in any way other than executing the tattoo and Victim requests the tattoo for this reason. If Recipient executes the tattoo in this case, he does not take advantage of the situation and respects Victim's autonomy as much as possible. Hence, Millum argues, and I agree, that Recipient permissibly executes the tattoo.

Millum made an important point: *Tattoo* shows that one may still permissibly tattoo another person even if that person has been subjected to third-party coercion. Unfortunately, Millum stops here. He does not use *Tattoo* to show, as I think he could, that there is a fundamental conflict between the *Permissibility Principle* and the *Coercion Principle.* Thus, to outline this conflict, I need to extend the analysis of *Tattoo* over what Millum himself says and, in particular, determine whether Recipient's execution of the tattoo is *narrowly* permissible or *merely widely* permissible. This is because the *Permissibility Principle* will only be triggered if Recipient, in fact, acts *narrowly* permissibly when executing the tattoo.

Recipient acts narrowly permissibly if and only if Recipient's execution of the tattoo does not wrong Victim, that is, violate Victim's right to bodily integrity. In such a version of *Tattoo*, and absent other reasons against tattooing, Recipient would also not engage in any wronging at all when executing the tattoo, despite the third party's coercion. By contrast, Recipient acts *merely widely* permissibly if Recipient's execution of the tattoo is justified, all things considered, but still wrongs Victim. On this understanding, executing the tattoo is widely permissible because sending Victim back to the mercy of Coercer would be even worse and wrong Victim even more seriously. But executing the tattoo still wrongs Victim (i.e. is narrowly impermissible) because it violates Victim's rights to bodily integrity, given the coercion in the background. Accordingly, Recipient acts permissibly, *not because* Recipient does not wrong Victim but because Recipient chooses the lesser of two evils.

So, which is the correct view? I claim that it is the first one, namely that Recipient's execution of the tattoo is *narrowly* permissible. This is because none of the features which accompanies narrow *impermissibility*, that is, wronging, is present in the interaction between Recipient and Victim. If a person is wronged by someone else, that person is entitled to demand an apology from the wrongdoer and may resent and potentially forgive him (Bennett, 2018, p. 209ff.; Darwall, 2006, ch. 5; Owens, 2012, ch. 2; Wallace, 2014, pp. 119–142). The wrongdoer, on the other hand, incurs an obligation to apologise, at a minimum. However, in *Tattoo*, Victim cannot justifiably resent Recipient for executing the tattoo, demand an apology, or offer to forgive Recipient. Moreover, Recipient is not obliged to apologise to Victim. After all, Recipient respected Victim's autonomy as much as he could and Victim requested the tattoo. Compare the interaction between Recipient and Victim with the interaction between Coercer and Victim, where it is clear that Coercer's threat wronged Victim. Victim can indeed justifiably resent Coercer, demand an apology, and perhaps eventually forgive him; and Coercer is certainly obliged to apologise. Therefore, it seems that only Coercer but not Recipient wrongs Victim. Recipient's execution of the tattoo is *narrowly* permissible (and not just *merely widely* permissible).

Hence, I will assume that Recipient's execution of the tattoo is narrowly permissible. On the basis of this extended analysis of *Tattoo*, I am now in a position to build further on Millum's insights and explain the inconsistency between the *Coercion Principle* and the *Permission Principle*. The *Coercion Principle* yields the following reasoning about *Tattoo*.

1. Coercion Principle: Coercion invalidates consent.
2. Facts in Tattoo: Victim is coerced into consenting.
3. Conclusion: Victim's consent is *invalid*.

However, once we agree that Recipient acts *narrowly permissibly*, applying the *Permissibility Principle* yields the opposite conclusion:

4. Permissibility Principle: Permissibly (*narrow*) executing a tattoo requires valid consent.
5. Verdict on Tattoo: Recipient acts *narrowly* permissibly in executing the tattoo.
6. Conclusion: Victim's consent is *valid*.[3]

Conclusions (3) and (6) are inconsistent. If we accept the facts and verdict in *Tattoo*, we face a dilemma: we need to reject either the

Permissibility Principle or the *Coercion Principle*. But the *Permissibility Principle* and the *Coercion Principle* are both highly plausible. Thus, how can we solve the dilemma?

6.2 Millum's Modified Permissibility Principle as a Potential Solution

Although Millum did not address the dilemma as I set it out, his statements may still allow us to form a potential solution. Millum accepts (1), the *Coercion Principle*: 'Victim's consent is always rendered invalid by third party coercion' (2014, p. 119). He also accepts (2): Victim is coerced into consenting. Finally, Millum concludes (3), that is, Victim's consent is invalid.

But Millum thinks Recipient still acts (*narrowly*) permissibly. Millum claims that 'illegitimate third-party coercion does not entail that it is impermissible to proceed with the act consented to even if it means that the consent is invalid' (2014, pp. 118–119). Whether or not Recipient may proceed on the basis of invalid consent depends, according to Millum, on 'the other options available to Recipient, and what Victim wants Recipient to do' (pp. 118–119). Developing these statements, Millum argues that, in cases of coerced and invalid consent, Recipient 'may proceed if doing so would constitute a reasonable joint decision of her and the victim of coercion' (p. 126). Joint decision-making 'involves each party taking the viewpoint of the other as seriously as her own and deciding on this basis what to do' (p. 121). If tattooing is based on such joint decision-making, 'Recipient thereby respects ... [Victim's] autonomy by giving her as much control over her consent decision as he is able' (p. 119). In such cases, 'a wrong has been committed by Coercer. But Recipient is not culpable for this wrong: he has done the best he could in non-ideal circumstances' (p. 119).

Hence, Millum claims that Recipient can execute the tattoo permissibly not only if he is given valid consent (option 1) but also if he is given invalid consent but acts on the basis of a reasonable joint decision (option 2). However, it is noteworthy that, in Millum's view, Recipient acts permissibly in *Tattoo* only if Victim actually *requests* the tattoo. In Millum's view, a request is still necessary to make a recipient's act permissible, and the absence of a request is sufficient to make Recipient's act impermissible.

Assuming that Recipient executes the tattoo narrowly permissibly then leads to the following solution to the dilemma. Millum's account can leave the first set of claims untouched:

1. Coercion Principle: Coercion invalidates consent.
2. Facts in Tattoo: Victim is coerced into consenting.
3. Conclusion: Victim's consent is *invalid*.

But Millum needs to change the second set of claims:

4. *Modified Permissibility Principle: Permissibly (narrow) executing a tattoo requires either (i) valid consent or (ii) a reasonable joint decision.
5. Verdict in Tattoo: Recipient acts narrowly permissibly in executing the tattoo.
6. *Modified Conclusion: Victim's consent is *either valid or invalid.*

On the *Modified Permissibility Principle*, the original conclusion (6), that is, that consent is valid, no longer follows: consent could be either valid or invalid and, as it happens, consent is invalid in *Tattoo* and Recipient acts narrowly permissibly due to basing his action on a reasonable joint decision. Hence, there is no contradiction anymore: conclusion (3) and modified conclusion (6*) are consistent with each other.

Unfortunately, this solution reconstructed from Millum's account remains unsatisfactory. Firstly, Millum's overall framework may ask for too much in one respect. Millum claims that, in the presence of third-party coercion, Recipient executes the tattoo permissibly if and only if doing so is based on a *reasonable joint decision,* and he explains that 'joint decision-making involves *each* party taking the viewpoint of the *other* as seriously as her own and deciding on this basis what to do' (2014, p. 121, emphasis added). Yet, there can be cases where Recipient's execution of the tattoo is *not* based on a reasonable joint decision, but Recipient may still proceed narrowly permissibly. To see this, consider the following case:

> **Manipulation:** Someone threatens Recipient with death if he tattoos Victim. Thus, if Recipient tattoos Victim, he will be killed, and if he does not, Victim will be beaten. To make Recipient proceed, Victim illegitimately manipulates Recipient into tattooing her: she uses emotional triggers and harnesses Recipient's decisional weaknesses.

In *Manipulation*, tattooing is not based on a reasonable joint decision. After all, Recipient faces greater harm than Victim would and, due to Victim's manipulation, it is not true that the decision-making 'involves each party taking the viewpoint of the other as seriously as her own and deciding on this basis what to do' (Millum, 2014, p. 121). But even if this is true, it would not follow that, *for this reason*, it is narrowly impermissible for Recipient to execute the tattoo, that is, that Recipient commits some wrong when proceeding on that basis. Hence, whether Recipient executes the *Tattoo* narrowly permissibly does not depend on whether doing so equally accounts for *both viewpoints*, that is, whether tattooing is based on a reasonable *joint* decision. It only depends on whether *Victim*'s viewpoint has been sufficiently accounted for, as it is *Victim* who will be subject to the tattoo. Millum's focus on a *joint* decision fails to capture this important point and, therefore, provides a misleading framework for evaluating when Recipient executes the tattoo narrowly permissibly.

In response, Millum could argue that his view only states a sufficient but not necessary condition for the narrow permissibility of Recipient's conduct. But there are two problems with this reply. (i) Millum's account would be incomplete. After all, we still need to know not only what is sufficient but also what is necessary for Recipient to act narrowly permissibly. (ii) This reply falsely suggests that, when there *is* a reasonable joint decision, part of the reason why Recipient does not wrong Victim is that Recipient sufficiently accounted for *his own* interests, for otherwise it would not be a *joint* decision. But accounting for *one's own* interests cannot (save in very exceptional cases) be part of the reason as to why one does not wrong *others*. Not wronging others depends on whether one sufficiently accounted for *their* interests. Thus, Millum's general focus on *joint* decisions does not offer an appropriate explanation (or, in other words, is *intensionally inadequate*), even when it delivers the correct verdict (e.g. no wronging).

Secondly and over and above Millum giving the wrong explanation of why Recipient acts narrowly permissibly in executing the tattoo, Millum's *Modified Permissibility Principle* also lacks justification for introducing a 'reasonable joint decision' as a concept distinct from valid consent. After all, a reasonable joint decision shares all the essential features of valid consent. Just like valid consent, a reasonable joint decision requires Victim's request for the tattoo, demands that Recipient not control Victim's decision-making, releases Recipient from the obligation not to interfere with Victim's body, and makes executing the tattoo narrowly permissible. Thus, it seems that Millum introduces a reasonable joint decision as something other than valid consent when it actually should be considered an instance of valid consent.

The first point of these criticisms and my example of *Manipulation* particularly target Millum's view in particular and his account of a 'reasonable joint decision'. However, the second point also applies to any other view that preserves the *Coercion Principle* and modifies the *Permissibility Principle* in some similar way. By way of explanation, even if other views reject Millum's 'reasonable joint decision' and adopt the correct view on when Recipient executes the tattoo in a narrowly permissible way (e.g. when Victim issues 'request X'), these versions will still lack justification for introducing 'request X' as something distinct from valid consent. After all, such 'request X' will still share all the essential features of valid consent. Just like valid consent, it will require Victim's request for the tattoo, demand that Recipient not control Victim's decision-making, release Recipient from the obligation not to interfere with Victim's body, and make executing the tattoo narrowly permissible. Thus, my critique applies more generally to any views that accept the *Coercion Principle* and aim to modify the *Permissibility Principle*. I therefore suggest rejecting Millum's solution alongside other views that also accept the *Coercion Principle* without modification. In the next section, I will provide an alternative solution that leaves the *Permissibility Principle* untouched.

6.3 My Proposal: Modifying the Coercion Principle

Shifting the Paradigm

The solution I want to propose operates under a paradigm which is different from the solution Millum provides and from what many authors in the debate on consent accept. Therefore, to explain my solution in contrast to these approaches, I first want to explain the paradigm behind Millum's solution, which I call the *Influence-Focus-View*.

The *Influence-Focus-View* holds that whether an influence invalidates consent depends solely on the nature, circumstances, and effect of the influence, but not who exerted it. People defending the *Influence-Focus-View* still diverge on what they think makes an influence consent-invalidating. Whereas some hold that an influence invalidates consent if it is substantially controlling (Feinberg, 1986; Nelson et al., 2011), others argue that an influence invalidates consent if the influencer lacks the right to exert it (Appelbaum et al., 2009). Yet, others hold that an influence needs to be both substantially controlling *and* illegitimate (Millum, 2014). However, all of them think that whether consent is valid depends only on the particular features of an influence, and not on who exerted it; and all of them also think that coercion is a paradigmatic case for an influence that invalidates consent. Hence, they all accept the *Coercion Principle*: once an influence qualifies as coercion, it invalidates consent, irrespective of who exerts the coercion.

However, the *Influence-Focus-View* is not without an alternative. The alternative I want to present in this chapter is what I call the *Recipient-Focus-View*. According to the *Recipient-Focus-View*, the validity of consent depends on the conduct of the person receiving consent rather than on third-party coercion alone. Most such views argue, more specifically, that consent is valid if the person receiving consent did not wrong Victim in order to receive consent, and invalid if he did wrong Victim in that way. Thus, the focus is on the person receiving consent rather than, as the *Influence-Focus-View* has it, on whether anyone, including third parties, coerces the person consenting.

As a result, the *Recipient-Focus-View* rejects the *Coercion Principle*, according to which coercion *always* invalidates consent. The *Recipient-Focus-View* holds whether coercion invalidates consent depends on the role of the consent-receiver, that is, Recipient. More specifically, most of these views hold that coercion *only* invalidates consent if Recipient committed some *wronging*, and as *Tattoo* showed, this does not always have to be the case.

But note: on such *Recipient-Focus-Views*, Recipient's wrong that invalidates consent is distinct from the wrong in acting on invalid consent. The former normally occurs *in the process of obtaining consent* and prior to Victim's consent, for example, when Recipient coerces Victim or collaborates with Coercer to extract consent.[4] Thus, the *Recipient-Focus-View* still accepts the traditional explanatory order: the invalidity of consent explains why acting on such consent is wrong, and not the other way around. The *Recipient-Focus-View* just adds that the reason why consent is invalid in the first place is always due to another, prior wrong committed by Recipient.

But how exactly can Recipient invalidate consent? What kinds of conduct are relevant? I suggest a tripartite account.

(i) **Exerting Coercion**
To begin with, Recipient wrongs Victim and invalidates consent when he himself exerts the coercion or collaborates with Coercer in exerting the coercion. Such cases are in fact the clearest examples of coercion invalidating consent.

(ii) **Exploiting Coercion**
In addition, Recipient wrongs Victim and invalidates consent when he exploits third-party coercion. Consider the following examples:

> **Tattoo Money:** Knowing that Victim would do anything to escape Coercer, Recipient charges five times the price for performing the tattoo. Otherwise, Recipient behaves in the same way as in *Tattoo*. Victim consents to the tattoo and to the payment.
>
> **Tattoo Sex:** Knowing that Victim would do anything to escape Coercer, Recipient tells Victim that he will perform the tattoo only if Victim has sex with him. Otherwise, Recipient behaves in the same way as in *Tattoo*. Victim consents to the tattoo and to sex.

In *Tattoo Money*, Recipient exploits the coercion by forcing Victim to pay an extortionate price. Recipient's conduct thereby wrongs Victim, makes the financial transaction voidable, and gives Victim a claim to compensation. In *Tattoo Sex*, Recipient exploits the coercion by forcing Victim to have sex with him. Recipient thereby also wrongs Victim, invalidates Victim's consent to the sex, and rapes Victim if he goes ahead.

Hence, exploiting coercion means that Recipient uses third-party coercion to force Victim to consent to something which even the coercing third party had not demanded from Victim, for example, an additional extortionate price (*Tattoo Money*) or sex (*Tattoo Sex*). In these cases, Recipient's additional demand is not necessary for Victim to escape Coercer's threat, imposes greater harm on Victim, and is not one that Recipient is entitled to make.

So understood, exploiting coercion is specific to the particular object of consent, that is, *what* Victim consents to. In *Tattoo Money* and

Tattoo Sex, Recipient's exploitation invalidates Victim's consent only to the extortionate price and to sex, but not to the tattoo. This is because exploitation requires a means–end link between Recipient's misconduct and what Victim consents to. And since Recipient exploited the coercion only with regard to the price and sex, but not the tattoo, which Victim would have consented to anyway, it is only Victim's consent to the price and to sex that is invalid.

Moreover, exploitation is more like 'taking advantage' rather than 'getting an advantage', that is, benefitting from what Coercer forced Victim to undergo. Exploiting, like taking advantage, requires that Recipient illegitimately harnesses the third-party coercion to obtain consent to something which even Coercer had not demanded from Victim. Therefore, however much Recipient otherwise benefits from executing the tattoo, such benefits *alone* do not imply that Recipient also exploits the coercion as I described it.

So understood, my view remains neutral with regard to Alan Wertheimer's account, according to which there can be instances of mutually advantageous and consensual exploitation. This is because I understand *exploitation*, specifically, as the illegitimate use of or reliance on third-party coercion, whereas Wertheimer understands exploitation more broadly as any conduct in which 'A takes unfair advantage of B' (1996, p. 10; 2012, p. 283), and Wertheimer also specifically requires the absence of coercion as a necessary condition for such a transaction to be consensual. Thus, even if one accepts my view in cases of third-party coercion, one would still be free to accept (or reject) Wertheimer's view on consensual exploitation in cases without coercion.

Yet, it is noteworthy that Wertheimer also relies on a distinction between different objects of consent similar to the one I presented in *Tattoo Sex* and *Tattoo Money*. In an example (called *Rescue*) in which A charges B an extortionate fee to free B's car, which would otherwise be stuck for hours, Wertheimer says:

> *Rescue* can involve at least two different types of moral transformation. Consider two questions: (1) does B's consent give A permission to tow B's car? (2) Does B's promise (consent) to pay A $200 obligate B to pay the full amount? I believe that the answer to (1) may be yes, because A has not coerced B and because B may be fully informed about the alternatives available to her and competent to choose among them. At the same time, the answer to (2) may be no.
>
> (2010, p. 112)

Thus, just as I distinguished between Victim's consent to the tattoo, on the one hand, and Victim's consent to the extortionate price or sex (in *Tattoo Money* and *Tattoo Sex*), on the other, Wertheimer distinguishes between two objects of consent as well.

(iii) Facilitating Coercive Success

Finally, Recipient wrongs Victim and invalidates consent when he facilitates coercive success, that is, when he denies Victim an alternative to acting on consent,[5] which would also allow Victim to avoid the threatened harm and not impose an unreasonable cost on Recipient (or others).[6] Consider the following example:

> **Mischievous:** As in *Tattoo*, except Recipient could make Coercer withdraw the threat simply by giving him a phone call. As Recipient knows, Coercer is the biggest fan of his tattoo art and would comply with anything Recipient tells him. Victim asks for help but Recipient refuses. Victim then consents to the tattoo and Recipient executes it.

Making Coercer withdraw the threat is an alternative to acting on consent, allows Victim to avoid the threatened harm, and does not impose an unreasonable cost. Hence, Recipient could easily enable Victim to return to the pre-coercion setting, in which Victim could avoid both the threatened harm *and* what Victim was forced to consent to. Denying Victim this alternative wrongs Victim, facilitates coercive success, and invalidates Victim's subsequent consent to the tattoo.

The key feature in cases like *Mischievous*, and the reason why I picked the formulation *facilitating* coercive success, is that Recipient has now control over Victim's situation that normally only Coercer has, that is, the control over whether Victim can return to the pre-coercion setting and avoid both evils, that is, the threatened harm and whatever results from complying with Coercer's demand. In other words, it is Recipient's own conduct that now determines whether Victim need to suffer anything at all. Therefore, if Recipient denies Victim a feasible alternative, he impedes Victim's return to the pre-coercion setting, slips into a role not unlike the one Coercer has, and thereby facilitates the ultimate success of the coercion.

Admittedly, there will be controversy over what counts as *unreasonable* costs,[7] *why exactly* Recipient ought to help Victim and thereby avoid facilitating coercive success,[8] and whether Recipient's help should be *legally* enforceable.[9] But at this point, I will not attempt to take a stance on these further questions. I only wish to defend my more general and *independent* claim that denying Victim a sufficiently costless alternative invalidates consent, and I take *Mischievous* to illustrate this point. What I can say, however, is that facilitating coercive success could be described, more specifically, as a violation of a duty to rescue, namely, a duty to help someone escape an immediate peril, rather than a general duty of beneficence.[10] Moreover, I would understand such a duty of rescue in cases of third-party coercion as a perfect (rather than imperfect) duty, because it correlates with Victim's claim-right that Recipient not facilitate coercive success.[11] There is such a claim-right because Recipient would wrong Victim when facilitating coercive success and people have claim-rights against being wronged.

An Alternative Solution Based on the Modified Coercion Principle

The last section claimed that Recipient invalidates Victim's consent when Recipient (1) exerts or collaborates in exerting the coercion, (2) exploits the coercion, or (3) facilitates coercive success. This section pulls these threads together and presents an alternative solution to the inconsistency of the *Coercion Principle* and the *Permissibility Principle.* This solution is based on a distinction between consent being 'obtained by' coercion and consent 'being merely motivated' by coercion.

Consent is 'obtained by' coercion, I argue, if and only if Recipient acts as in (1), (2), or (3). 'Obtain' implies the involvement of Recipient and that Recipient uses or illegitimately relies on the constraint on Victim's situation to receive consent to a particular interaction, as is the case in standard two-party scenarios of coercion as well as in my examples of *Tattoo Money*, *Tattoo Sex*, and *Mischievous.*

These cases differ significantly from the original *Tattoo* case, in which Recipient did not exert coercion, exploit coercion, or facilitate its success. I therefore argue that, in *Tattoo*, consent was 'merely motivated by' coercion. Consent is merely motivated by coercion if a person's reason for consenting is to prevent a threat from being carried out, but the threat came from a third party, and Recipient neither contributed to it nor wronged Victim in any of the three ways outlined. Thus, the contrast between 'obtained by' and 'merely motivated by' reflects a shift of perspective: the former looks at how *Recipient* uses or illegitimately relies on coercion to receive consent, and the latter looks at what *Victim*'s reasons for consenting are.

The distinction between consent being obtained by coercion and consent being merely motivated by coercion also disambiguates the *Coercion Principle.* It is not true that consent is invalid if a person is coerced into consenting. Whether coercion invalidates consent depends on whether consent was, more specifically, 'obtained by' coercion. Adopting this view provides the following alternative solution to the dilemma at hand. It is now the first set of claims that requires change:

1. *Modified Coercion Principle: Consent is invalid if obtained by coercion, and valid if merely motivated by coercion.
2. *Specified Facts in *Tattoo*: Victim's consent is merely motivated by coercion.
3. *Modified Conclusion: Victim's consent is *valid.*

The second set of claims, on the other hand, can be left untouched:

4. Permissibility Principle: Permissibly (narrow) executing a tattoo requires valid consent.
5. Verdict in *Tattoo*: Recipient narrowly permissibly executes the tattoo.
6. Conclusion: Victim's consent is *valid*.

As a result, there is no longer any contradiction. Modified conclusion (3*) and conclusion (6) are consistent with each other. Thus, there is an alternative solution to the dilemma that does not require any of Millum's assumptions.

Moreover, this solution, following a *Recipient-Focus-View* and based on the *Modified Coercion Principle*, avoids the flaws that I argued Millum's solution, based on the *Modified Permissibility Principle*, suffers from.

To begin with, unlike Millum's solution, my view delivers the correct result not only for *Tattoo* but also for *Manipulation*. In the latter case, Recipient did not obtain consent by means of coercion, notwithstanding the fact that the final agreement between Recipient and Victim was not a reasonable joint decision. After all, Recipient neither exerted coercion nor took advantage of it. Therefore, my view holds that Recipient executes the tattoo narrowly permissibly and reaches the correct result in this case.

Moreover, unlike Millum's solution and any other version of the *Influence-Focus-View*, my view avoids introducing a concept distinct from valid consent, for example, a reasonable joint decision or 'request X', when doing so lacks justification. The *Modified Coercion Principle* only asks for adjusting the validity condition concerning coercion. In this regard, my solution avoids the second flaw of an *Influence-Focus-View* and thereby displays greater theoretical parsimony.

For these reasons, my *Modified Coercion Principle*, as a distinct version of a *Recipient-Focus-View*, presents a better solution to the inconsistency of the *Coercion Principle* and the *Permissibility Principle* than Millum's account.

An Important Further Challenge

There is a strong objection to my view, in fact to *any* Recipient-Focus-View, and this objection arises from cases in which there is no interaction between the person giving and the person receiving consent. Consider the following example:

> **Envelope:** Recipient receives an envelope containing a note with a username and password for online banking, inviting Recipient to log on. The envelope also contains a thumbnail drive. On it, Recipient finds a reliable and accurate video of Victim writing the note at gunpoint. Yet, Recipient's actual logging on is not necessary for Victim to escape being shot. Victim has already escaped

> Coercer when the letter reaches Recipient, and (let us assume) Recipient knows this. Still, Recipient does not know who Victim is, has no possibility to contact or interact with Victim, and hence no possibility of offering Victim anything.

Here, Recipient cannot permissibly log on, and Victim's consent to Recipient logging on is invalid. *Envelope* is a particularly challenging case for any version of the *Recipient-Focus-View* precisely because there is no interaction between consent-receiver and consent-giver. It seems that any *Recipient-Focus-View*, which makes the validity of consent dependent on some wrongdoing of Recipient, needs to identify an instance of Recipient wrongdoing that is distinct from and *prior* to the wrongdoing of acting on consent, precisely because the Recipient's wrongdoing is supposed to explain why consent is invalid and acting on consent is wrong in the first place. Yet, in *Envelope*, there is no such prior time at which Recipient could wrong Victim. Thus, a successful reply to *Envelope* will advance our understanding of *Recipient-Focus-Views* more generally.

My own view offers a solution. I argued that consent is invalid when Recipient 'facilitates coercive success', that is, when Recipient denies Victim an alternative to acting on consent, which would also allow Victim to avoid the threatened harm and not impose an unreasonable cost. Usually, an alternative is another way to escape the threatened harm, and Recipient would normally be able to offer that alternative before Victim consents. However, in my view, an alternative can take other forms too, even the form of an *omission*. And in *Envelope*, it does: simply by *not logging on* can Recipient make it the case that Victim not only avoids the physical injury, that is, the threatened harm, but also the exposure of the bank account, that is, what Victim was forced to consent to. Moreover, not logging on does not impose unreasonable costs on Recipient (or anyone else), and Recipient should assume that Victim would ask Recipient not to log on if able to communicate freely. Hence, if Recipient logs on, he 'facilitates coercive success' and consent is therefore invalid.

Thus, when logging on (and this is critical), Recipient commits *two* wrongs simultaneously: he facilitates coercive success *and* acts on invalid consent. These are *distinct* wrongs because facilitating coercive success, when there is a feasible alternative, is wrongful independently of whether consent is involved.[12] Yet, they are *not independent* wrongs because the facilitation of coercive success explains why consent is invalid in the first place and acting on it wrong. In other words, the facilitation of coercive success may not be *temporarily* prior to acting on invalid consent, but it is *explanatorily* prior.

Let me illustrate this point with a story. Greek mythology tells us that the moment King Midas touches food, he turns it into gold and renders it inedible. The food's becoming gold and its becoming inedible happen at the same time. Yet, one explains the other: the food is inedible *because* it is golden, rather than the food is golden because it is inedible. Thus, the story of Midas supports the distinction between temporal and explanatory priority: two things may happen at the same time, yet one explains the other.

My *Recipient-Focus-View* proposes a very similar picture for *Envelope*: the moment Recipient acts on consent, he facilitates coercive success and renders consent invalid. Thus, just as the conversion into gold explains the inedibility of food, the facilitation of coercive success explains the invalidity of consent. The fact that everything happens at the same time does not preclude this explanatory order. Hence, this version of the *Recipient-Focus-View* can deal with cases like *Envelope* by endorsing the distinction between temporal and explanatory priority, and making only the latter a requirement for wrongdoing to invalidate consent.

However, readers may point to some unconventional implication of my proposal, namely that Victim's consent is either valid or indeterminate up until the moment when Recipient logs on. Those who find this implication implausible can opt for an alternative, which is also based on my view of 'facilitating coercive success'.

So far, I have assumed that the validity of consent depends on Recipient's conduct in the sense that Recipient's conduct, and not the third party's coercion, *invalidates* consent. Yet, alternatively, one could also argue that the validity of consent depends on Recipient's conduct in the sense that it can *revalidate* consent, that is, make an otherwise invalid token of consent valid again. Applied to *Envelope*, this view would consider Victim's coerced consent invalid from the beginning and claim that, if Recipient acts on that consent without thereby 'facilitating coercive success', as I defined it, then Recipient revalidates consent, namely, he makes Victim's otherwise invalid consent valid again. In *Envelope*, Recipient cannot log on without facilitating coercive success, hence cannot revalidate consent. Yet, in another version of *Envelope*, in which logging on is necessary to save Victim, Recipient may log on without facilitating coercive success and thereby revalidate consent.

This view is a hybrid version of an *Influence-Focus-View* and a *Recipient-Focus-View*. On the one hand, it concedes to the *Influence-Focus-View* that, in cases without interaction between consent-receiver and consent-giver, coercion always invalidates consent, irrespective of who exerts it. On the other hand, this view sides with the *Recipient-Focus-View* in claiming that the validity of consent crucially depends on Recipient, precisely because the validity of consent ultimately depends on whether Recipient facilitates coercive success when acting on consent.

This hybrid view gives us the right result in *Envelope* again: consent is invalid. Moreover, it remains true to my substantial claims about 'facilitating coercive success' and to the view that the validity of consent crucially depends on Recipient. Finally, this hybrid view can describe Victim's consent as invalid from the moment Victim gives it. Yet, this hybrid view also makes a critical concession to the *Influence-Focus-View* and thereby relinquishes part of *Recipient-Focus-Views*.

Both of my proposed solutions are based on my account of what it means to 'facilitate coercive success' and consistent with my overall framework. However, I opt for the first of these two solutions because it is closer to how I defined my view and because it does not have to make a concession to the *Influence-Focus-View*. Yet, readers with a diverging opinion could still adopt the second solution while also embracing my overall approach to consent and third-party coercion.

The fact that my view holds a solution, or even *two* solutions, to cases like *Envelope* makes it also clearly distinct from other *Recipient-Focus-Views*, since cases like *Envelope* have not been discussed in the literature and other *Recipient-Focus-Views* seem unable to deal with them. Consider Mollie Gerver's account as another elaborate version of a *Recipient-Focus-View*.

Gerver claims that where consent is invalid and 'where the consent-seeker is aware of the threat, the consent-seeker implies a threat himself' (2021, p. 265). She says 'that agents can fail to obtain valid consent despite engaging in no coercion (issue not at least an implicit threat) themselves ... is incorrect' (p. 261). But *Envelope* shows that this is wrong. In *Envelope*, consent is invalid but Recipient does not issue any threat, either explicit or implicit.

Thus, Gerver's view, unlike mine, is either inapplicable to *Envelope* or suggests that consent is valid due to the absence of a threat from Recipient. The conclusion that consent is valid is unacceptable. But claiming that Gerver's account is not supposed to apply to cases like *Envelope* is also an undesirable response, for it would render Gerver's view incomplete and suggest that *Recipient-Focus-Views* might be mistaken altogether if they cannot apply to such cases. The competing view, what we may call *Influence-Focus-View*, which holds that coercion always invalidates consent, can apply across all these different cases.

Another alternative version of a *Recipient-Focus-View* comes from Tom Dougherty, who also claims that a person's consent can be valid even if there was coercion from a third party. Dougherty claims:

> If X [i.e. Victim] sincerely performs a speech-act that authorizes Y [i.e. Recipient] to perform A as an extension of X's own agency in circumstances that are beyond the control of Y, then Y has X's valid consent to perform A.
>
> (2019, p. 11)

Applied to *Tattoo*, Victim's consent is valid on Dougherty's view because the third party's coercion is beyond Victim's and Recipient's control, and Recipient's execution of the tattoo can be seen as an 'extension of Victim's agency'. 'Extension of Victim's agency' means that 'if Victim were directly able to control [Recipient's] behavior with their own choices, then Victim would choose that [Recipient execute the tattoo]' (Dougherty, 2019, p. 11). In Dougherty's view, such an 'extension of Victim's agency' is a sufficient (yet not a necessary) condition for valid consent. This is another *Recipient-Focus-View* as it makes the validity of consent to depend on Recipient's action, rather than on third-party coercion alone.

Dougherty's view gives us the right result in *Tattoo*, that is, that Victim's consent is valid. Yet, it is too demanding in other cases. Consider the following example:

> **No Hero:** Recipient has two options to rescue Victim from third-party coercion. Both options involve the execution of a particular tattoo. However, one option comes with great costs for Recipient, that is, suffering severe physical harm, and the other option comes with no costs for Recipient. If Victim were able to control Recipient's behaviour directly with her own choices, (let us assume) Victim would choose that Recipient take the first option as this option involves a smaller and less painful tattoo for Victim. Yet, Recipient cannot be expected to bear such high costs, and as a matter of fact, Recipient only offers the second option. Victim eventually consents to it.

In this case, Recipient's execution of the tattoo is *not* an extension of Victim's agency in Dougherty's sense, for if Victim were able to control Recipient's behaviour directly with her own choices, Recipient would take the first option, not the second. Yet, if Victim consents to the second option and Recipient executes it, Victim's consent is still valid and Recipient acts permissibly. This is because denying Victim the first option does not wrong Victim. There is a limit to the costs that Recipient can be expected to bear for the sake of Victim.

Hence, even if Recipient's conduct falls short of Dougherty's 'extension of agency', consent can still be valid. We should therefore add to Dougherty's view that not only the extension of Victim's agency but also Recipient's conduct in *No Hero* is sufficient for valid consent. My own view can step in here and explain that consent is valid in *No Hero* because Recipient did not obtain consent by means of coercion, namely, because Recipient did not exert coercion, exploit coercion, or facilitate coercive success as I defined it.

Thus, there are two key differences between Dougherty's view and my view: (i) what I consider to be sufficient for valid consent (i.e. that consent is not 'obtained by coercion') is less demanding than what Dougherty considers to be sufficient (i.e. the 'extension of Victim's agency'), and this is why my view delivers the correct result in *No Hero*; (ii) unlike Dougherty, I provide both sufficient *and necessary* conditions for valid consent in cases of third-party coercion. For these reasons, I argue, my view is preferable to, or at least importantly supplements, Dougherty's proposal.[13]

I therefore conclude that my solution to *Envelope* not only sets my view apart from Gerver's and Dougherty's views but also advances our understanding of *Recipient-Focus-Views* more generally, by demonstrating how *Recipient-Focus-Views* can deal with cases like *Envelope*.

6.4 Conclusion

I argued that there is a fundamental conflict between what I call the *Permissibility Principle* and the *Coercion Principle*, and I proposed a modification of the *Coercion Principle* as a solution. This solution is based on the view that coercion invalidates consent if consent was 'obtained by' coercion but not if 'merely motivated by' coercion. I argued that this solution best resolves the inconsistency between the two principles and also challenges how we currently think about consent more generally. I took the current paradigm to be what I call the *Influence-Focus-View*, according to which there is no relevant difference between two- and three-party cases when identifying those influences that invalidate consent. The validity of consent always depends solely on the features of the exerted influence, but not on who exerts it. However, if my solution based on the *Modified Coercion Principle* is correct, the *Influence-Focus-View* is false. Whether an influence invalidates consent does not just depend on whether it is coercive or, more generally, illegitimately controlling. Rather, the validity of consent depends on the person receiving consent. For this reason, I defended what I call the *Recipient-Focus-View*, I explained how my particular version of it differs from alternative versions of this approach, and I showed how my view can deal with particularly difficult cases like *Envelope* that have hitherto seemed unsurmountable for *Recipient-Focus-Views*.

So understood, my arguments defend another key element of my proposal, ICCJ, namely what I call the third distinctive view of ICCJ, that is, the view that it is ultimately only the consent-receiver's influences, or his conduct more generally, that can invalidate consent, even in cases where the influences are exerted by third parties. The influences of third parties, and their strength and illegitimacy, may inform what the person receiving consent is obliged to do in order to maintain the voluntariness of a person's consent, but they cannot directly negate the voluntariness of consent. In Part Three, I will address a real-life situation of third-party pressure in the context of living organ donation and thereby confirm that this view can withstand scrutiny in clinical practice too.

Conclusion of Top-Down Defence of ICCJ

I now conclude my Top-Down defence of ICCJ. I defended the three main distinctive views of ICCJ, as mentioned at the beginning of Chapter 3. I first explained ICCJ's answer to the question of *how* exactly influences like causation and manipulation cause and thereby invalidate consent.

According to ICCJ, an influence such as coercion causes and thereby invalidates consent (if it does) when it induces a certain type of motivation, regardless of whether it does so directly or through deviant causal chains. I further specified this view in terms of what I call the *Bad-Reasons-View.* I then addressed the question of *which* influences invalidate consent. I argued for ICCJ's position according to which only 'interpersonally unjustifiable' influences invalidate consent. In so doing, I rejected value-neutral views and alternative moralised views of voluntariness. Finally, I showed that ICCJ restricts *whose* influences (or conduct) invalidate consent. ICCJ holds that it is ultimately only the consent-receiver's influences, or his conduct more generally, that can invalidate consent, even in cases where the influences are exerted by third parties.

I therefore hope to have provided sufficient support for the three main characteristics of my proposal, ICCJ. In the next part, I will proceed to the Bottom-Up defence of ICCJ, showing that ICCJ also successfully deals with three key challenges in clinical practice. I aim to confirm further those aspects that I have already argued for in my Top-Down defence. But my main objective will be to argue for the specific principles of ICCJ, which I have not explicitly supported so far. I will start with a chapter on nudging and manipulation with the objective of claiming that a correct assessment of these influences will lead us to the specific principles on which ICCJ is based. I will then discuss challenges in clinical trials, including the case of Rambha mentioned in the Introduction, as well as the challenges inherent in living organ donation, where people's decision-making is subject to a variety of different kinds of pressure.

Before I proceed, however, it is worth separating ICCJ from what seems to be a close contender, namely Miller and Wertheimer's *Fair Transaction View.* According to this, 'A is morally permitted to proceed on the basis of a consent transaction if A has treated B fairly and responds in a reasonable manner to B's token or expression of consent or what A reasonably believes is B's token or expression of consent' (2010, p. 81).

This view overlaps to some extent with ICCJ. I agree with Miller and Wertheimer that 'the transformative power of B's consent (or behavior) is a function of the transactional circumstances under which B chooses (including the behavior of A) rather than the specific mental states that characterise or motivate B's choice' (p. 94). I also agree that we need a moralised account and that third-party coercion alone does not invalidate consent.

Yet, there are also considerable differences. First, in cases of third-party coercion, I hold that there can be duties to assist, the violation of which invalidates consent, whereas Miller and Wertheimer do not mention any such duties. Second, Miller and Wertheimer argue, which I reject, that the consent-receiver's misconduct can make it impermissible to proceed with the consented-to action, even if such misconduct does not affect the consent-giver's decision-making at all. The following example from their paper illustrates this:

> Nondisclosure. A intentionally fails to disclose information about the risks of a surgical procedure because he fears that B will wrongly overestimate the importance of those risks. Unbeknownst to A, B has consulted with another physician and has a full grasp of the risks. B signs the consent form because she wants A to perform the surgery.
>
> (Miller & Wertheimer, 2010, p. 100)

> Because A has not treated B fairly and because A does not know that B's consent is fully informed, we believe that A is not permitted to proceed even though B's consent is fully informed and thus compatible with LK/AA. Once again, this case demonstrates that B's mental state is not the key to morally transformative consent: The consent transaction between A and B must be fair.
>
> (p. 100)

Although I agree that A treated B unfairly, the consent-receiver's misconduct did not have an impact on the other person's consent at all. Thus, in my view, it cannot preclude the morally transformative effect of the interaction.

Third, Miller and Wertheimer reject the framework of 'valid consent', presenting their *Fair Transaction View* as an alternative. By contrast, I still work within the framework of valid consent. My proposal, ICCJ, still adheres to voluntariness as a necessary condition of valid consent and considers validity to be the appropriate framework within which to assess the moral effect of consent.

Finally, Miller and Wertheimer focus on fairness, which is a very general term, and do not specify in greater detail what it means. In fact, they remain content to present their view as a 'preface' to be spelled out on another occasion. By contrast, I offer a much more specific view based on the notion of interpersonal justification. Moreover, ICCJ does not feature a principle of justice (only principles of autonomy and beneficence) and, as such, differs from an account of fairness that incorporates the notion of justice.

Notes

1 Main parts of this chapter were previously published with open access in Kiener, Maximilian (2021) "Consenting Under Third-Party Coercion", The Journal of Moral Philosophy 19, 361–389.
2 Thus, in this chapter, I will not consider forms of 'minor coercion' or influences other than illegitimate and severe threats. Cf. Dougherty (2021).
3 Note that this second set of claims does not reverse the correct explanatory order. I do not claim that the permissibility of tattooing explains the validity of consent. Rather, I only aim show that, *once* we accept that tattooing is permissible, it follows that consent must have been valid too.
4 I say 'normally' as there are some exceptional cases in which the wronging temporarily coincides with acting on invalid consent. I will discuss such a case (*Envelope*) later in this chapter.

5 To clarify: I here mean *Recipient* acting on consent, for example, by executing the tattoo.

6 Including 'others' is important as helping Victim may sometimes impose unreasonable costs on others, and not Recipient. If so, Recipient is not required to help.

7 Demanding views could hold that one is obliged to help as long as one does not sacrifice something of (comparable) moral significance (Singer, 1972, 2010) or does not jeopardise one's own prospects for a minimally flourishing life (Fabre, 2006, chs. 1 and 2). Less demanding views may only require to accept moderate costs (Barry & Øverland, 2013), only a slight sacrifice (Scanlon, 1998, p. 224), or no genuine costs at all (cf. Ferzan, 2017).

8 For instance, is there a *sui generis* duty of justice (Miller, 2020) or a duty from a implicit social contract (Valentini, 2015)?

9 See Fabre (2006, ch. 2); Ferzan (2017); Whelan (1991).

10 I do not talk about a duty of beneficence because beneficence, unlike rescue, is too broad. As Beauchamp (2019) explains, beneficence is understood 'to include effectively all norms, dispositions, and actions with the goal of benefiting or promoting the good of other persons'. Yet, in cases like *Mischievous*, the situation is much more specific and closer to situations of rescuing, that is, helping someone escape an immediate peril.

11 Many think that the correlation with a claim-right makes a duty perfect rather than imperfect. See, for instance, O'Neill (1990, p. 189). On the difference between perfect and imperfect duties more generally, see Rainbolt (2000); Schroeder (2014).

12 Note that proponents of the *Influence-Focus-View*, who are likely to challenge my view with *Envelope*, already accept that there are two distinct wrongs in such cases. See Millum (2014). Thus, I here only rely on an assumption that my opponents share too.

13 For these reasons, my view also gives a different explanation for why there was invalid consent in Dougherty's case *False Fear*, discussed at the end of Chapter 4, where Ally consented to Leo using her bread-making machine only because she falsely believed that she would otherwise face retaliation. In my view, consent is invalid, not because Leo's conduct fails to be an 'extension' of Ally's agency but rather because, in acting on consent, Leo would deny Ally an alternative to acting on consent, which would also allow Ally to avoid the (falsely) perceived harm and not impose an unreasonable cost on him.

References

Appelbaum, P. S., Lidz, C. W., & Klitzman, R. (2009). Voluntariness of consent to research: A conceptual model. *Hastings Center Report, 39*(1), 30–39.

Barry, C., & Øverland, G. (2013). How much for the child? *Ethical Theory and Moral Practice, 16*(1), 189–204.

Beauchamp, T. (2019). The principle of beneficence in applied ethics. In *The Stanford encyclopedia of philosophy*. Retrieved from https://plato.stanford.edu

Bennett, C. (2018). The alteration thesis: Forgiveness as a normative power. *Philosophy & Public Affairs, 46*(2), 207–233. doi:10.1111/papa.12117.

Darwall, S. (2006). *The second-person standpoint: Morality, respect, and accountability*. Cambridge, MA: Harvard University Press.

Dougherty, T. (2015). Yes means yes: Consent as communication. *Philosophy & Public Affairs, 43*(3), 224–253.

Dougherty, T. (2019). Why does duress undermine consent? *Noûs, 55*(2), 317–333. doi:10.1111/nous.12313.

Dougherty, T. (2021). Sexual misconduct on a scale: Gravity, coercion, and consent. *Ethics, 131*(2), 319–344.

Fabre, C. (2006). *Whose body is it anyway? Justice and the integrity of the person*. Oxford: Oxford University Press.

Feinberg, J. (1986). *The moral limits of the criminal law. Volume 3: Harm to self*. New York: Oxford University Press.

Ferzan, K. K. (2017). Omissions, acts, and the duty to rescue. In D. K. Nelkin & S. C. Rickless (Eds.), *The ethics and law of omissions* (pp. 217–234). New York: Oxford University Press.

Ferzan, K. K. (2018). Consent and coercion. *Arizona State Law Journal, 50*, 951.

Gerver, M. (2021). Consent and third-party coercion. *Ethics, 131*(2), 246–269.

Kiener, M. (2020). Coercion. In *The Routledge encyclopedia of philosophy*. Retrieved from https://www.rep.routledge.com

Kiener, M. (2021). Consenting under third-party coercion. *Journal of Moral Philosophy, 19*, 361–389.

Mayr, E. (2019). Blame for constitutivists: Kantian constitutivism and the victim's special standing to complain. *Philosophical Explorations, 22*(2), 117–129.

Miller, D. (2020). The nature and limits of the duty of rescue. *Journal of Moral Philosophy, 17*(3), 320–341.

Miller, F., & Wertheimer, A. (2010). Preface to a theory of consent transactions: Beyond valid consent. In F. Miller & A. Wertheimer (Eds.), *The ethics of consent: Theory and practice* (pp. 79–105). New York: Oxford University Press.

Millum, J. (2014). Consent under pressure: The puzzle of third party coercion. *Ethical Theory and Moral Practice, 17*(1), 113–127.

Nagel, T. (1986). *The view from nowhere*. New York; Oxford: Oxford University Press.

Nelson, R. M., Beauchamp, T., Miller, V. A., Reynolds, W., Ittenbach, R. F., & Luce, M. F. (2011). The concept of voluntary consent. *American Journal of Bioethics, 11*(8), 6–16.

O'Neill, O. (1990). *Constructions of reason: Explorations of Kant's practical philosophy*. Cambridge: Cambridge University Press.

Owens, D. (2012). *Shaping the normative landscape*. Oxford: Oxford University Press.

Rainbolt, G. (2000). Perfect and imperfect obligations. *Philosophical Studies, 98*(3), 233–256.

Scanlon, T. (1998). *What we owe to each other*. Cambridge, MA: Belknap Press of Harvard University Press.

Schaber, P. (2018). Consent and wronging a person. In P. Schaber & A. Müller (Eds.), *The Routledge handbook of the ethics of consent* (pp. 55–64). Abingdon, Oxon; New York, NY: Routledge.

Schroeder, S. A. (2014). Imperfect duties, group obligations, and beneficence. *Journal of Moral Philosophy, 11*(5), 557–584.

Singer, P. (1972). Famine, affluence, and morality. *Philosophy & Public Affairs, 1*(3), 229–243.

Singer, P. (2010). *The life you can save: How to play your part in ending world poverty*. London: Picador.

Tadros, V. (2016). *Wrongs and crimes*. Oxford: Oxford University Press.
Thompson, M. (2004). What is it to wrong someone? A puzzle about justice. In R. J. Wallace, P. Pettit, S. Scheffler, & M. Smith (Eds.), *Reason and value themes from the moral philosophy of Joseph Raz* (pp. 333–384). Oxford: Clarendon Press.
Valentini, L. (2015). Social Samaritan justice: When and why needy fellow citizens have a right to assistance. *American Political Science Review, 109*(4), 735–749.
Wallace, R. J. (2014). Emotions and relationships. In D. Shoemaker & N. Tognazzini (Eds.), *Oxford studies in agency and responsibility, Volume 2: 'Freedom and resentment' at 50* (pp. 119–142). Oxford: Oxford University Press.
Wertheimer, A. (1996). *Exploitation*. Princeton: Princeton University Press.
Wertheimer, A. (2010). *Rethinking the ethics of clinical research: Widening the lens*. New York; Oxford: Oxford University Press.
Wertheimer, A. (2012). The obligations of researchers amidst injustice or deprivation. In J. Millum & E. J. Emanuel (Eds.), *Global justice and bioethics* (pp. 279–304). New York; Oxford: Oxford University Press.
Whelan, J. M. (1991). Charity and the duty to rescue. *Social Theory and Practice, 17*(3), 441–456.

Part 3

The Practice of Voluntary Consent

7 Nudging and Manipulation

Introduction

In 2021, it was reported that about thirty-eight million people are infected with HIV. Yet, many of them are unaware of their status and unable to ensure they do not spread the disease or even just protect their own health (UNAIDS, 2021). Unfortunately, in some regions of the world, still far too few people consent to HIV screening, and with each passing day people die (Thornton, 2008). So, how could we increase HIV screening and thereby save lives? [1]

Montoy and colleagues (Montoy, Dow, & Kaplan, 2018) highlighted a powerful response. They no longer asked patients whether they wanted to have HIV screening on top of their other blood tests. They just made HIV screening the default option. But this change from an opt-in system ('you can have the test if you like') to an opt-out system ('you will be tested unless you decline', where declining only required a brief 'no') had a considerable effect: it increased testing by almost 24%, more than any of the financial incentives commonly used (Montoy et al., 2018). Other studies have found an even greater impact of such default settings (cf. Johnson & Goldstein, 2003).

On the one hand, Montoy's default setting seems innocuous. Montoy neither changed the set of options, nor did he make any option more costly to choose. In addition, *something* had to be the default option, and if one of those options could have such positive effects, choosing it seems to be justified on grounds of beneficence.

On the other hand, Montoy's default setting seems problematic. The reason why 24% of people, who would otherwise *not* have consented, eventually consented was not because they had better reasons to do so. Montoy took advantage of a feature of their psyche called the *status quo bias*, that is, people's inherent tendency to accept the default option rather than deviate from it (cf. Dean, Kıbrıs, & Masatlioglu, 2017; Kahneman & Tversky, 1972; McKenzie, Liersch, & Finkelstein, 2006). Although consent was not irrational, it was certainly arational in the sense that the reason for it (i.e. that they were simply too lazy to depart from the default) could no longer count as a justification, even from their own

DOI: 10.4324/9781003301417-10

point of view. Hence, Montoy targeted people's psychology rather than engaging in an open discussion. He steered them in a particular direction.

Montoy's case illustrates a serious challenge for consent. Often, people make medical decisions that are regrettable for some reason: for example, they decide not to undergo what is in their interests and conducive to public health (e.g. HIV screening, vaccination), they decide not to undergo optimal medical treatment, they decide not to enrol in clinical trials that are urgently needed for scientific progress, or they decide not to allow junior doctors to examine them, whose training may be impeded as a result.

However, in all these cases, people could be subtly influenced into making a different decision. Fifty years of behavioural psychology have revealed several ways to exploit different mechanisms in people's psyches. Most recently, Thaler and Sunstein developed what they call 'nudging' to explain how people's decision-making can be influenced without resorting to either rational persuasion or coercion.

But this situation creates an urgent question: do people still voluntarily consent to a medical procedure if others harness their psychological mechanisms or flaws? Answering this question is critical. We cannot afford to leave to chance how people's decision-making will be affected, given how effective and ubiquitous those influences are. We need to protect people's autonomy, particularly in a medical context where people are already vulnerable and, vis-à-vis medical professionals, find themselves in relations of great asymmetry. But we also need to explore the great potential which influences like Montoy's provide, that is, the potential to save lives.

In this chapter, I will argue that my proposal, ICCJ, provides the correct approach to the assessment of nudging and manipulation. More specifically, my main objective will be to argue for ICCJ's specific principles of *Assisted Decision-Making*, *Equal Moral Standing*, and *Trusted Partner*. I will show that the correct assessment of nudging and manipulation leads to these exact principles, and in so doing, I will add a further key component in my support of ICCJ.

But before I proceed, a few clarifications are in order. Firstly, and as before, I will assume that when an influence invalidates consent – in other words, vitiates consent – consent no longer renders the performance of a medical procedure permissible. More specifically, without valid consent, performing a medical procedure would wrong the patient, for example, by amounting to battery, assault, or (as it can be the case in legal proceedings) negligence.

Secondly, I will continue to focus on only one condition of valid consent, namely *voluntariness*, that is, the condition that requires a consenter's decision to be sufficiently free from external control, for example, coercion, and potentially also from internal impediments such as addiction. Voluntariness itself is a *necessary* condition of valid consent and only provides sufficient conditions for valid consent together with the requirements of competence (i.e. the possession of certain mental capacities) and information (i.e. being informed about relevant details of a medical procedure).

Finally, I will rely on a rather wide notion of 'nudging', or what I will also call 'non-persuasive influences'. What I have in mind is close to what Beauchamp and Childress (2013) call 'manipulation', or what Blumenthal-Barby (2012) calls 'non-argumentative' influences. I will assume that these influences are characterised, negatively speaking, by the fact that they are *neither* rational persuasion *nor* coercion and, positively speaking, by the fact that they trigger certain psychological mechanisms such as biases, heuristics, or mental shortcuts. I consider this wide approach important to capture the great variety of non-persuasive influences that exist and avoid cutting the debate short by a definitional stop.

7.1 The Conditions of Easy Resistibility, Transparency, and Rationality

The main ethical concern about permissible nudging has been whether nudging undermines the influenced person's autonomy. Whereas some deny that it does by pointing out how nudges can preserve substantial freedom of choice (Saghai, 2013), others are more sceptical and claim that the influenced person's decision-making will often be subverted (Ploug & Holm, 2015). However, most scholars neither fully reject nor embrace nudging. Rather, they claim that nudging is permissible (and autonomy-preserving) under certain specific conditions. Amidst the numerous proposals, the debate has moved towards a set of three key conditions: easily resistibility, transparency, and rationality.

Easy Resistibility

Thaler and Sunstein claimed that nudges 'must be easy and cheap to avoid' (2009, p. 6), thereby providing the basis of what has now been developed into a two-part condition of easy resistibility. There is firstly a straightforward or *resilience-based* interpretation of easy resistibility: a nudge is resistible if and only if the person influenced does not experience psychological pressure beyond a certain low threshold, and therefore, acting against this influence does not require special fortitude, resilience, or other mental effort. Secondly, scholars also proposed a *skill-based* interpretation: a nudge is easily resistible on this understanding if and only if one does not need any special psychological skills to resist it (Saghai, 2013). This interpretation is relevant because, on some occasions, resisting a nudge requires psychological expertise on how such a nudge works and how it could be resisted, for example, in cases of subliminal advertising. Whereas some thought that this requirement of easy resistibility can indeed be met by some or even many nudges (Blumenthal-Barby & Burroughs, 2012; Engelen, 2019a, 2019b; Saghai, 2013), others were more sceptical about nudges ever being easily resistible in the relevant sense (Bovens, 2009, pp. 209–210; Hausman & Welch, 2010, p. 128; Wilkinson, 2013, p. 345). Yet, on both sides of the debate, people accepted easy resistibility as condition of permissible nudging.

Transparency

In addition, many emphasised the significance of transparency. For instance, Hansen and Jespersen claim that 'the distinction between transparent and non-transparent nudges ... serves as a basis for distinguishing the manipulative use of nudges from other types of uses' (2013, p. 6), and Bovens even argues that 'every Nudge should be such that it is in principle possible for everyone who is watchful to unmask the manipulation' (2009, p. 217). Admittedly, there is still controversy over what exact type of transparency is required (e.g. transparency about every particular nudge, transparency about nudging being generally practised, or transparency about the intention behind the nudging) and also about whether nudging can ever be sufficiently transparent. Yet, both proponents of nudging (Blumenthal-Barby & Burroughs, 2012, pp. 347, 357; Engelen, 2019a, p. 52; Ivanković & Engelen, 2019; Schmidt, 2019, p. 533) and critics of nudging (Calo, 2013, p. 795; Dubov, 2015, p. 497; Greenspan, 2003, p. 163; Grüne-Yanoff & Hertwig, 2016, p. 177; Hausman & Welch, 2010; Wilkinson, 2013) accept some form of transparency as a condition of permissible nudging.

Rationality

Finally, scholars have argued for a condition of rationality. Schmidt argues that 'nudging not only is compatible with rational agency but can even support it' (2019, p. 511), whereas Conly criticises nudging precisely on the grounds that when we nudge other people, 'rather than regarding people as generally capable of making good choices, we outmanoeuvre them by appealing to their irrationality' (2013, p. 30). Most scholars have focused on a condition of *process* rationality rather than *outcome* rationality. A person demonstrates process rationality if and only if the 'decision-making procedure should yield accurate results somewhat reliably and not just accidentally' (Schmidt, 2019, p. 512). By contrast, a person demonstrates outcome rationality if and only if, as a matter of fact, he ends up doing what a rational person would do. Whether the process leading to that result was rational, too, is immaterial to outcome rationality. As in the case of transparency, the correct view on rationality and its relation to nudging has remained controversial. Yet, both proponents of nudging (Cohen, 2013, p. 5; Engelen, 2019b; Hanna, 2015, pp. 622–624; Hansen & Jespersen, 2013, pp. 14–15; Houk, DiSilvestro, & Jensen, 2016, p. 21; Schmidt, 2019, p. 511) and critics of nudging (Conly, 2013, p. 30; Grüne-Yanoff, 2012, pp. 636–637; Hausman & Welch, 2010, p. 134; Ploug & Holm, 2015, pp. 34–37) accept some form of rationality requirement as a condition of permissible nudging, that is, a requirement that, roughly, nudging should neither subvert a person's procedural rationality nor exploit already existing irrationality.

These debates on easy resistibility, transparency, and rationality have provided rich resources for any ethical inquiry of nudging. However, scholars have mostly focused on public policy and the general permissibility of nudging, giving short shrift to the more specific question about how nudging affects the validity of people's medical consent. So, to what extent can the three conditions help us assess the validity or, more specifically, the voluntariness of medical consent too? In other words, to what extent can we use a *general* theory of nudging, based on these three conditions, to model a *specific* theory of nudging, tasked to explain the voluntariness of medical consent?

7.2 The Three Conditions Applied to Questions of Voluntary Consent

In what follows, I shall devise two cases to challenge the three conditions of easy resistibility, transparency, and rationality. The first case, *Racial Bias*, will suggest that the three conditions are not necessary to guarantee voluntary consent, whereas the second case, *TV Bully*, will suggest that they are not sufficient either.

Case 1: Racial Bias

Betty is diagnosed with early-stage cervical cancer. Her physician, who happens to be Black, recommends surgery, which would almost certainly cure her. Yet, Betty refuses and says, 'Anyone knows that people with cancer are sick, feel bad, and lose weight' and adds that, as a matter of fact, she feels very well. She continues to believe that she is healthy despite clear evidence to the contrary. Betty's disbelief in the diagnosis is further reinforced by a strong racial bias that prevents her from trusting a Black doctor (Faden & Faden, 1977).

In this case, Betty relies on a 'representative heuristic': since she does not look and feel like the typical ill patient, she does not believe that she is ill (Krawczyk & Rachubik, 2019). Moreover, Betty is subject to a severe form of 'confirmation bias', which means 'that information is searched for, interpreted, and remembered in such a way that it systematically impedes the possibility that the hypothesis could be rejected' (Oswald & Grosjean, 2004, p. 80). Betty's 'hypothesis' is a deep racial bias, that is, the view that Black people are neither intelligent nor trustworthy on medical matters. To confirm this view, she interprets her doctor's statement as false and prioritises her own feeling of being healthy. Finally, Betty may even have been subject to what has been described as the 'backfire effect': the more her physician presents evidence contrary to what she believes, the more she clings on to her own mistaken beliefs (Nyhan & Reifler, 2013).

So far, the story is true. But now, let us go beyond the facts and stipulate that Betty has a second, even stronger confirmation bias. Suppose Betty has the firm belief that white men belonging to her religious community are almost infallible. As a result, and to confirm her high opinion of these white men, Betty will consider statements from them always true and authoritative.

Suppose Betty's physician knows this and therefore asks a nurse, who is a white man and belongs to Betty's religious community, to tell her that she needs to take the medical evidence very seriously, but nothing more. The nurse should only talk about the significance of the evidence and make clear that, based on *this* information, Betty should then make her own decision about whether to undergo surgery. Here, the nurse triggers Betty's second confirmation bias, silences the effects of the previous representative heuristic, and thereby exerts a clear non-persuasive influence. Yet, *none* of the aforementioned three conditions would be satisfied in this case.

Transparency: Betty is not at all aware that the medical team arranged the situation to exploit her confirmation bias and make her appreciate the medical evidence.

Easy Resistibility: The lack of transparency prevents Betty from becoming aware of the influence and triggering her propensity to act against it. Moreover, Betty is so indoctrinated and biased that she would believe or do almost anything that the nurse tells her.

Rationality: Betty lacks process rationality: her deliberation is not a reliable procedure by which to arrive at a rational decision. Even on the least demanding accounts of process rationality, that is, the views claiming that the 'decision-making procedure should yield accurate results *somewhat reliably* and not just accidentally' (Schmidt, 2019, p. 521, emphasis added), Betty's deliberation will be procedurally irrational. Trusting a person because of their sex, skin colour, and membership of a religious community is not at all a reliable procedure in medical matters. It is only in these manipulated circumstances that her bias will lead to an acceptable result. Therefore, even if Betty displays outcome rationality, that is, appreciating the evidence is what a rational person would do, the nurse's influence induced a specific kind of (procedural) irrationality in a major part of her deliberation.

Hence, if one relies on the three main conditions from the literature, at least in the general versions I referred to, the influence on Betty will come out as clearly impermissible, and if these conditions are also applied to determine the validity of consent, the influence on Betty will have to be seen as invalidating her consent too. However, this conclusion is too hasty. We should distinguish at least two variants of *Racial Bias*.

In variant 1, and contrary to what the medical team intended, the impact of the nurse's influence does not stop at making Betty appreciate the evidence. Betty thinks that the nurse also required her to consent. As a result, Betty completely defers to the perceived authority of the nurse and consents to the procedure without deliberating herself. Betty's decision may be *in accordance with* the available evidence but not *because of* the evidence. In such a case, I concede, Betty's consent may be non-autonomous and invalid.

However, the situation could be different. Suppose, in variant 2, and aligning with what the medical team intended, the impact of the nurse's influence *does* stop at making Betty appreciate the evidence. Betty realises that appreciating the evidence is all the nurse wants her do and that she is free to make her own decision about whether to consent. In fact, after being nudged into considering the evidence in this non-transparent, irresistible, and irrationality-exploiting way, Betty suddenly sees that she has missed something extremely important, realises how stubborn she has been, and is now determined to base her decision on the available medical facts. Thus, the nurse's influence shaped Betty's perception of the situation only up to this point of enlightenment. From there onwards, the nurse's influence loses its grip on Betty's decision-making, and Betty is solely guided by her recognition of the available evidence. As a result, when Betty eventually consents, she consents not only *in accordance with* the evidence (as in variant 1) but also *because of* the evidence.

Thus, the nurse's influence can no longer sufficiently explain why Betty consented. To explain Betty's consent, we need to refer, unlike in variant 1, to Betty's own deliberation about the medical facts and how surgery will cure her disease. Exploiting Betty's confirmation bias only enabled her to appreciate critical evidence but left her free to make any decision she wanted. It enabled Betty to deliberate over how to protect her values and interests but did not unduly control her decision-making about whether to consent. For these reasons, Betty's consent is still a valuable expression of her autonomy, and the subsequent performance of the surgery will not amount to battery or assault. But if so, consent must have been voluntary and valid too, despite the fact that the nurse's influence, which pushed Betty into focusing on a specific set of considerations and without which Betty would not have consented, was still non-transparent, irresistible, and irrationality-exploiting.[2]

Thus, the three conditions, if applied to consent, deliver the wrong result: an influence can violate them all, yet still not invalidate consent. (From here onwards, I will only refer to variant 2 of *Racial Bias*.)

However, one may object that Betty was not nudged in the relevant sense after all. She was nudged into *considering the evidence* but not nudged into *consenting*, and it is only nudging into consenting that is relevant here. This objection makes an important point. There is indeed a relevant difference between influencing people into considering evidence and influencing people into consenting, and I will address this point explicitly in due course. However, we should not discard the influence on Betty as irrelevant at this early point in our inquiry, both because a person's perception of the evidence is an important part in her motivation to consent and because some nudges into considering evidence (as opposed to nudges into consenting) can invalidate consent. For instance, suppose a physician nudges his patient into considering certain pieces of the evidence by making them very salient to her while ensuring that other evidence is less salient. In this case, the physician would also not directly nudge the patient into consenting but rather only nudge her into considering the evidence in a certain way. Yet, the nudge would not be unproblematic and would be capable of invalidating subsequent consent.[3] Hence, the nudge on Betty remains within the ambit of influences that a satisfactory view has to account for.

Case 2: TV Bully

Alan is publicly known for claiming that people are morally obliged to serve as volunteers in clinical research. Yet, Alan himself has never participated in a trial himself because he is highly averse to undergoing medical procedures. Clinical investigator Carl harbours a grudge against Alan for that reason and wants to end Alan's (as he sees it) hypocritical behaviour. To do so, Carl decides to surprise Alan during a TV interview. Unbeknownst to Alan, Carl arranges matters so that they will both appear on a particular live show. When the moment comes, Carl confronts Alan in front of the audience and asks him to participate in his clinical trial, a situation which will likely cause Alan embarrassment if he declines. Under the heat of the studio lights and the audience's expectations, Alan declares that he will participate.

Carl employs a number of non-persuasive influences. To begin with, he exploits what is called the spotlight effect, that is, people's tendency to overestimate how much attention they receive from others (Gilovich 2000), by asking Alan *during a TV interview*. Moreover, Carl also relies on the hot–cold empathy gap in Alan, that is, the tendency to underestimate how much one's decision in a situation of agitation differs from what it would be if made with a relaxed state of mind (Loewenstein 2005), by creating a situation of surprise and potential embarrassment and asking Alan to make an immediate decision during the interview. In addition, Carl plays on the affect heuristic, that is, people's tendency to act in ways that produce pleasant rather than unpleasant feelings (Barnhill, 2014, p. 56; Slovic, Finucane, Peters, & MacGregor, 2007), by giving him the opportunity to win the audience's approval rather than their disappointment.

Carl's various non-persuasive influences make Alan consent to participate in the trial. Note, however, that Carl does not change the incentive structure. He does not make not consenting to participating in the trial more costly for Alan because the public, let us assume, would have expected Alan to make a decision about his own trial participation in the coming weeks anyway. Carl simply pushed Alan in a carefully crafted environment designed to nudge him into consenting.

So understood, this case can satisfy the three aforementioned conditions.

Transparency. Let us assume that Alan knows Carl very well. He immediately recognises what Carl is doing when they both meet on TV, as well as which exact influences Carl is employing. Hence, Carl's influences are all fully token-transparent, to use Boven's expression, and such token transparency seems to be *the* or at least *one* of the most demanding types of transparency discussed in the literature on nudging.

Rationality. Although the array of Carl's non-persuasive influences will have an arational impact on Alan's decision-making, Alan is aware of them, reflects on whether to follow the push of these influences, and thereby arrives at his decision in a way that is a sufficiently reliable procedure for a rational decision. Thus, Alan's decision-making will still 'yield accurate results somewhat reliably and not just accidentally' (Schmidt, 2019, p. 512).

Easy Resistibility. But is Carl's influence really easily resistible? Admittedly, the average person may, in fact, *not* be able to resist an influence like Carl's easily as doing so seems to require great psychological effort, given how much pressure one might feel during a public TV interview. However, the situation could be different for Alan. Suppose Alan is a seasoned interviewee who knows how to dodge questions. Although Alan consents, perhaps partly because he is tired after a long day and does not want to displease his opponent, Carl, once again, he still has the ability to manoeuvre his way out of those nudges relatively easily and decline to participate or refuse to make a decision during the interview.

Hence, in this scenario, the three conditions are all satisfied and, therefore, the traditional view suggests that Carl's nudging was permissible. Moreover, if applied to consent, the traditional view also suggests that Alan's consent remains perfectly valid. But these judgements are wrong. To begin with, Carl still *illegitimately influenced* Alan. Carl *influenced* Alan by deliberately crafting the context in which Alan eventually decided to consent, and this context, namely, the range of non-persuasive influences, happened to play a key causal role in the events leading to Alan's consent. Such influence is *illegitimate* because, firstly, it still amounts to manipulation in the morally pejorative sense which Noggle and others think is characteristic of manipulation more generally, that is, it decreases the quality of the target's decision-making (Noggle, 1996, 2020).[4] Carl decreases the quality of Alan's decision-making by (i) subjecting Alan to arational influences which he would otherwise be free from and the sole purpose of which is to promote Carl's interests over Alan's, and (ii) by cutting short Alan's process of deliberation: in the absence of Carl's intervention, Alan would have taken more time to think about the matter and may have figured out an even better solution to avoid participating without incurring public embarrassment.

Secondly, Carl's influence is also illegitimate because it is essentially a trap. Carl went behind Alan's back to arrange the situation so as to surprise Alan on live TV. Although the nudges themselves were fully token-transparent when they happened, Carl did not tell Alan about his intentions before the interview and tricked him into a situation designed to make him consent.

Finally, Carl's influence is illegitimate because he violates a professional obligation that clinical investigators owe their prospective volunteers. Investigators like Carl are obliged to respect people's autonomy in making medical decisions, which requires that they promote or at least not sabotage people's decision-making as Carl did. Particularly in the context of clinical research, where medical procedures hold no medical benefit for those participating in a trial, respect for autonomy is especially important and implies, at a minimum, an especially strong negative duty not to interfere with a person's autonomous decision-making (Berg & Applebaum, 2001, p. 279; Boddington, 2012, p. 178; Nelson-Marten & Rich, 1999, p. 81; Pellegrino, 1992).

Hence, the traditional view that the three conditions are sufficient to rule out impermissible nudging is mistaken. Whatever else we may think about *TV Bully*, Carl acts wrongly in nudging Alan and is therefore liable to, at least, certain disciplinary sanctions.

But the problem with the traditional view is not just that it fails to identify impermissible nudging. It also fails to identify consent-invalidating nudging. This is because Carl not only illegitimately influences Alan, he also – more specifically – renders Alan's consent *invalid*, or at least this is what two plausible approaches to consent suggest. To begin with, David Owens claimed that influences invalidate consent when they *wrong* the consenter (Owens, 2007, 2012, chs. 2 and 7), and let us assume that we can understand 'wronging' here with the needed qualifications as developed in Chapter 5 (i.e. wrong due to the exertion of pressure). In *TV Bully*, Carl wrongs Alan in the relevant consent-invalidating way by violating the negative duty not to sabotage Alan's decision-making. This is a very significant duty in medical contexts and fundamental to the relationship between clinical investigators and prospective trial participants. Thus, on a plausible view of consent, Alan's consent is invalid.

Moreover, in his contractual theory, Samuel Pufendorf claimed that consent is invalid if the recipient 'disqualified' himself in the process of obtaining that consent (Pufendorf, 1998; Liber III Cap VI: §X–XI).[5] 'Disqualification' means the violation of a norm that is constitutive of the role one occupies in receiving another person's consent. In *TV Bully*, Carl receives Alan's consent in his role as a clinical investigator. Yet, in the very process of obtaining that consent, Carl violates norms central to this role, namely, he violates the aforementioned negative duty not to sabotage people's decision-making and thereby 'disqualifies' himself as a recipient of Alan's consent. Thus, in Pufendorf's view too, Alan's consent to Carl is invalid.

Hence, on two plausible views concerning invalid consent, that is, an adjusted version of Owen's wronging view and Pufendorf's disqualification view, Carl not only illegitimately influenced Alan, he also invalidated Alan's consent. Therefore, the three conditions seem to deliver the wrong result again: they can all be satisfied, yet consent is still invalid.

Yet, I admit that, in some contexts outside medicine, consent could be classified as voluntary even if obtained by the means Carl employed. But it seems reasonable to set the threshold higher in the medical context, given the importance we attach to our bodily integrity and the special obligations of medical professionals.

Potential Response to Racial Bias *and* TV Bully

Thus, I have now presented two examples, *Racial Bias* and *TV Bully*, which were designed to put pressure on the three conditions, that is, easy resistibility, transparency, and rationality. The first example, *Racial Bias*, suggested that the three conditions are not necessary to guarantee voluntary consent, whereas the second example, *TV Bully*, suggested that they are not sufficient either. However, these two examples are complex and far from the ordinary. For this reason, they are not meant as decisive arguments against the three conditions. I only use them as test cases, designed to reassess the three conditions in certain ways. But can the three conditions be rescued for the assessment of voluntary consent?

Transparency

When discussing nudging in public policy, Thaler and Sunstein argued that, at least *hypothetically* speaking, governments must be prepared to justify their nudging practices in public (2009, p. 243ff). Building on this thought, a modified transparency condition might opt for a disjunctive view, requiring an influence to be either actually transparent *or* such that, *hypothetically* speaking, it *could* be made transparent and thereby justified to those affected by it. Thus, to defend transparency, one could introduce *hypothetical* transparency as a further and – for the validity of consent – sufficient requirement.

This view seems to be promising as a way of accommodating our intuitive response to *Racial Bias*: even though the medical team did not actually make their influence transparent to Betty, they could – hypothetically speaking – later do so and justify it to Betty on the grounds that it assisted Betty in pursuing her own conception of the good. So understood, the influence on Betty satisfies the requirement of (hypothetical) transparency and accounts for my first case, *Racial Bias*.

But this response comes at a cost. What matters in the end is not the possibility of making the influence *transparent* but rather whether, in so doing, one could also *justify* it, and in particular justify it *to Betty* and in terms of Betty's own values. So, it is this (interpersonal) justification, and not transparency, that is doing the actual normative work and determines whether the influence invalidates consent. If anything, transparency could be a *test* (for interpersonal justification): since only suitably justifiable influences could be made transparent to Betty without her feeling legitimate resentment, we can use hypothetical transparency as a test to separate justifiable from unjustifiable influences.

A similar conclusion, namely that it is not transparency that is doing the actual normative work, seems to arise when considering my other example, *TV Bully*. Here, Carl's influences are actually and fully transparent. Yet, such transparency does not speak in favour of Carl's influence being permissible, or compatible with Alan's voluntary consent. Here, transparency only *excludes* other potential problems associated with *non*-transparency, for example, problems of deceit. Thus, in *TV Bully*, transparency seems to be best understood not as a condition of permissibility of voluntary consent itself but rather as a way of ensuring that certain other problems do not arise. I therefore conclude that transparency, although still significant, should not be seen as a genuine condition of valid consent. Rather, in its hypothetical form, it is a *test* for justifiability; and in its actual form, it *excludes* certain other challenges to valid consent. So understood, we can rescue the significance of transparency while at the same time accounting for the intuitively correct assessment of my two examples.

Rationality

What about rationality? Is there a way to defend it as a condition of influences preserving valid consent? To answer this question, I will first need to outline three striking differences between *Racial Bias* and *TV Bully*.

(1) In *Racial Bias*, the influence on Betty targeted her appreciation of the evidence, as opposed to her decision to consent. Thus, the influence may have made Betty's deliberation about why she should consider the evidence irrational, but it did not make Betty's subsequent deliberation about whether to consent in any way irrational. After all, she consented for correctly appreciated health reasons. By contrast, the influence on Alan directly targeted his decision to consent rather than his appreciation of already existing evidence.

(2) In *Racial Bias*, the influence did not make Betty's deliberation worse than it would *otherwise* have been. In any case, Betty would have been subject to the confirmation bias in one way or another. By contrast, in *TV Bully*, Carl's influences made Alan's deliberation subject to certain psychological heuristics and biases that would otherwise *not* have affected his decision.

(3) In *Racial Bias*, the influence supported Betty in pursuing only her own conception of the good, that is, by enabling her to make a decision in light of all the relevant facts together with her own individual values. Thus, Betty's rationality was fully in service of her own ends. By contrast, in *TV Bully*, Alan's rationality was put to the service of Carl's ends. The influences changed the situation so that Alan's procedural rationality would inevitably promote Carl's goal of trial recruitment too. Thus, in some way, these influences hijacked Alan's rationality.

On the basis of these three differences, one could modify the rationality requirement so that it will be met in *Racial Bias* and violated in *TV Bully*. This modified rationality requirement would hold that an influence invalidates consent if it (i) controls the decision to consent, as opposed to the appreciation of correct and balanced evidence, (ii) renders the subject's reasoning (considerably) less rational than it would otherwise have been, and (iii) forces a subject's procedural rationality into serving other people's ends at the expense of his own. So understood, the influence on Betty does not violate this requirement, whereas the influences on Alan do. Hence, in this suggested modified version, the rationality requirement can successfully deal with my examples of *Racial Bias* and *TV Bully* and therefore be potentially retained as an actual condition for influences preserving valid consent.

This modified rationality condition is a novel addition to the ethics of nudging. Yet, aspect (ii) has also a possible basis in the existing literature, at least if we classify the various rationality objections against nudging into two different groups.[6] On the one hand, scholars argued that nudging *subverts* rationality. For instance, it was held that nudging 'perverts decision-making' (Wilkinson, 2013, p. 349), 'perverts people's rationality and thus makes them less rational' (Engelen, 2019b, p. 206), or 'undercuts people's rational agency' (Schmidt, 2019, p. 515). I take it that the thought here is that nudging induces forms of irrationality in people's decision-making that would otherwise not arise. On the other hand, however, scholars also argued that nudging *exploits* irrationality. For instance, Bovens argued that in cases of nudging 'some pattern of irrationality is being exploited' (2009, p. 209), and Conly holds that, as nudgers, 'rather than regarding people as generally capable of making good choices, we outmanoeuvre them by appealing to their irrationality' (2013, p. 30). I take it that the thought here is *not* that nudging creates *additional* and otherwise non-existing irrationality, but rather that it exploits, harness, or appeals to already existing irrationality in people's decision-making. Although many people gloss over this distinction between subverting and exploiting irrationality, it can be drawn, and since it accounts for the needed clause (ii) in my modified rationality requirement, it is highly morally significant.

Easy Resistibility

Finally, let me test whether the condition of easy resistibility could be defended. At first, this seems very difficult. The condition of easy resistibility did not fare well in my two examples. The influence on Betty was very hard to resist, yet it did not invalidate her consent. By contrast, the influence on Alan was, at least *for him*, easy to resist but still invalidated his consent. Hence, these cases suggest that easy resistibility cannot be made a condition of valid consent.

However, the condition of easy resistibility fares much better in more ordinary cases. For instance, if Alan was not such an experienced interviewee, Carl's influence would have been hard to resist indeed. Here, the lack of easy resistibility would have tracked Carl's influence as consent-invalidating. Moreover, a severe threat, for example, a threat of bodily harm, is often also very hard to resist and a paradigmatic example of an influence that invalidates consent. Thus, *these* cases suggest that easy resistibility can indeed be used when assessing whether a person's consent is valid.

To account for this mixed result, I suggest that easy resistibility should be seen, not as a *condition* for valid consent, but rather as an *imperfect proxy* for something else that is such a condition, namely the absence of illegitimate control. Let me elaborate.

I understand 'illegitimate control' as the exertion of pressure on the consenter that deprives him or her of a fair opportunity to make a free decision. Here are a few examples: someone illegitimately controls the consenter's decision-making and removes a fair opportunity when he renders not consenting costly in a significant way (e.g. by imposing a penalty as in cases of threats), when he exploits the consenter's already existing decisional weakness (e.g. by harnessing the consenter's situation of tiredness, anxiety, agitation, or other similar state) or even creates such a weakness in the first place, when he actively diminishes the consenter's *emotional* capacities for decision-making (e.g. by shaming him for his body in order to obtain consent to cosmetic surgery) (Eyal, 2014), when he actively diminishes the consenter's *cognitive* capacities for decision-making (e.g. by distracting the consenter or appealing to phobic tendencies to obtain consent) (Noggle, 2018, p. 169), or when he excludes the consenter from important parts of the decision-making (e.g. by working on the consenter's unconscious psychological tendencies, as in certain cases of 'priming').

This list of examples of illegitimate control is not exhaustive, yet it still elucidates what illegitimate control comprises. In all of these examples, the influence from the person receiving consent (i.e. the consentee) wrongs the person giving consent (i.e. the consenter) during the process of obtaining consent. By 'wronging' I mean violating a claim that the consenter can make on the conduct of the consentee when the latter obtains his consent. What counts as a wronging therefore depends on the context and, more specifically, the norms governing the relation between the consenter and the consentee. For instance, in the medical context, it is fundamental to the patient–physician relationship that the patient is entitled to respect for his autonomy and promotion of his well-being. Thus, these two principles of respect for autonomy and beneficence can explain why a physician wrongs the patient when he exerts certain influences, for example, penalises, shames, or distracts the patient. I will further elaborate on the relevant principles and claims in the medical context when developing my own view in Section 7.3. At this point, it suffices to leave the elaboration of 'illegitimate control' at this general level, that is, as the exertion of pressure that violates a claim the consenter can make on the conduct of the consentee.

So understood, illegitimate control tracks consent-invalidating influences: in Betty's case, there was no illegitimate control: she was not deprived of fair opportunity to make a free decision about whether to consent, but only enabled to make a decision based on her own value and on the facts. If anything, Betty's standing in the decision-making process has been strengthened. By contrast, in Alan's case, there was illegitimate control: independent of the pressure Alan actually experienced, Carl set up a trap for Alan, made Alan's decision-making worse than it would otherwise have been, and violated an important professional obligation that he has *qua* clinical investigator. Finally, there is also clear illegitimate control in cases of threats, as threats penalise non-compliance and remove options to which the consenter is otherwise entitled.

However, even if illegitimate control is doing the actual normative work in the assessment of valid consent, easy resistibility can still serve as a proxy. This is because, *normally*, influences that are not easy to resist are also those that are likely to usurp too much control over another person's decision-making and thereby exert illegitimate control. Normally, being threatened comes with great pressure, being shamed comes with great pressure, and so on. Yet, the qualification *normally* is important because easy resistibility is only an *imperfect* proxy, as my examples about Betty and Alan show. Hence, the best way to defend the significance of easy resistibility against my two examples is to describe it as an imperfect proxy for illegitimate control.

But note that this conclusion is not restricted to the realm of non-persuasive influences. It can also be supported in the context of other types of influences, for example, threats and offers. To see this, suppose I offer you £1 million in exchange for your sofa and you really need the money to pay your mortgage. Such an offer is very hard to resist as it requires great resilience or insensitivity to financial gain. Yet, other things being equal, your consent to selling the sofa remains voluntary and valid, precisely because my offer did not illegitimately control your decision-making, that is, it did not deprive you of a fair opportunity to make a free decision. Contrast this case with another scenario where I threaten to beat you unless you sell the sofa to me. It may be easier for you to resist this threat than to decline my previous offer. Yet, even if this is the case and you happen to be the person who can resist threats more easily than offers, your consent to selling is forced, involuntary, and can be voided, and this is because the threat of physical harm constitutes the kind of illegitimate control that invalidates a person's consent.[7] Thus, the distinction between resistibility and illegitimate control is of more general importance and should be part of any inquiry into the voluntariness of consent.[8] Therefore, I can reach one further final conclusion: even if a clever reader finds a way to deny that Carl's influence was easily resistible for the seasoned interviewee Alan, this would be a dead end, because it would commit to the false view that easy resistibility determines whether consent is voluntary.

7.3 The Three Conditions Within a Framework of Interpersonal Justification

Thus, suitably modified, the three conditions can still help us assess voluntary consent. Yet, the required modifications are substantial and lead to a rather complicated solution, including many nuanced distinctions and the downgrading of transparency and resistibility from genuine conditions to a mere test and proxy. In this section, I therefore want to account for my results within a simpler and more elegant approach, namely the following: nudging invalidates medical consent if and only if it cannot be *interpersonally justified*. In so doing, I will again defend the core idea behind my proposal, ICCJ, and also, most importantly, use my discussion of nudging to further support the specific principles of ICCJ that I developed in Chapter 3.

Outline of Interpersonal Justification

Let me recapitulate my central ideas behind interpersonal justification. Interpersonal justification, as I understand it, is an adequate reply to the question 'Why is it permissible for *you* (*qua* physician) to obtain consent from *me* (*qua* patient or trial participant) in this way?' To answer this question, the person receiving consent, that is, the physician or trial investigator, needs to show that their influence on the person giving consent is permissible in light of the claims that the person giving consent can make on them *qua* the person receiving consent. Hence, I focus on the interpersonal justification of an influence *from* the person giving consent *to* the person receiving it. But I only require hypothetical justification. It is not necessary for the physician to provide an actual answer to the aforementioned question, or for the patient actually to ask it.

So understood, interpersonal justification contrasts with justification *all things considered*, which is much broader and requires that something is permissible in light of *all the relevant* moral considerations, and not just the claims the person giving consent can make on the conduct of the person receiving consent. Moreover, it is worth noting that interpersonal justification is not a trivial consequence of justification all things considered. It is *not* the case that the physician's conduct will be, firstly, justified on grounds unrelated to the patient and then, only as a consequence, be justifiable to anyone, including the patient. The grounds for interpersonal justification will always be relative to the person consenting and the claims this person can make on the person receiving consent.

The idea of interpersonal justification plays an important role in other philosophical debates. Most importantly, in the debate about contractualism, scholars asked what we *owe to each other* (Scanlon, 1998), thereby also alluding to the aspect of what can be justified *to certain others* rather than justified all things considered. Moreover, philosophers often distinguish between *wrongdoing* and *wronging* (Dougherty, 2015, p. 232; Mayr, 2019, pp. 118–124; Tadros, 2016, p. 201; Thompson, 2004, pp. 333–335) and thereby rely on a similar contrast too: wrongdoing consists in the performance of an action that is impermissible *in light of all the morally relevant facts*, whereas wronging consists in the performance of an action that is impermissible *in light of what is owed to a particular person*, for example, impermissible because it violates a right one owes to that person. Thus, my contrast between interpersonal justification and justification all things considered has a basis in the philosophical literature more generally.

My discussion of nudging leads to this idea of applying interpersonal justification. To begin with, my discussion of transparency explicitly highlighted it. Here, it was key that an influence could not only hypothetically be made transparent but also *justified to the person affected*, that is, *interpersonally justified*. In addition, regarding rationality, I claimed that an influence needs to respect the consenter's entitlement to pursue their own conception of the good. This entitlement is at least partly a claim of non-interference which the consenter can make on the conduct of others, for example, the physician. Therefore, respecting this claim is a means to ensure interpersonal justifiability. Finally, regarding easy resistibility, I argued that easy resistibility is a proxy for the absence of illegitimate control, and I explained that illegitimate control consists in the violation of claims the consenter can make on the conduct of the consentee, that is, those claims that also shape interpersonal justification. Thus, interpersonal justification may be the unifying consideration behind the complicated modifications of the three conditions and lead to a more elegant approach to voluntary consent.

However, to make full use of this idea of interpersonal justification in the assessment of consent, I need to specify it further. What exactly does interpersonal justification require in the context of valid consent? What precisely are the claims the consenter can make on the conduct of the person receiving consent? And what are the principles that need to be satisfied for an influence to be interpersonally justifiable in a way that preserves the validity of consent?

Fortunately, the modified three conditions can provide further guidance on these questions too and thereby explicitly support ICCJ's principles outlined in Chapter 3.

The Principles of Interpersonal Justification

To begin with, my discussion of hypothetical transparency seems to point to a principle of trust. By way of explanation, when we trust another, we can neither spell out the precise terms which the trusted person should act on nor completely control or monitor the trusted person's conduct. In fact, the very point of trust is the reliance on a person's benevolence in situations where we are unable to control or monitor that person. But as

I have explained elsewhere, trust also always comes with the *proviso of hypothetical transparency*:

> Even though a trusting person refrains from 'the precise spelling out of terms' (Greenspan, 2003, p. 161) which the trusted person may operate on, trust always comes with the proviso that the trusted party's relevant actions as well as 'the motives of the trusted party have to be able to be made transparent to the one who extends trust' (Ibid.). This proviso is respected only if full transparency did not lead to the trusting person being justified in feeling resentment or insulted.
> (Kiener, 2018, p. 193)

Hence, acting in ways that could hypothetically be made transparent is a way of honouring a person's trust, and therefore the significance of hypothetical transparency, as I explained earlier, could be accounted for by a wider principle of trust. However, trust not only requires hypothetical transparency. It also requires that the trusted person does not abuse their superior position of power more generally, independently of whether doing so would actually be transparent to the trusting person. Thus, including this further aspect, the modified condition of transparency supports ICCJ's principle of *Trusted Partner*:

> **Trusted Partner:** The medical professional is obliged to honour the consenter's trust, that is, to act in ways which (i) could be made hypothetically transparent without causing justified resentment in the consenter and (ii) do not abuse a superior position of power relative to the consenter.

So understood, *Trusted Partner* allows influences to remain non-transparent as long as transparency would not lead to justified resentment and thereby accounts for my conclusion in Betty's case, but *Trusted Partner* still proscribes even fully transparent influences when they unduly dominate the consenter, that is, it proscribes Carl's influence on Alan, where Carl clearly exploited his superior position of power to dominate Alan's decision. Hence, *Trusted Partner* does not only build on my earlier results on hypothetical transparency but also accounts for the intuitively correct results in my examples. Therefore, we can use it as first pillar in an account of consent and interpersonal justification.

Secondly, in my discussion of the condition of rationality, I claimed that it was key whether an influence forces a person's rationality into serving of other people's ends, or whether it allows a person to pursue their own ends and conception of the good. Building on this insight and being inspired by John Rawls' important work on people's entitlement to pursue a conception of the good, I suggest that my discussion then leads to this second principle of interpersonal justification, which I also already outlined earlier:

Equal Moral Standing: The medical professional is obliged to respect the consenter's entitlement to form, revise, and rationally pursue a conception of the good.

As I explained in Chapter 3, I call this principle *Equal 'Moral' Standing* because it is about people exercising what Rawls calls a *moral power*: the capacity to 'form, revise, and rationally pursue a conception of the good' (2005, p. 30). And I call it *Equal* Moral Standing because it obliges physicians to acknowledge that patients, despite being in an asymmetrical relationship to physicians in other respects, are still on a par with them regarding the entitlement to pursue a conception of the good. So understood, *Equal Moral Standing* builds on the insights from the discussion of rationality and accounts for my earlier results. It captures the fact that, in Alan's case, the influences were problematic because Alan's rationality was pushed into serving other people's interests while also capturing my view in Betty's case that the influence was less problematic because the medical team allowed her to pursue her own values.

Finally, recall my discussion of easy resistibility, where I argued that the psychological impact of an influence alone cannot determine whether an influence invalidates consent. What matters is the presence or absence of illegitimate control. This discussion seems to point to the following third and last principle of interpersonal justification, which I call *Assisted Decision-Making:*

Assisted Decision-Making: The medical professional is obliged not to illegitimately control but only to assist his or her patient's decision-making.

As already explained in Chapter 3, *Assisted Decision-Making* focuses on illegitimate control rather than easy resistibility and thereby builds on my previous conclusions. However, *Assisted Decision-Making* also goes beyond my previous discussion by specifically permitting influences that *assist* a person's decision-making. To assist a patient's decision-making, a medical professional can frame medical information in a way conducive to understanding, actively help the patient to clarify views and options, make recommendations, and even push a patient into considering relevant evidence, as in Betty's case. How much and which assistance is appropriate depends on what a person consents to and the wider circumstances. More serious medical procedures may require greater assistance than less serious procedures would. Moreover, in some cases, assistance may require joint deliberation, whereas in others, for example, emergency cases with little time for a decision, assistance should take the form of a straightforward recommendation. On this basis, *Assisted Decision-Making* identifies the influence on Betty not as illegitimately controlling but rather as assisting, while it marks the influence on Alan as illegitimately controlling. The key features of *Assisted Decision-Making* are that, firstly, it explicitly allows influencing patients in ways conducive to their decision-making while at the same time setting clear boundaries in doing so; and secondly, it rejects a mere psychological focus and considers influences as exerting illegitimate control even if they are easily resistible, as in the case of the seasoned interviewee Alan.

Thus, the three conditions lead us to the view that an influence is interpersonally justified if and only if it is consistent with the more general principles of *Trusted Partner*, *Equal Moral Standing*, and *Assisted Decision-Making*. Hence, in my view, the person giving consent can claim that the person receiving it abide by these principles, and if he fails to do so when influencing the person giving consent, his influence will invalidate consent. Admittedly, the three principles overlap with each other in certain respects, but they still all have their distinctive role. *Trusted Partner* accounts especially for the significance of hypothetical transparency, *Equal Moral Standing* for the importance of not forcing people's rationality into serving other people's ends, and *Assisted Decision-Making* for the important distinction between resistibility and illegitimate control. On this basis, we arrive at the following hierarchical scheme in the assessment of voluntary consent.

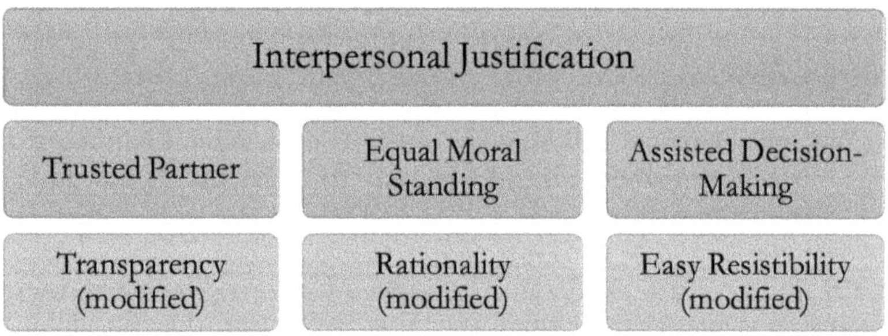

Figure 7.1 Three-layer model of interpersonal justification.

On the top, there is the most general idea of interpersonal justification: nudging undermines voluntary consent if and only if it fails to be interpersonally justifiable to the consenter. On the next level, there are three more specific mid-level principles that explain what interpersonal justification requires, namely that an influence be consistent with the demands of *Trusted Partner*, *Equal Moral Standing*, and *Assisted Decision-Making*. Finally, at the bottom, there are the modified conditions of transparency, rationality, and easy resistibility, from which I developed the principles at the second level. The three conditions at the bottom are more specific than the mid-level principles at the second level and can provide further guidance in clinical practice. However, a proper assessment of voluntary consent requires that transparency, rationality, and easy resistibility are always interpreted in the light of the idea of interpersonal justification and its more general principles of *Trusted Partner*, *Equal Moral Standing*, and *Assisted Decision-Making*. Hence, by incorporating the three conditions within this framework of interpersonal justification, my hierarchical model can retain the significance of the three conditions in the context of consent.

This is an important result because it supports not only the general approach in this book, that is, the idea of assessing consent in terms of interpersonal justification, but also the more specific principles which I attached to interpersonal justification. But before I conclude, let me address an objection and provide some clarification.

Objection and Clarifications

Suppose a physician wants to harm her patient she knows is inclined to buy into an anti-vaxx conspiracy theory. The physician makes the patient focus heavily on the potential side-effects of the vaccine by tapping into his irrational fears via some well-designed nudges, for example, by exaggerating his fear that governments use vaccines to harm its citizens. In this case, the physician's nudges may seem to be interpersonally justifiable to that patient because they trigger what are, *by the patient's own lights*, reasonable grounds for refusing the vaccine. Yet, this appears to be a case of impermissible or even consent-invalidating nudging.

Fortunately, my view is compatible with this intuition and does not imply that influences are interpersonally justifiable if they trigger what patients already accept. This is because interpersonal justification rests on three principles which do not fully depend on the perspective of the patient. In this case at hand, the physician would at least violate *Assisted Decision-Making* as she clearly subverts rather than enhances her patient's decision-making. After all, the physician would reinforce a false belief as the ground for consent, and this is inconsistent with respect for patient autonomy as well as her professional duty to act beneficently. Thus, although interpersonal justification requires specifically focusing on the claims the consenter has against the consentee, rather than moral norms in general, it does not imply that an individual consenter always knows what his claims against the consentee are or that he always knows when, or can always decide if, something violates such a claim.

But let me vary this example. In an allegedly true case, a physician meets a woman described as a 'conspiracy theory magnet'. When the woman refuses vaccination on the grounds of conspiracy theories, the physician asks her:

> Have you considered the possibility that anti-vaccine propaganda could be an attempt by the Russians or the Chinese to weaken the health of the United States population?[9]

The woman looks shocked, remains silent for a moment, and eventually consents to the vaccination. This case differs from the previous one as the physician makes the patient consent to beneficial and potentially urgently needed medical treatment.

My view offers a nuanced take on this case. Suppose the physician just asked the quoted rhetorical question to make the woman aware that her beliefs actually support a variety of inconsistent conclusions. As a result, the physician's question makes the woman realise that her beliefs are ill-founded and she consequently stops believing in any of those conspiracy theories. Here, the physician's intervention is interpersonally justifiable: it enhanced the woman's decision-making and allowed her to make her own decision in the end.

But alternatively, it could also happen that the rhetorical question makes the woman immediately adopt that other conspiracy theory: she is now fully convinced that the Russians or the Chinese try to weaken the health of the US population and therefore consents. Let us assume that the physician does not object to this false belief but on the contrary reinforces it, for example, by making a certain website that endorses this conspiracy theory very salient to her or even by pretending to believe it himself. In this scenario, vaccination may still be in the best interests of the woman. Yet, according to my view, this intervention qualifies as impermissible and consent-invalidating, because the nudges fail to treat the woman as an equal in the decision-making process (they steer her towards a decision without strengthening her standing in the process) and encourage the woman to base her decision on a false belief, thereby sabotaging her decision-making. This appears to lead to a violation of *Equal Moral Standing* and *Assisted Decision-Making*, which would render the nudge interpersonally unjustifiable in my view.[10]

7.4 Conclusion

The permissibility of nudging in public policy is often assessed in terms of the conditions of transparency, rationality, and easy resistibility. I credited this debate for producing important resources for any ethical inquiry into nudging, but also pointed out that scholars have not directly focused on a different and very important question, namely when nudges negate the voluntariness of medical consent. I then presented two cases designed to show that the three conditions are neither necessary nor sufficient for voluntary consent to a medical procedure. I conceded that, suitably modified, the three conditions remain significant in the assessment of voluntary consent, but these modifications result in a rather complicated solution. I have proposed a tidier solution, namely, that an influence invalidates medical consent if and only if it cannot be *interpersonally justified.* I used the three modified conditions not only to motivate the idea of interpersonal justification but also to further specify the principles it involves. This resulting hierarchical view is especially attractive because it builds on already existing insights from the debate on nudging, it updates those insights with an eye to medical consent, and it finally unites them in an elegant and simple framework.

These conclusions provide further support for ICCJ, my key proposal in this book. The discussion of nudging and manipulation explicitly supported the focus on interpersonal justification and the three principles ICCJ rests on. More specifically, in my discussion of resistibility and illegitimate control, I could further support the view that the voluntariness of consent cannot be understood in psychological terms only (e.g. resistibility) but needs to include moral judgements about the influences on a person's decision-making (e.g. on the *illegitimacy* of control).

Before I conclude, however, I wish to return to Montoy, that is, the HIV test example from the beginning of this chapter. ICCJ will likely consider Montoy's nudge consistent with voluntariness. If Montoy sets the default as he did and refrains from making it more costly or difficult for people to refuse screening, and if he refrains from using other reinforcing nudges (e.g. priming, shaming), he can interpersonally justify the default nudge to his patients. Announcing the default openly makes it a point for discussion, does not compromise the decision-making process, and thereby aligns with *Assisted Decision-Making*. Actively asking people to make a decision does not compromise their ability or opportunity to pursue a conception of the good and thereby aligns with *Equal Moral Standing*. Finally, Montoy did not use non-transparency or a position of power to *dominate* his patients' decision-making and thereby aligns with *Trusted Partner*. Hence, even if Montoy's default was a steering nudge and did not aim to enhance people's decision-making, it failed to violate any of ICCJ's principles and was therefore consistent with voluntary consent.

Notes

1 Parts of this chapter have previously been published with open access in Kiener, Maximilian (2021), "When do Nudges Undermine Voluntary Consent?", Philosophical Studies 178(12), 4201–4226."

2 To clarify: in variant 2, the nurse still exploits Betty's irrationality because he still triggers Betty's confirmation bias: Betty considers the medical evidence *relevant* to her decision about whether to consent *only because* this white man belonging to her religious community told her so. As a result, there is still an important part in Betty's decision-making that is procedurally irrational: selecting evidence in the way Betty does is in no way a reliable procedure when making medical decisions.

3 See, for instance, Noggle (2018) on the use of 'salience nudges'.

4 It is worth noting that some people explicitly explained how some techniques of manipulation work very transparently while still reducing the quality of their target's decision-making (Barnhill, 2014; Gorin, 2014a, 2014b).

5 In analysing the validity of consent transactions, Pufendorf focuses on the recipient of consent and says that consent is invalid if there is something 'quod ineptum ipsum reddit ad ius acquirendum' (1998: Liber III Cap VI: §X). Pufendorf then affirms this view in §XI, that is, if there is something that 'disqualifies him as a recipient of a right' (My translation. Thanks to Elvira Seibert-Kiener for advice on the translation.)

6 I owe this distinction to Thomas Douglas (unpublished manuscript).
7 For a related claim, see Wertheimer (2013).
8 I discuss related claims on pressure and consent in the context of living organ donation in Kiener (2020).
9 This case has been reported as a true event. www.boredpanda.com/pediatrician-anti-vaccination-parent-conspiracy-theory/?utm_source=google&utm_medium=organic&utm_campaign=organic. I simplified this case by focusing on the woman consenting to her own vaccination rather than deciding whether her child should be vaccinated.
10 Here, the physician's influence may not only negate the voluntariness of consent but also undermine *informed* consent.

References

Barnhill, A. (2014). What is manipulation? In C. Coons & M. Weber (Eds.), *Manipulation: Theory and practice* (pp. 51–72). Oxford: Oxford University Press.

Beauchamp, T. L., & Childress, J. F. (2013). *Principles of biomedical ethics.* New York: Oxford University Press.

Berg, J. W., & Applebaum, P. S. (2001). *Informed consent: Legal theory and clinical practice* (2nd ed.). Oxford; New York: Oxford University Press.

Blumenthal-Barby, J. S., & Burroughs, H. (2012). Seeking better health care outcomes: The ethics of using the 'nudge'. *American Journal of Bioethics, 12*(2), 1–10.

Boddington, P. (2012). *Ethical challenges in genomics research: A guide to understanding ethics in context.* Berlin: Springer.

Bovens, L. (2009). The ethics of nudge. In T. Grüne-Yanoff & S. Hansson (Eds.), *Preference change approaches from philosophy, economics and psychology.* (pp. 207–219). Dordrecht; London: Springer.

Calo, R. (2013). Code, nudge, or notice. *Iowa Law Review, 99*(2), 773–802.

Cohen, S. (2013). Nudging and informed consent. *American Journal of Bioethics, 13*(6), 3–11.

Conly, S. (2013). *Against autonomy: Justifying coercive paternalism.* Cambridge: Cambridge University Press.

Dean, M., Kıbrıs, Ö., & Masatlioglu, Y. (2017). Limited attention and status quo bias. *Journal of Economic Theory, 169*, 93–127.

Dougherty, T. (2015). Yes means yes: Consent as communication. *Philosophy & Public Affairs, 43*(3), 224–253.

Dubov, A. (2015). Ethical persuasion: The rhetoric of communication in critical care. *Journal of Evaluation in Clinical Practice, 21*(3), 496–502.

Engelen, B. (2019a). Ethical criteria for health-promoting nudges: A case-by-case analysis. *American Journal of Bioethics, 19*(5), 48–59.

Engelen, B. (2019b). Nudging and rationality: What is there to worry? *Rationality and Society, 31*(2), 204–232.

Eyal, N. (2014). Nudging by shaming, shaming by nudging. *International Journal of Health Policy and Management, 3*(2), 53–56.

Faden, R., & Faden, A. (1977). False belief and the refusal of medical treatment. *Journal of Medical Ethics, 3*(3), 133–136.

Gilovich, T., Medvec, V. H., & Savitsky, K. (2000). The spotlight effect in social judgment: An egocentric bias in estimates of the salience of one's own actions and appearance. *Journal of Personality and Social Psychology, 78*(2), 211–222.

Gorin, M. (2014a). Do manipulators always threaten rationality? *American Philosophical Quarterly, 51*(1), 51–61.

Gorin, M. (2014b). Towards a theory of interpersonal manipulation. In C. Coons & M. Weber (Eds.), *Manipulation: Theory and practice* (pp. 73–97). Oxford: Oxford University Press.

Greenspan, P. (2003). The problem with manipulation. *American Philosophical Quarterly, 40*(2), 155–164.

Grüne-Yanoff, T. (2012). Old wine in new casks: Libertarian paternalism still violates liberal principles. *Social Choice and Welfare, 38*(4), 635–645.

Grüne-Yanoff, T., & Hertwig, R. (2016). Nudge versus boost: How coherent are policy and theory? *Minds and Machines, 26*(1–2), 149–183.

Hanna, J. (2015). Libertarian paternalism, manipulation, and the shaping of preferences. *Social Theory and Practice, 41*(4), 618–643.

Hansen, P. G., & Jespersen, A. M. (2013). Nudge and the manipulation of choice: A framework for the responsible use of the nudge approach to behaviour change in public policy. *European Journal of Risk Regulation, 4*(1), 3–28.

Hausman, D. M., & Welch, B. (2010). Debate: To nudge or not to nudge. *Journal of Political Philosophy, 18*(1), 123–136.

Houk, T., DiSilvestro, R., & Jensen, M. (2016). Smoke and mirrors: Subverting rationality, positive freedom, and their relevance to nudging and/or smoking policies. *American Journal of Bioethics, 16*(7), 20–22.

Ivanković, V., & Engelen, B. (2019). Nudging, transparency, and watchfulness. *Social Theory and Practice, 45*(1), 43–74. doi:10.5840/soctheorpract20191751.

Johnson, E. J., & Goldstein, D. (2003). Do defaults save lives? *Science 302*(5649), 1338–1339.

Kahneman, D., & Tversky, A. (1972). Subjective probability: A judgment of representativeness. *Cognitive Psychology, 3*(3), 430–454.

Kiener, M. (2018). Truth-telling and respect for autonomy. *AJOB Neuroscience, 9*(3), 193–194. doi:10.1080/21507740.2018.1496169.

Kiener, M. (2020). Consent and living organ donation. *Journal of Medical Ethics, 41*.

Kiener, M. (2021). When do nudges undermine voluntary consent? *Philosophical Studies, 178*(12), 4201–4226.

Krawczyk, M. W., & Rachubik, J. (2019). The representativeness heuristic and the choice of lottery tickets: A field experiment. *Judgment and Decision Making, 14*(1), 51.

Mayr, E. (2019). Blame for constitutivists: Kantian constitutivism and the victim's special standing to complain. *Philosophical Explorations, 22*(2), 117–129.

McKenzie, C. R., Liersch, M. J., & Finkelstein, S. R. (2006). Recommendations implicit in policy defaults. *Psychological Science, 17*(5), 414–420.

Montoy, J. C. C., Dow, W. H., & Kaplan, B. C. (2018). Cash incentives versus defaults for HIV testing: A randomized clinical trial. *PloS One, 13*(7), e0199833.

Nelson-Marten, P., & Rich, B. A. (1999). A historical perspective of informed consent in clinical practice and research. *Seminars in Oncology Nursing, 15*(2), 81–88. doi:10.1016/S0749-2081(99)80065-5.

Noggle, R. (1996). Manipulative actions: A conceptual and moral analysis. *American Philosophical Quarterly, 33*(1), 43–55.

Noggle, R. (2018). Manipulation, salience, and nudges. *Bioethics, 32*(3), 164–170.

Noggle, R. (2020). Pressure, trickery, and a unified account of manipulation. *American Philosophical Quarterly, 57*(3), 241–252. doi:10.2307/48574436.

Nyhan, B., & Reifler, J. (2013, October). Which corrections work? Research results and practice recommendation. New America Foundation, 1–15.

Oswald, M., & Grosjean, S. (2004). Confirmation bias. In R. Pohl (Ed.), *Cognitive illusions. A handbook on fallacies and biases in thinking, judgment and memory* (pp. 79–96). Hove; New York, NY: Psychology Press.

Owens, D. (2007). Duress, deception, and the validity of a promise. *Mind, 116*(462), 293–315. doi:10.1093/mind/fzm293.

Owens, D. (2012). *Shaping the normative landscape*. Oxford: Oxford University Press.

Pellegrino, E. D. (1992). Beneficence, scientific autonomy, and self-interest: Ethical dilemmas in clinical research. *Cambridge Quarterly Healthcare Ethics, 1*(4), 361–369. doi:10.1017/S0963180100006551.

Ploug, T., & Holm, S. (2015). Doctors, patients, and nudging in the clinical context: Four views on nudging and informed consent. *American Journal of Bioethics, 15*(10), 28–38.

Pufendorf, S. (1998). *Samuel Pufendorf. Gesammelte Werke*. Berlin: Akademie Verlag.

Rawls, J. (2005). *Political liberalism*. New York: Columbia University Press.

Saghai, Y. (2013). Salvaging the concept of nudge. *Journal of Medical Ethics, 39*(8), 487–493.

Scanlon, T. (1998). *What we owe to each other*. Cambridge, MA: Harvard University Press.

Schmidt, A. T. (2019). Getting real on rationality: Behavioral science, nudging, and public policy. *Ethics, 129*(4), 511–543.

Slovic, P., Finucane, M. L., Peters, E., & MacGregor, D. G. (2007). The affect heuristic. *European Journal of Operational Research, 177*(3), 1333–1352.

Tadros, V. (2016). *Wrongs and crimes*. Oxford: Oxford University Press.

Thaler, R. H., & Sunstein, C. R. (2009). *Nudge: Improving decisions about health, wealth and happiness*. London: Penguin Books.

Thompson, M. (2004). What is it to wrong someone? A puzzle about justice. In R. J. Wallace, P. Pettit, S. Scheffler, & M. Smith (Eds.), *Reason and value themes from the moral philosophy of Joseph Raz* (pp. 333–384). Oxford: Clarendon Press.

Thornton, R. L. (2008). The demand for, and impact of, learning HIV status. *American Economic Review, 98*(5), 1829–1863.

UNAIDS. (2021). *UNAIDS World AIDS Day report*. Retrieved from https://www.unaids.org/sites/default/files/media_asset/2021-global-aids-update_en.pdf.

Wertheimer, A. (2013). Should 'nudge' be salvaged? *Journal of Medical Ethics, 39*(8), 498. doi:10.1136/medethics-2012-101061.

Wilkinson, T. M. (2013). Nudging and manipulation. *Political Studies, 61*(2), 341–355.

8 Payment in Clinical Trials

Introduction

Let me now return to Rambha Gajre, whose case I already mentioned in the Introduction. Rambha is a young mother from India and worried about her son. He is seriously ill and needs life-saving treatment, but Rambha cannot pay for it. She has so little money that she struggles to pay her rent and has been threatened with eviction. To earn enough money for the rent and her son's treatment, Rambha consents to paid participation in a clinical trial. Such participation may be highly intrusive, potentially involve exploitation, and be the consequence of unjust circumstances. Yet, Rambha enrols and explains her situation as follows:

> Many people commit suicide and I didn't want to become one of those and I didn't want people to think I did it to avoid repaying [i.e. paying the rent]. I have two young kids, 10 and 12 years old. What would become of them? ... I am helpless, I have to do this [i.e. paid trial participation] .... They don't really force us, but I don't have a choice.
>
> (Quote from Wertheimer, 2014, pp. 280–281)

In this chapter, I will focus on the question of whether, and if so, under what conditions the offer of payment invalidates a person's consent to participation in a clinical trial. Concerns about consent and voluntariness arise when payments not only reimburse participants for their expenses (e.g. travelling costs to the research facility, parking costs, etc.) but also compensate for time and inconvenience and thereby exert an incentivising influence.[1] Such concerns become reinforced once the background conditions of a participant are as dire as in Rambha's case.

Cases like Rambha's pose the strongest challenge to ICCJ's position that the voluntariness of consent is neither a 'psychological' concept indicative of the inner states of a person's mind nor a 'circumstantial' concept indicative of a person's set of options. I therefore need to defend my proposal in the face of such challenging cases. I will argue that ICCJ not only correctly determines the voluntariness of consent in such cases but also

DOI: 10.4324/9781003301417-11

best protects people like Rambha, including in cases of heightened risks and illegitimate treatment of research participants.

When addressing the question of whether offering payment invalidates consent, I will start from the presumption that *it does not* because consent to financial transactions is normally voluntary, and I will then test whether this presumption can be defeated in the context of paid trial participation. This presumption is only a minimal Archimedean point. It does not rely on any theoretical or libertarian commitments but rather, if anything, only on what seems true in everyday life. We voluntarily consent to work in exchange for money, even if the situation is less than perfect, for example, when we consent to work in order to avoid becoming homeless. So, the key question becomes what could be so special about clinical trials that makes people's consent involuntary.

8.1 Clinical Trials and Payment for Participation

A *clinical trial* is any investigation involving human subjects that is carried out to advance scientific knowledge about the effects of medicines or therapies (Hackshaw, 2009). The role of a *human subject* can involve exposure to certain medication or treatment during a period of time when one is also being monitored. The medication or treatment will be initiated at the beginning of the investigation and could be one the participant had not received before ('interventional' trials), or it can involve mere monitoring, where medication or treatment, if people receive it at all, has been prescribed prior to and independently of the investigation ('observational' trials).

Among interventional trials, Phase I trials 'are conducted to examine the biological and pharmacological actions of a new treatment (usually a new drug), and its side-effects' (Hackshaw, 2009, p. 31). Often, participants need to stay overnight in research units and undergo several diagnostic procedures; sometimes participants will also be infected with a bacterial or viral illness (e.g. typhus or COVID-19) to test a new therapeutic strategy or vaccine; and sometimes participants will have to take drugs in increasing doses. By contrast, Phase II and III trials no longer aim to find new forms of treatment but rather 'provide enough evidence to warrant a change in practice' (Hackshaw, 2009, p. 57), that is, a change from current routine to a new form of treatment already tested in Phase I trials. Whereas Phase I trials usually involve only healthy participants, Phase II–III trials mostly involve patients whose illnesses investigators want to focus on.

In most countries, a clinical trial has to receive approval from a research ethics committee before it can be initiated. In the UK, the law states that 'a trial shall be initiated only if an ethics committee and the licensing authority comes to the conclusion that the anticipated therapeutic and public health benefits justify the risks'.[2]

'Risks' means the likelihood that participants will experience adverse effects on their health as a result of trial participation. On the basis that the 'rights, safety, and well-being of the trial subjects are the most important considerations and shall prevail over interests of science and society',[3] risks exceeding a certain degree or inflicting serious harm are absolutely excluded. Other risks can be justified only if they are not 'disproportionate to [their] ... potential benefits'.[4] On the other hand, 'benefits' are either therapeutic advantages for the participant or scientific progress as a result of the trial.[5] Payment for participation, however much the participant welcomes it, is *not* considered a benefit.[6] The research ethics committee must come to the conclusion that a trial has a favourable risk–benefit ratio independent of payments (Jackson, 2019, ch. 8; Mason, Laurie, & Aziz, 2011, ch. 19).

Henceforward, I shall only focus on healthy participants in Phase I trials, that is, trials like Rambha's, where ethical questions around payment arise most clearly and forcefully. Moreover, I shall rely on the empirical evidence that monetary offers do not distort a person's judgement about trial participation in any considerable way and will only focus on the pressure they exert on a person's decision-making (Bentley & Thacker, 2004; Halpern, Karlawish, Casarett, Berlin, & Asch, 2004), asking whether such pressure could negate voluntariness and thereby invalidate consent.

8.2 Three Challenges to Voluntary Consent

Scholars argued that a necessary, yet not sufficient, condition for payment to invalidate consent arises when prospective participants are already very badly situated, financially speaking. In particular, people sometimes struggle to satisfy their own and their loved ones' basic needs, that is, needs concerning the minimal provision of healthcare and the economic resources for food and shelter. In such situations, paid trial participation may become their best or only option to satisfy these needs, and it will normally be very difficult to resist, that is, it may take great psychological effort or resilience to decline participation. As Vanderpool explained, in such situations, the offer of paid trial participation may even be 'virtually irresistible' (2005, p. 18).[7]

Rambha is in such a situation. She has great difficulty paying for her son's medical treatment and securing shelter. Moreover, paid trial participation has become by far her most feasible option to satisfy these needs. Finally, the offer of paid participation is very hard to resist for Rambha and exerts a strong influence on her decision-making.

Such situations are often considered a necessary condition for payments to negate voluntariness. Yet, there is also agreement that such situations are not sufficient to negate voluntariness and invalidate consent. For instance, if Rambha could earn enough money simply by watering flowers, instead of participating in a trial, and also enjoys gardening work, the moral unease about what she is being paid to do would vanish. Hence, a further condition has to be added if payments for research participation are to invalidate consent. Three proposals deserve particular attention.

Challenge 1: Aversion

In separate papers, Vanderpool as well as Grant and Sugarman suggest that payments can invalidate consent if, in addition to the difficulties in satisfying basic needs, participants are offered money to do something they are *averse* to (Grant & Sugarman, 2004, pp. 727–728; Vanderpool, 2005, p. 18).

'Being averse' goes beyond people's refusal to do something without payment, that is 'what they otherwise would refuse' to do (Vanderpool, 2005, p. 18). It concerns what people 'would *strongly* prefer not to do' (p. 18, emphasis added). Assuming this line can be drawn, Vanderpool presents the example of an impecunious college student who is averse to painful muscle biopsies but still consents to undergo them in exchange for money. Grant and Sugarman add examples of situations where 'the aversion is a principled one or a matter of moral scruple' (2004, p. 728). For instance, a religious person may be 'averse' to donating sperm (p. 736 fn 20).

For certain procedures, aversion is a matter of individual disposition: some consider muscle biopsies a minor inconvenience, while others panic at the very thought of it. For other procedures, aversion is very widespread, for example, when procedures become 'physically invasive, upset the customary boundaries of privacy, or involve areas of the body generally associated with feelings of shame' (Grant & Sugarman, 2004, pp. 729–730). However, in any case, aversion to a procedure does not already mean that undergoing that procedure is risky or harmful.

But to clarify: neither Vanderpool nor Grant and Sugarman claim that mere aversion to a medical procedure invalidates consent. Peter may be highly averse to dental surgery because it will be painful. Yet, he consents to it to free himself from some illness. James may be highly averse to receiving a blood transfusion because of religious beliefs, yet consents to it as part of his leukaemia treatment. Peter and James overcame their aversions after reflecting on their situation, and doing so was a genuine exercise of their autonomy.

The situation becomes morally problematic and potentially invalidates consent, Grant and Sugarman argue, when one attempts to 'overcome' another person's aversion by means of a monetary offer (2004, p. 729). Furthermore, problems arise when (i) a person's resistance to undergo certain procedures is 'reasonable' (p. 729), (ii) the monetary offer 'ought to be resisted in some sense' (p. 729; Vanderpool, 2005, p. 18), and (iii) a person's acceptance of the offer would therefore go 'against his or her better judgment' (Grant & Sugarman, 2004, pp. 727–729, 734). Let me elaborate on these aspects in turn.

(i) A person's resistance is *reasonable* when it is necessary to protect his interests and justified on the basis of the overall situation. So understood, Peter's resistance is *unreasonable*: although declining dental surgery allows him to avoid pain, foregoing urgently needed treatment lacks a plausible justification. By contrast, the impecunious college student's resistance is *reasonable*: not enrolling in the trial protects his interest in avoiding biopsies, and other things being equal, prioritising such an interest over financial gain is justifiable. Similarly, the religious person's resistance is reasonable because prioritising religious commitments over financial gain can be justified.

(ii) Sometimes, however, a person may not only *reasonably* resist certain medical procedures, he also *ought* to resist and decline an offer to the contrary. For instance, the impecunious college student ought to resist the offer of payment, at least when the trial involves 'undignified procedures, embarrassing situations, and degrading experiences' (p. 729) and fails to pay a sufficient amount of money. Moreover, the religious person ought to resist an offer if his important religious commitments are of such paramount importance to him that no financial gain could ever justify their violation. Grant and Sugarman are particularly concerned with cases similar to that of the religious person and argue:

> The ethical problem is multiplied where the aversion is a principled one or a matter of moral scruple. To deliberately induce religious people to work on the sabbath by offering large incentives would involve an attempt to get them to act against what they see as their duties; it would be a form of bribery.
>
> (p. 728)

And they add:

> Respect for persons ... requires respect for certain of their values, beliefs, and preferences. It requires refraining from making seductive offers, offers that ought to be resisted.
>
> (p. 729)

(iii) If a person's resistance is 'reasonable' and the monetary offer 'ought to be resisted in some sense' (p. 729), then accepting such an offer conflicts with at least *a* better judgement, that is, the justified judgement that one ought to resist such an offer. Such a judgement could be better in an objective sense, independent of the person's endorsed values and preferences, or in a subjective sense, based on a person's own values and preferences. In the former case, the person accepting the offer disagrees with the objective standard and thereby acts against an objectively better judgement. In the latter case, the person agrees with the subjective standard but still acts against it, that is, acts akratically: despite knowing what is best, he acts against *his* better judgement. When these three conditions are met, Vanderpool and Grant consider payments to be instances of 'manipulation' or 'undue influence.'

The emphasis on a person's resistance being reasonable or unreasonable is noteworthy because payments can sometimes turn previously *reasonable* resistance into *unreasonable* resistance. Recall the impecunious college student. Suppose he is offered very little money to conquer his aversion. Here, his resistance seems reasonable, and he ought not to accept the offer. But if he is offered so much money that he can pay the tuition fees for his entire degree, his continued resistance may become *unreasonable*, and there are strong reasons for him to enrol. The same is true of Rambha: it may be quite reasonable for her to overcome a physical aversion to muscle biopsies if she could thereby earn enough money to secure shelter and pay for her son's treatment.

If this line of reasoning is correct, two conclusions follow. Firstly, *raising payments* can remove the problem of incentivising people to overcome a *reasonable* aversion. As a result, one should sometimes only be concerned about *low* rather than *high* payments. Secondly, if offering more money removes the problematic aspect of such payments, then there was no problem with the *voluntariness* of consent in the first place. This is because these payments would not be problematic due to their incentivising effect on consent, which – as I argued in Chapter 5 – is necessary to negate voluntariness. They would have been problematic because they were not large enough.

But even if the subject's resistance remains reasonable on *moral or religious* grounds, even if any financial incentive ought to be resisted, and even if enrolling conflicts with the subject's better judgement, the offer of payment still fails to invalidate consent. To see this, suppose an investigator offers money to the potential participant, Jack, but enrolling in the trial would violate duties Jack has towards work: he works in a kitchen and, given the risk of infection, enrolling in the trial would transgress rules of hygiene. Suppose Jack has a reasonable and strong aversion to enrolment – for example, it could be a moral aversion to harming others – the monetary offer ought to be resisted because Jack would otherwise depart from his values and preferences, and enrolling would therefore be against his better judgement, objectively as well as subjectively. But if he does enrol, his consent can still be voluntary. If the investigator performs the trial procedure, he will not assault Jack.

This is a case of principled or moral aversion to violating duties rather than aversion to physical pain. In this respect, it is similar to the case of the religious person who is averse to donating sperm. Thus, can we conclude that if financial incentives do not invalidate Jack's consent, then they will also not invalidate the consent of the religious person?

Grant and Sugarman may reject this comparison on the grounds that, in the case of aversion on religious grounds, the person's aversion is more fundamentally connected to his core values and identity than in the case of Jack transgressing rules of hygiene. Thus, even if Jack's consent is voluntary, the religious person's consent may not be.

However, this response is misleading. Suppose that the religious person decides to donate sperm and contacts the investigators after seeing the advertisement of the trial. In this case, it is disrespectful to exclude him on the grounds that his aversion to donating sperm is so fundamental to his core values and identity. Doing so would deny him the authority to decide whether to surmount his aversion in exchange for money or not. In fact, once core values are at stake, the disrespect seems even greater than before. Therefore, it is not *offering money* that is disrespectful (as Grant and Sugarman would argue), but rather *excluding people* and only allowing those to enrol who can show that they do not harbour any aversion. Thus, the difference between Jack and the religious person does not justify treating them differently with regard to the voluntariness of their consent.

Hence, *Challenge 1: Aversion* cannot explain when payments invalidate consent, and this conclusion teaches a first, more general lesson: the voluntariness of consent is not a psychological concept indicative of the inner states of a person's mind. Voluntariness is not willingness, and involuntariness is not aversion or reluctance. Thus, so far, ICCJ is correct in rejecting psychological explanations of voluntariness.

Challenge 2: No Acceptable Alternative

Joan McGregor argues that payments invalidate consent if there is *no acceptable alternative* to paid trial participation. This means that trial participation is a person's *only* and not just her best way to satisfy basic needs, and therefore, not participating would leave her in an unacceptably bad position. McGregor speaks of 'desperate situations' (2005, p. 25) where a 'lack of options' makes even the direst proposal 'the only eligible choice' (p. 25). McGregor's proposal is stricter than Vanderpool's and Grant's, where a person may still have other acceptable options to earn money.

If payment from research participation is the only acceptable alternative, McGregor argues, then a financial offer becomes 'coercive' and invalidates consent (p. 25). Rambha is in such a situation: trial participation is her only way to earn the money needed to avoid eviction and cover her son's treatment.

McGregor's view is a specification of Serena Olsaretti's account, and therefore, looking at Olsaretti can help to find the strongest version of this view. According to Olsaretti,

> A choice is voluntary if and only if it is not forced, and it is forced if and only if it is made only or primarily because the alternative to it is unacceptable, where the standard for the acceptability of options

> is an objective standard of well-being, and unacceptable options are those which, by that standard, fall below a certain threshold.
>
> (2016, p. 444)

Olsaretti claims that people act involuntarily if they do something *only or primarily because* the alternative to it is unacceptable. The italicised phrase is important because it shows that people may sometimes act voluntarily even if they lack an acceptable alternative: they act voluntarily as long as they decide to do something for reasons that are independent of the fact that there is no acceptable alternative to it. On the other hand, people may *not* act voluntarily even if there *are* acceptable alternatives. This is the case if the person reasonably thinks there is no acceptable alternative, for example, when a person hands over money to a robber after being threatened with a realistic toy gun. Thus, on Olsaretti's view, a person's motivation is critical to the voluntariness of her action.

Olsaretti then claims that the 'standard for the acceptability of options is an objective standard of well-being' (2016, p. 444). An option is acceptable if and only if it satisfies core aspects of a person's well-being. An example of an *unacceptable* option is dying a painful death, but also being evicted from one's home or seeing one's son suffer or die, as in Rambha's case.

Finally, Olsaretti explicitly applies her view to medial consent. She claims that voluntariness is necessary for the validity of 'consent to ... surgery' (2016, p. 443), that is, 'whether or not it is permissible ... for him [i.e. the physician] to carry out the operation' (p. 445). And she adds that the significance of voluntariness for consent is part of a wider 'justificatory role' (p. 443) that voluntariness plays: on any satisfactory account, voluntariness 'must be able to undergird attributions of responsibility, as people's voluntary choices – for example, the choice of entering a contract, that of making a promise, or that of consenting to an interference – can change their and others' entitlements and obligations' (p. 443).

But so understood, this view faces an obvious challenge. In medical contexts, the lack of acceptable alternatives does not automatically invalidate consent. To see this, consider the fictitious case of Peter who has been diagnosed with a serious illness. If he does not undergo major surgery, he will die a painful death. Although Peter is afraid of the surgery, he eventually consents, but only for want of an acceptable alternative.

Clinical practice considers consent from people like Peter voluntary and valid, and such a view is indeed justified. This is because consenting to a medical procedure only because one lacks an acceptable alternative can be a genuine exercise of a person's autonomy as well as a promotion of his well-being. Peter may have wished never to be in the situation he finds himself in now. But *once* he is in that situation, selecting the option he prefers most allows him to take control of his life and decision. Moreover, selecting the option he prefers most also allows him to promote his well-being, and assuming that people are usually better judges than others of what is good for them, Peter's choice will likely advance his well-being more than others' choices would.

However, on Olsaretti's and McGregor's views, Peter's consent is involuntary. Death is clearly an unacceptable option. So, how could they respond? Olsaretti identifies the problem and claims:

> The fact that the patient's consent is intentional and informed may suffice to authorize the surgeon's operation, and perhaps also to justify holding the patient to compensate the surgeon for some of the costs the surgeon has to incur.
>
> (2016, pp. 445–446)

This is an unsatisfying response. If consent is intentional and well-informed, it does not follow that it is also voluntary, and Olsaretti does not claim otherwise. Hence, Olsaretti is committed to saying that Peter's consent is involuntary but valid, thereby abandoning voluntariness as a necessary condition for the validity of consent. This implication is not only contrary to the orthodox link between validity and voluntariness, it is also at odds with her own claims about voluntariness playing a 'justificatory role' with regard to the question of 'whether or not it is permissible ... for him [i.e. the physician] to carry out the operation' (Olsaretti, 2016, p. 445). Hence, I suggest rejecting Olsaretti's and McGregor's views in the context of treatment.

Therefore, if this second view, which I termed *No Acceptable Alternative*, is to explain when payments invalidate consent, there has to be a significant difference between patients like Peter and trial participants like Rambha. The obvious candidate for such a difference is the combination of monetary considerations figuring in Rambha's but not Peter's decision and those monetary considerations incentivising something that fails to benefit the consenting person's health, that is, Peter medically benefits from the surgery, whereas Rambha does not medically benefit from the trial procedures. With these points in mind, let me reconsider the arguments from well-being and autonomy that justified considering Peter's consent to be voluntary and valid.

Well-Being

The well-being of a person depends on her health and the satisfaction of basic needs. Trial participation often involves a trade-off. The procedures may negatively affect a person's health, but the money she earns can help to satisfy other interests. Depending on how health-related and economic interests are balanced, trial participation may or may not be detrimental to a person's overall well-being. Therefore, considerations relating to the well-being of research participants can differ from those relating to the well-being of the terminally ill patient.

Considerations of well-being only make a significant difference in some trials, but not in others. Suppose Rambha enrols in a trial testing the effect of certain physical exercises on the quality of sleep. Such a risk-free trial does not compromise any of her health-related interests. Yet, it may help to satisfy other important interests, for example, by allowing her to pay the rent and cover her son's medical treatment. Hence, enrolment seems conducive to Rambha's overall well-being, whereas being denied access to the trial would make Rambha worse off. In the latter case, she would be deprived of what is her only option to pay for her son's treatment and secure shelter. Therefore, in this scenario, undergoing a procedure only for want of an acceptable alternative can still promote a person's well-being.

The situation may be different when clinical trials become more intrusive or risky. However, risk and intrusiveness are additional considerations and not part of Olsaretti's and McGregor's views. In fact, Olsaretti and McGregor exclusively focus on the unacceptability of foregoing the opportunity of paid trial participation, rather than the level of risk or harm involved in participation. Therefore, they lack the means to reject the argument from well-being on the grounds of risk and intrusiveness.

Hence, both Peter *and* Rambha can promote their well-being by undergoing procedures to which they lack an acceptable alternative.

Autonomy

But what about the argument from autonomy? Is there a significant difference in this regard between Peter and Rambha?

Payments for research participation broaden people's earning potential and thereby promote 'positive autonomy': money enables people to do things they would otherwise be unable to do. The proscription of payments, on the other hand, excludes financial influences and thereby promotes 'negative autonomy': it keeps decisions free from the interference of other people's offers. Since positive and negative autonomy cannot be simultaneously maximised, a sound balance is required.

On this basis, McGregor and Olsaretti could claim that considering Rambha's consent to be valid unduly prioritises positive autonomy over negative autonomy. Therefore, the argument from autonomy only supports the validity of Peter's but not Rambha's consent.

To evaluate this response, let us consider a paradigm case of a wrong prioritisation of positive and negative autonomy. It is uncontroversial that a person ought not to have the power to transfer the title of his property to a burglar while being threatened with death. Allowing transfer of the title only when one's decision is kept free from the interference of the burglar (negative autonomy) is clearly required, whereas enabling the person to organise his life by entering a binding agreement under such circumstances (positive autonomy) lacks justification. This is because the burglar's threat severely wrongs a person and dominates his decision-making.

Rambha's situation is very unlike the burglar example. The offer of payment does not wrong Rambha but rather provides the means to improve an otherwise unacceptable situation. Moreover, Rambha is not dominated as the person in the burglar example is. Participation allows her to regain control over her situation. Finally, investigators did not cause Rambha's situation. Thus, allowing Rambha to consent to paid trial participation is very different from the burglar case and consistent with a sound balance of positive and negative autonomy.

Hence, there is no difference between Peter's and Rambha's situation that could explain why only Peter, but not Rambha, consents voluntarily. Thus, *Challenge 2: No Acceptable Alternative* fails to explain when payments invalidate consent.

This conclusion provides a second, more general lesson: the voluntariness of consent is not merely a 'circumstantial' concept reporting on a person's set of options. Therefore, a person's background situation, just as a person's psychological preferences, cannot determine the voluntariness of consent. Thus, ICCJ is also correct in refusing to explain the voluntariness of consent in terms of a person's background circumstances.

Digression: Voluntariness and Exploitation

At this point, it is worth pausing to consider the relation between voluntariness and exploitation. This is because, throughout this book and in this chapter, I have discussed various aspects related to exploitation, and I am now in a position to consider them more systematically.

Exploitation means taking unfair advantage of someone. It differs from abuse and discrimination. Exploitation requires that the exploiter benefit in some way, whereas abuse and discrimination do not necessarily require that the wrongdoer benefit (Wertheimer, 1996).[8] Moreover, exploitation differs from coercion. As Feinberg explains: 'Exploiters are typically opportunists; they extract advantage from situations that are not of their own making. Coercers, on the other hand, are typically makers rather than mere discoverers and users of opportunities' (1986, p. 184).

Yet, despite its distinctive profile, exploitation often blends into other types of influence. A threat can be both coercive and exploitative, as when it extracts an unfair advantage from its target. Moreover, as Feinberg explains, exploitation can comprise 'forms of noncoercive "using" or "playing upon" another person [and] involve a great miscellany of manipulative techniques [including] ... inducements, ... flattery, ... alluring portrayals or seductive suggestions' (1986, p. 181). In such cases, the exploiter would take advantage of his target's traits, including virtues and vices, the propensity to make decisions in a certain way, and so on. Finally, exploitation can present itself through offers, as when offers take advantage of a person's lack of alternatives and/or extract an undue benefit (e.g. exploitative working conditions).

For these reasons, it is not surprising that many of my examples in this book could be described as involving some form of exploitation. In Chapter 5, I used the example of *Discrimination*, where, motivated by racism, clinical investigator Daniel gave participant Peter lower compensation than he did for others. Daniel can be said to have exploited Peter because he took unfair advantage of Peter's position of vulnerability. Moreover, also in Chapter 5, I featured the example of *Last Minute Rescue*, where clinical investigator Roger offered to help Peter escape criminal prosecution if he would participate in his trial. Roger exploited Peter's background situation: he made use of Peter's desire to escape prosecution to boost recruitment for his trial. Chapter 6 discussed *Tattoo Sex*, where Recipient offered to help Victim escape third-party coercion only if Victim would have sex with him. Recipient exploited Victim by taking unfair advantage of Victim's subjection to severe coercion from another party. In *Racial Bias*, from Chapter 7, the medical team took advantage or exploited Betty's bias to make her appreciate relevant evidence. Furthermore, in *TV Bully*, from Chapter 7, the consent-receiver Carl exploited Alan's situation of potential distress and thereby obtained consent. Finally, in this chapter, I presented further cases of potential exploitation. It may be argued that investigators exploited Rambha's dire background situation to increase enrolment in their clinical trials. Perhaps they even endorsed the rationale of the company iGATE Clinical Research, Inc., behind why they conduct clinical trials in India: 'A huge population with a diversity of diseases that are untreated – yes, that is the "India Advantage"' (quoted from Wertheimer, 2012, p. 285). The 'India Advantage' means the opportunity to benefit from the poor conditions in which some people in India find themselves.

These examples illustrate the many guises of exploitation. Yet, consent was involuntary in only some of them (e.g. *Tattoo Sex*, *TV Bully*) and voluntary in others (e.g. *Discrimination*, *Racial Bias)*. So, how exactly does exploitation affect voluntary consent? I suggest two individually necessary conditions and, with some qualification, jointly sufficient conditions to determine whether exploitation invalidates consent.

First, exploitation invalidates consent only if it is wrong due to the pressure it exerts on a person's decision-making. In Chapter 5, I claimed that an influence negates the voluntariness of consent only if it is wrong due to how it incentivises consent or, respectively, disincentivises the refusal of consent, as opposed to other grounds for wrongness. For instance, influences that are wrong because they discriminate are not of the kind that negate voluntariness. This claim is helpful in the context of exploitation because exploitation is often wrong quite independently of any incentivising effect on consent. This explains why consent was not invalid in *Discrimination*. Moreover, it explains why paying people too little for their participation in clinical trials, although exploitative, does not negate the voluntariness of their consent.

Second, exploitation invalidates consent only if it constitutes an instance of *taking unfair advantage* of someone rather than *taking advantage of unfairness*. Often intuitions about exploitation are triggered in both kinds of case, but Wertheimer reminds us that they are different and provides a good example: 'If A hires B, who has been unjustly fired from his previous job by C, then A is taking advantage of C's unfairness to B. But unless the terms of A's offer are unfair, A has not taken unfair advantage of B' (2012, p. 284). In this case, B can still validly consent to A's job offer, despite the unfairness or even lack of alternatives in the background. Thus, to invalidate consent, the consent-receiver needs to take *unfair* advantage in some sense, rather than merely benefitting from the unfairness or injustice the consent-giver is already subject to. This focus on the consent-receiver aligns with my *Recipient-Focus-View* from Chapter 6. Based on this condition, one can rule out cases like *Racial Bias* from Chapter 7, where investigators took advantage of a serious bias in a person but did not do so unfairly or unjustifiably.

However, to render the two conditions jointly sufficient, we need to modify the second condition. As pointed out in Chapter 7 on nudging, I do not rely on the notion of 'fairness' as Miller and Wertheimer do. Thus, for exploitation to invalidate consent, it needs to take advantage of someone in a way that is *interpersonally unjustifiable* rather than merely *unfair*. This is an important difference, but it still leaves the core of the second condition in place. For exploitation to invalidate consent, there has to be some flaw in the way the consent-receiver obtains consent rather than merely a flaw in the background situation against which the consent-receiver obtains some benefit.

However, there is often a thin line between (permissible) advantage-taking of unfairness and taking unfair (respectively interpersonally unjustifiable) advantage. Consider Rambha's case again and what iGATE Clinical Research, Inc., said about research in India: 'A huge population with a diversity of diseases that are untreated—yes, that is the "India Advantage"' (quoted from Wertheimer, 2012, p. 285). Here, investigators certainly take advantage of unfairness, that is, the unfairness or desperation people in India face due to the lack of medical care. Yet, we need to fill in further details to determine whether they also take *unfair* (respectively interpersonally unjustifiable) advantage. So far, I have argued that, for investigators to take such unfair advantage, more is needed than for a person like Rambha just to be asked to overcome an aversion, or for her just to lack acceptable alternatives. Invalid consent requires that investigators violate some further important norms. Whether this can be the case in situations of increased risks will be my focus in the next section. But for now, I can state that the fact that something is an instance of exploitation is, in itself, of limited relevance to the question of whether it invalidates consent. Rather, and just like other influences, it needs to be evaluated on general grounds, and the two conditions I stated here can guide this evaluation.

Challenge 3: Risk

Finally, let me focus on a third challenge to voluntary consent in the context of paid trial participation. Nelson et al. argue that payments invalidate consent if participants are offered money to do something where there is 'a risk of harm of sufficient seriousness' and the payment is 'irresistibly attractive' (2011, p. 9).

The 'seriousness' of risk is a function of the probability that harm will occur and the kind of harm at stake, for example, harm of a bruise or harm of renal failure. 'Irresistibility' refers to the great psychological effort it would take to decline research participation, but it does not mean a psychological *inability* to decline the offer. In other words, people would find it very hard to decline an offer but would, in principle, still be able to do so.

Elaborating on their view, Nelson et al. claim that payments to undergo risky procedures invalidate consent because these payments are 'manipulative' (2011, p. 9). I take the core thought to be that payments are 'manipulative' not because they side-step a person's rational deliberation but because they incentivise a person to act against some of her important interests. But why exactly would such a 'manipulative' incentive invalidate consent? Unfortunately, Nelson et al. do not provide an answer. Building on their claims, the following line of thought seems to present the strongest version of their position.

High risks affect the situation in three ways. Firstly, as Nelson et al. explain, when risks are high, payments need to exert a strong influence to make a person consent. Secondly, although Nelson et al. do not say this, when risks are high, payments are more likely to incentivise what is contrary to important interests of a participant and become anti-beneficent and, to this extent, illegitimate. Finally, as Nelson et al. imply, when risks are high, the test for valid consent is more exigent, for example, informed consent may require more information, and less severe influences compromise voluntariness. (This point repeats my claim about raising stakes I made in my comparison of consent and responsibility in Chapter 5.) Hence, payments for participation in risky trials may invalidate consent because they are strong and illegitimate influences which fail to meet the higher standards required for consent to serious medical procedures.[9]

However, this kind of argument presupposes that risks are possible to detect, as the following case illustrates:

Unknown Risk: Investigator Sarah wants to develop a new vaccine, but the envisaged trial bears such high risks of toxicity that exposing people to them cannot be justified.[10] Unfortunately, neither Sarah nor the research ethics committee know about these risks and could not possibly have detected them. Rambha enrols in exchange for money.

Due to the unjustified risks of the trial, payments incentivise undergoing procedures that conflict with the required protection of participants' health and are therefore anti-beneficent. Yet, no matter how high such risks are, payments do not invalidate consent. This is because the mere presence of high risks neither increases the pressure on Rambha's decision-making, as Rambha did not know about them, nor leads to Sarah violating her specific obligations of beneficence. Investigators violate their obligations of beneficence only if they knowingly or negligently act against a person's important health interests, but not when they act with due diligence. Moreover, clinical research will inevitably bear the danger of unknown risks, and if such risks materialise, they are better understood as creating additional claims for compensation rather than as invalidating consent to procedures already performed.[11] Hence, to invalidate consent, investigators must have at least had a chance to find out about unjustified risks.

However, even when investigators know about risks, monetary offers do not automatically invalidate consent. Consider the following case:

Deviant Scientist: Investigator Sarah wants to test a new drug, but the envisaged trial would involve unjustified risks, which Sarah is aware of. Sarah fakes the documents submitted to the research ethics committee, but tells Rambha everything about the risks. Moreover, she bribes Rambha to remain silent and offers further substantial payment if she participates. Rambha enrols.

Performing the procedures in *Deviant Scientist* is impermissible because it violates the restrictions on clinical research that aim to protect the participants' health. These restrictions are paternalistic, that is, they aim to prevent people from harming themselves, and the deliberate violation of them *alone* makes conducting the trial illegitimate.

But their violation alone does not invalidate participants' consent. For instance, Sarah's colleague George may be so intrigued by the prospect of contributing to scientific progress that he also enrols. Even though the procedures remain impermissible, George can give his voluntary consent and thereby prevent Sarah from committing the kind of wrong that would occur without his voluntary consent.

Therefore, to evaluate *Deviant Scientist* appropriately, we need to distinguish between impermissibility due to the deliberate violation of paternalistic restrictions and impermissibility due to the consent of participants being involuntary. If Rambha's consent is involuntary, it will be due to the aspects that distinguish her situation from George's, that is, that she does not share the scientific objective of Sarah's trial and, unlike George, is under high pressure to enrol, given her dire circumstances.

In what follows, I will accept that performing the procedures in *Deviant Scientist* is impermissible for the former reason and only focus on the voluntariness of Rambha's consent. Thus, can Sarah's offer invalidate Rambha's consent, given that it is now a strong and illegitimate influence?

Rambha's consent will be involuntary in only one variation of *Deviant Scientist*, that is, when Sarah illegitimately reduces Rambha's options before offering payment. Suppose Sarah could either conduct the one risky trial or two safe trials to promote her scientific objective. But Sarah eventually opts for the one risky trial to accelerate her research and save money, thereby subordinating Rambha's interest in protecting her health to the comparatively minor scientific interests in saving time and money. In such a situation, Sarah acts illegitimately and Rambha is entitled to the safe trials because investigators are obliged to act beneficently and respect participants' interests where this is possible and feasible.[12] Hence, if Rambha consents to the risky trial only because the option of safe trials is withheld from her, then Sarah illegitimately constrained Rambha's situation and the pressure on Rambha's decision-making therefore invalidates her consent.

But now suppose that, to protect participants' health appropriately, Sarah needs to engage in animal testing first or is required to conduct the safer trials in places where Rambha could not participate, or suppose a safer trial would require greater resources not available at the moment. In these situations, offering the risky trial does not withhold another option from Rambha, and if Sarah and Rambha agree that it is better for them both to select the risky trial, payments do not invalidate consent. In such a situation, Sarah would only make another option available to Rambha and not control Rambha's situation in the way necessary to invalidate consent. After all, Sarah cannot enhance Rambha's control over her situation in any way other than allowing her to enrol in exchange for money. Furthermore, rejecting Rambha as a participant and only enrolling George may amount to greater disrespect than allowing her to enrol alongside George.

Hence, the voluntariness of Rambha's consent does not depend on whether payments are strong and illegitimate influences, when illegitimacy is due to the deliberate violation of a paternalistic restriction. Instead, it depends on whether Sarah illegitimately reduced Rambha's options in order to pressure Rambha into consenting.

Sometimes, however, risks can create yet another situation where consent is invalid, as the following case exemplifies:

> **Adverse Effect:** Rambha is halfway through a trial when the procedures cause severe side-effects and reach a level of risk that makes continued participation inconsistent with the protection of her health. Sarah informs Rambha about the situation and tells her that she will not receive any compensation if she withdraws. Rambha remains enrolled.

Adverse Effect shares with *Deviant Scientist* the fact that Sarah knows about unjustified risks, that she deliberately violates a paternalistic restriction, and that she incentivises Rambha to forego the required protection of her health. *Adverse Effect* differs from *Deviant Scientist* in that Rambha is now already halfway through the trial and the trial procedures caused severe side-effects as well as further risks for Rambha. This difference is significant because now (i) Rambha ought to receive full compensation without further participation, whereas she was not entitled to any compensation without participation in *Deviant Scientist*; (ii) withholding compensation violates Rambha's right to withdraw from a trial, and (iii) it therefore also invalidates her consent to continued participation.

(i) Rambha ought to receive full compensation because investigators would otherwise violate an obligation they owe her, that is, the obligation not to incentivise a course of action that imposes serious risks on her health. As any difference in payment between Rambha's continued participation and her withdrawal would, in fact, incentivise Rambha to pursue such a course of action, paying the full amount is the only way in which investigators can avoid violating their obligation.

(ii) When Rambha ought to receive full compensation, withholding payment penalises her withdrawal: it withholds from Rambha what she is entitled to. Penalising withdrawal also violates Rambha's right to withdraw from a trial. As a widely accepted official document on clinical conduct, the *CIOMS Guide* explains: the right to withdraw requires that someone be able to withdraw consent 'without penalty or loss of benefits to which he or she would otherwise be entitled'.[13]

(iii) Influences which violate the right to withdraw consent also invalidate consent to continued participation. As I argued in Chapter 5, this is because the protection afforded by the right to withdraw consent is implied not only by the general principle of self-determination, but also by the requirement that consent be voluntary. For if an influence violates a person's right to withdraw consent, it qualifies as a controlling influence and is therefore incompatible with consent continuing to be voluntary. Hence, if withholding compensation incentivises Rambha to consent to staying enrolled, her consent will be involuntary for that reason.

Therefore, increased risks *can* lead to a situation where certain modes of payment, for example, payment upon completion only, invalidate consent to continued participation in a clinical trial. And this conclusion also applies when participants become ill during a trial, without the trial procedures having caused the illness. In such cases too, threatening to withhold payment violates the obligation not to incentivise a course of action that imposes serious risks on a participant's health and thereby invalidates continued consent.

To conclude: unjustified risks do not invalidate consent if investigators could not have detected them, as shown in *Unknown Risk*. If investigators know about these risks, consent is invalidated only if investigators illegitimately reduce a person's options in order to penalise withdrawal.[14]

Hence, *Challenge 3: Risk* led my discussion to certain scenarios where Rambha's consent was indeed involuntary, even if risks alone could not invalidate consent.

This conclusion provides us with a third general lesson: the voluntariness of consent does not directly depend on the features of a medical procedure, for example, its risks. However, the voluntariness of consent is sensitive to the interaction between investigator and participant and, therefore, can be understood (at least partly) as an 'interpersonal concept' requiring the absence of illegitimate control within the investigator–participant interaction. If the investigator takes advantage of their position of power to dominate or penalise a participant's decision, such illegitimate control invalidates consent, and the presence of risks is relevant here: it may affect the moral quality of the investigator–participant interaction. Thus, ICCJ's focus on interpersonal justification aligns with this conclusion too.

8.3 ICCJ on Paid Trial Participation

In discussing the three main challenges to the voluntariness of consent, I claimed that payments invalidate consent only in certain cases of increased risk. But this discussion also provided important lessons about voluntary consent more generally, namely, that the voluntariness of consent is neither a *psychological* concept indicative of some inner states of a person nor a *circumstantial* concept indicative of a person's option set; rather, it is an *interpersonal* concept requiring the absence of controlling influences on the participant in her interaction with the investigator.

I already indicated that ICCJ accords with these three claims. Now, I wish to elaborate on my support of ICCJ and also include ICCJ's specific principles as providing the correct approach to voluntary consent in the context of paid trial participation.

With respect to *Challenge 1: Aversion*, Vanderpool and Grant claimed that payments invalidate consent if participants are offered money to do something they are averse to, and they presented the cases of an impecunious college student and a religious person as examples. ICCJ follows the result that this position is false and explains the voluntariness of consent with reference to the principles fundamental to the consenter–consentee relationship, thereby avoiding an explanation of voluntariness in psychological terms (first lesson).

In situations of aversion, payments are in accordance with *Assisted Decision-Making* as they do not compromise a person's decision-making, leave the final decision-making authority to participants, and still allow the investigator to assist participants in their deliberation about whether to enrol. Moreover, *Assisted Decision-Making* can account for cases where people *unreasonably* but still *voluntarily* consent to trial participation (e.g. Jack, who would violate duties at work, the religious person, or the impecunious college student may all unreasonably yet still voluntarily consent to enrolment). *Assisted Decision-Making* can account for these cases as it explicitly distinguishes between the voluntariness of a decision and its reasonableness. To recall: as *Assisted Decision-Making* emphasises that the person consenting has the final say, it is possible that his decision remains unreasonable or ill-judged in some way. Yet, a person ought to be respected in his decision-making and, other things being equal, can still consent voluntarily.

Furthermore, payments are in accordance with *Equal Moral Standing* as they respect people's entitlement to pursue a conception of the good and decide whether it is worth overcoming an aversion in exchange for money. In fact, *Equal Moral Standing* explicitly claims that people can valuably pursue a conception of the good even when they eventually consent to something with great reluctance or aversion. Investigators offering payments in these circumstances do not impose their own values on the person consenting, and they do not restrict but rather expand that person's options to pursue a conception of the good. By contrast, excluding someone from clinical trials on the basis of his aversion would impose values on a person that he currently does not endorse and restrict his options to pursue a conception of the good. As a result, such exclusion would express a negative judgement about a person's ability to make a reasoned decision and compromise his equal moral standing.

Finally, payments are in accordance with *Trusted Partner* as they satisfy both central norms of trust, that is, the *proviso of hypothetical transparency* and *loyalty in power*. In situations of aversion, there is no concern over transparency and investigators do not abuse their position of power when offering payment in exchange for trial participation.

With respect to *Challenge 2: No Acceptable Alternative*, ICCJ explains why McGregor and Olsaretti are mistaken when they claim that payments invalidate consent if participants enrol only for want of an acceptable alternative. ICCJ thereby aligns with the second lesson and does not consider voluntary consent to be a circumstantial concept.

ICCJ's commitment to respecting a person's autonomy requires that people be allowed to enrol in trials when they find themselves in dire circumstances. Respect for autonomy requires allowing Rambha to make her own decision as long as she is not under any wrongful or dominating influence.

Moreover, ICCJ's commitment to beneficence requires acknowledging that people's well-being depends not solely on their physical well-being but also on the satisfaction of other important needs, to which paid trial participation can contribute.

On this basis, payment to people in situations without acceptable alternatives is consistent with ICCJ's more specific principles. It is consistent with *Assisted Decision-Making* because the investigator can still actively assist but not control a person's decision-making. Investigators would in no way restrict but only expand a person's option and refrain from controlling a person's otherwise available options.

Moreover, obtaining consent in situations without acceptable alternatives is also consistent with *Equal Moral Standing*. In fact, *Equal Moral Standing* explicitly holds that people can valuably pursue a conception of the good when there are only very few options to choose from. Once the situation has become dire, it may even become particularly important for a person to be able to select what aligns best with her values and preferences. Thus, the offer of paid trial participation may be a significant contribution to a person's ability to pursue her conception of the good.

In addition, obtaining consent from a person in situations without an acceptable alternative is also consistent with *Trusted Partner*. Investigators would neither use non-transparency nor their position of power to dominate a person's decision-making and thereby avoid betraying the trust that prospective participants can expect them to honour.

With respect to *Challenge 3: Risk*, ICCJ also accounts for the third lesson concerning the significance of the interpersonal interaction between investigator and participant. To begin with, ICCJ explains why *unknown* risks cannot invalidate consent. ICCJ focuses on the actual interaction between consenter and consentee and on what the latter could be expected to have known. Accordingly, it holds that consent can be invalidated only if the person receiving consent violated a norm she could be expected to abide by.

Furthermore, ICCJ also explains why *known* risks invalidate consent if investigators thereby also illegitimately withhold a further option from a prospective participant. In the respective version of *Deviant Scientist*, Sarah completely ignores Rambha's standpoint when she subordinates Rambha's critical interest in the protection of her health to the comparatively minor scientific interests in saving time and money. Therefore, neither on the basis of the obligation to respect Rambha's autonomy nor on the basis of the obligation to act beneficently can Sarah justify to Rambha how she obtains her consent to paid trial participation.

As a result, Sarah violates *Assisted Decision-Making* because reducing Rambha's option illegitimately constrains Rambha's situation in such a way that creates undue pressure and compromises her opportunity to make a free decision. Sarah's conduct is also particularly serious because she aims to make Rambha do what greatly differs from her otherwise existing preference and because Rambha lacks any feasible means to protect herself against Sarah's dominance.

Moreover, Sarah also violates *Trusted Partner* because she abuses her professional power over which trials to conduct and dominates Rambha's decision-making. This is also a particularly serious instance as Sarah greatly relies on her position of power, and Rambha is in a very weak position.

However, ICCJ holds that Rambha's consent is voluntary in the first version of *Deviant Scientist*, where Sarah does not withhold any options from Rambha. Here, Sarah does not illegitimately constrain Rambha's situation, ignore Rambha's standpoint, or subordinate Rambha's critical interest in the protection of her health to comparatively minor scientific interests. Sarah allows Rambha to decide on her own and expands rather than restricts Rambha's available options. Thus, Sarah can interpersonally justify to Rambha how she obtains her consent to paid trial participation, and Rambha's consent is voluntary for that reason.

Finally, ICCJ's focus on the interpersonal interaction between participant and investigator accounts for cases where modes of payment penalise withdrawal and thereby invalidate consent. In *Adverse Effect*, Sarah cannot interpersonally justify to Rambha how she maintains Rambha's consent to continued participation because interpersonal justification requires taking seriously the interests of the person consenting and thereby opposes the subordination of the legitimate participants' interests to scientific interests.

Sarah violates *Assisted Decision-Making* because penalising withdrawal illegitimately threatens to harm Rambha if she does not consent, renders non-consent costly in a significant way, weakens Rambha's standing in the decision-making, and thereby unduly controls rather than supports Rambha in her decision-making. This is also a particularly serious incident because Rambha is entitled to compensation, there are serious risks for her health, and she is in very weak position compared to Sarah.

Sarah also violates *Trusted Partner* because she abuses her position of power to dominate Rambha's decision-making and thereby betrays the trust participants must be able to bestow upon her.

Hence, ICCJ maintains that Sarah invalidates Rambha's consent in *Adverse Effect*, and on this basis, ICCJ opposes certain modes of payment, for example, payment upon completion of a trial only.

8.4 Conclusion

This chapter focused on the question of whether, and if so, under what conditions paying research subjects invalidates their consent to participation. I answered that paying participants invalidates consent only in certain cases of increased risks when investigators illegitimately withhold an option of safer trials or penalise withdrawal. In all other cases, payments do not invalidate consent. On this basis, I supported three more general claims, namely that the voluntariness of consent is neither a 'psychological' concept indicative of the inner states of a person's mind nor a 'circumstantial' concept indicative of a person's set of options. Rather, it is an 'interpersonal' concept requiring the absence of illegitimate control *within* the investigator–participant interaction. I showed not only how my proposal, ICCJ, explicitly incorporates these three lessons but also how its specific principles, that is, *Assisted Decision-Making*, *Equal Moral Sanding*, and *Trusted Partner*, adequately guide an assessment of voluntary consent in a variety of cases and challenges. I can therefore support my proposal, ICCJ, in the context of paid trial participation too, another key challenge in clinical practice.

Notes

1 Hence I will focus on whether *high* payments are problematic and exclude concerns about too low payments from the scope of this chapter, which are discussed in Phillips (2011) and Belfrage (2016).
2 The Medicines for Human Use (Clinical Trials) Regulation 2004, Schedule 1, Part 2. See also Arrangement of Regulations, Part 3, 12; EU Directive 2001/20/EC, Article 3, 2(a); Convention for the Protection of Human Rights and Dignity of the Human Being with Regard to the Application of Biology and Medicine: Convention on Human Rights and Biomedicine, Article 16 (iii); Additional Protocol to the Convention on Human Rights and Biomedicine, Concerning Biomedical Research, Article 7.
3 Medicines, Schedule 1, Part 2. See also EU Directive 2001/20/EC, Article 4(h), Article 5(h); Convention Article 2; Additional Protocol Chapter II Article 3.
4 Additional Protocol Article 6, 1.
5 The EU Directive 2001/20/EC, Article 3, 2(a). Medicines, Schedule 1, Part 2. Convention, Article 17. Additional Protocol, Article 6 (2), 15 (2).
6 See *The Belmont Report*, Part C, C.2; International Ethical Guidelines for Biomedical Research Involving Human Subjects (henceforth the *CIOMS Guide*), Guideline 8.
7 I interpret Vanderpool as stating, not a psychological inability to resist but rather refers to the extraordinary psychological effort it would take to turn down the offer of paid trial participation.
8 The exploiter's benefit does not need to be large and can take many forms (beyond financial advantage), that is, it could just be a person's consent or acquiescence, or it could ultimately concern a third party too.
9 Note that this challenge is different from other challenges discussed in the literature, where risks and harms are sometimes considered to be *indirectly* relevant to voluntariness. Consider the debate on consent to something *harmful*: in the legal cases *R v Carriere* [1987] and *R v Brown* [1994], people consented to a violent fist-fight and very painful sadomasochistic sex, respectively. The judges deliberated whether there was something else in the background that pressured them into consenting to these things that they thought an 'ordinary' person would never consent to. See also V. Bergelson (2007); V. Bergelson (2018); Hart (1963, p. 33). A similar rationale could apply to consent to *risky* procedures. If the risk is one that, to use Nelson et al.'s words, 'the person would not ordinarily assume' (2011, p. 9), there may be the suspicion that something else pressures her into consenting to it. Assumptions about background pressure are reasonable, but do not show that risk itself could ever negate the voluntariness of a person's action. I will therefore not discuss this approach in detail.
10 See Straus (2012, pp. 111–119), who presents a real example of unanticipated high risk in a clinical trial.
11 Particularly in Phase I trials, it is impossible to anticipate all the risks because it is only through such trials that science can detect and assess risks of certain new forms of treatment. See Straus (2012, p. 110).
12 See my argument for obligations of beneficence in clinical research in Chapter 3.
13 *CIOMS Guide*, Guideline 9. Other documents echo this position. See section 2.2.1 in Part 1 of this book.

14 Unfortunately, neither the ethics literature nor policy documents have discussed how investigators can penalise withdrawal. Neither the relevant EU Directive, nor the Convention, nor the Additional Protocol, nor Medicines say anything about modes of payment. The documents referred to are: (1) EU Directive 2001/20/EC. (2) Convention for the Protection of Human Rights and Dignity of the Human Being with Regard to the Application of Biology and Medicine: Convention on Human Rights and Biomedicine. (3) Additional Protocol to the Convention on Human Rights and Biomedicine, Concerning Biomedical Research. (4) The Medicines for Human Use (Clinical Trials) Regulation 2004. An exception is the *CIOMS Guide*, which says that participants who withdraw because they became ill during the trial should receive as much money as they would have received upon completion. See the *CIOMS Guide*, Guideline 7. However, the CIOMS Guide does not offer any justification for this view and only presents it as a policy recommendation.

References

Belfrage, S. (2016). Exploitative, irresistible, and coercive offers: Why research participants should be paid well or not at all. *Journal of Global Ethics, 12*(1), 69–86.

Bentley, J. P., & Thacker, P. G. (2004). The influence of risk and monetary payment on the research participation decision making process. *Journal of Medical Ethics, 30*(3), 293–298.

Bergelson, V. (2007). The right to be hurt: Testing the boundaries of consent. *George Washington Law Review, 165*(75), 212–213.

Bergelson, V. (2018). Consent to pain. In P. Schaber & A. Müller (Eds.), *The Routledge handbook of the ethics of consent* (pp. 199–210). Abingdon, Oxon; New York, NY: Routledge.

Feinberg, J. (1986). *The moral limits of the criminal law. Volume 3: Harm to self.* New York: Oxford University Press.

Grant, R. W., & Sugarman, J. (2004). Ethics in human subjects research: Do incentives matter? *Journal of Medicine and Philosophy, 29*(6), 717–738 .

Hackshaw, A. K. (2009). *A concise guide to clinical trials.* Chichester and Hoboken, NJ: Wiley-Blackwell/BMJ Books.

Halpern, S. D., Karlawish, J. H., Casarett, D., Berlin, J. A., & Asch, D. A. (2004). Empirical assessment of whether moderate payments are undue or unjust inducements for participation in clinical trials. *Archives of Internal Medicine, 164*(7), 801–803.

Hart, H. L. A. (1963). *Law, liberty and morality.* London: Oxford University Press.

Jackson, E. (2019). *Medical law: Text, cases, and materials* (5th ed.). Oxford: Oxford University Press.

Mason, J. K., Laurie, G. T., & Aziz, M. (2011). *Mason and McCall Smith's law and medical ethics* (8th ed.). New York: Oxford University Press.

McGregor, J. (2005). Undue inducement as coercive offers. *American Journal of Bioethics, 5*(5), 24–25.

Nelson, R. M., Beauchamp, T., Miller, V. A., Reynolds, W., Ittenbach, R. F., & Luce, M. F. (2011). The concept of voluntary consent. *American Journal of Bioethics, 11*(8), 6–16.

Olsaretti, S. (2016). Voluntariness, coercion, self-ownership. In D. Schmidtz & C. Pavel (Eds.), *The Oxford handbook of freedom* (pp. 439–455). Oxford: Oxford University Press.

Phillips, T. (2011). Exploitation in payments to research subjects. *Bioethics, 25*(4), 209–219.

Straus, S. (2012). Unanticipated risk in clinical research. In J. Gallin & F. Ognibene (Eds.), *Principles and practice of clinical research* (pp. 109–126). London: Elsevier/Academic Press.

Vanderpool, H. Y. (2005). A quartet of criticisms. *American Journal of Bioethics, 5*(5), 16–19.

Wertheimer, A. (1996). *Exploitation*. Princeton: Princeton University Press.

Wertheimer, A. (2012). The obligations of researchers amidst injustice or deprivation. In J. Millum & E. J. Emanuel (Eds.), *Global justice and bioethics* (pp. 279–304). New York; Oxford: Oxford University Press.

Wertheimer, A. (2014). Poverty, voluntariness, and consent to participate in research. In T. Meyers (Ed.), *Poverty, agency, and human rights* (pp. 272–298). New York: Oxford University Press.

Legal Cases

- *R v Brown* [1994] 1 AC 212 HL.
- *R v Carriere* [1987] 35 CCC (3d) 276, 286–87 (Can).

International Documents

International Law

- Additional Protocol to the Convention on Human Rights and Biomedicine, Concerning Biomedical Research (2005). https://rm.coe.int/168008371a.
- Convention for the Protection of Human Rights and Dignity of the Human Being with Regard to the Application of Biology and Medicine: Convention on Human Rights and Biomedicine (1997). https://rm.coe.int/168007cf98.
- EU Directive 2001/20/EC. https://ec.europa.eu/health/medicinal-products/clinical-trials/clinical-trials-directive-200120ec_en.

National Law (UK)

- The Medicines for Human Use (Clinical Trials) Regulations (2004). www.legislation.gov.uk/uksi/2004/1031/pdfs/uksi_20041031_en.pdf.

International Documents (Not Legally Binding But Very Widely Accepted)

- *The Belmont Report* (1978). https://videocast.nih.gov/pdf/ohrp_belmont_report.pdf.
- International Ethical Guidelines for Biomedical Research Involving Human Subjects (*CIOMS Guide*) (2002). www.cioms.ch/publications/layout_guide2002.pdf.

9 Living Organ Donation

Introduction

Nashville, USA, Vanderbilt Transplantation Centre[1]. Sarah is 15 years old and suffers from cystic fibrosis, a genetic disorder that damages a person's lungs and reduces the quality and length of her life considerably. Currently, there is no known cure. As Sarah's condition is worsening, her parents, James and Debby, consider donating parts of their lungs to her, which would greatly improve her condition, and approach the medical team about this. James and Debby undergo tests and will soon receive the results.[2]

Whereas some people feel very gratified if they can donate and help their child, others are extremely frightened and secretly hope not to be compatible. In interviews, the latter admit to be 'scared to death' (Forsberg, Nilsson, Krantz, & Olausson, 2004, p. 375) and 'terrified all the way down' (p. 375).[3] Some even say that 'it feels like having a gun put to your head, it's like being taken hostage, so what can you do, there is absolutely nothing ... this is a decision about life and death, it's not about getting a pay rise or buying a car. This is real life drama' (p. 374). Yet, many of the most frightened eventually feel compelled to donate because they see themselves as under a moral obligation, experience implicit social pressure, or are subject to outright third-party coercion. Empirical evidence shows that, in one form or another, 'pressure to donate is a reality' (Eggeling, 1999, p. 20) (see also Al-Khader, 2005; Crowley-Matoka, Siegler, & Cronin, 2004; Forsberg et al., 2004; Lennerling, Forsberg, & Nyberg, 2003).

These situations pose a serious challenge to the voluntariness of consent: is a person's consent to surgery still voluntary if given under any of these conditions of pressure? After all, the standards for consent must be very high: someone would be consenting to a procedure that is risky, highly intrusive, and lacking in any medical benefit for him.

Given the need for organs and the ubiquity of pressure, this is a very urgent question. Yet, it has not received sufficient attention in the literature on living organ donation. The current literature offers a fair amount of qualitative interview data, revealing donors' motivations

DOI: 10.4324/9781003301417-12

and experiences as well as several policy recommendations on how to assist people in their decision-making (Al-Khader, 2005; Biller-Andorno, 2011). However, there is very little ethical analysis of the voluntariness of consent. So, what can we say about voluntariness in this context?

In addressing this question, I shall further support my proposal, ICCJ, and in particular its rejection of psychological views of voluntariness, its specific principles, as well as its endorsement of a *Recipient-Focus-View*, that is, the view that consent ultimately depends on the consent-receiver, even if influences are exerted by third parties. In so doing, I will show that ICCJ provides the correct approach to this third key challenge in clinical practice. I proceed as follows: in the Sections 9.1–9.4, I will make four claims about voluntariness in the context of living organ donation before I show, in Section 9.5, that my proposal, ICCJ, accounts for all of them.

9.1 Voluntariness Is Not Willingness

Recall Sarah's situation at Vanderbilt Transplantation Centre. Suppose that the tests reveal that both of her parents, James and Debby, are eligible to donate parts of their lungs to Sarah. But whereas Debby is happy to proceed, James is extremely frightened and would strongly prefer not to undergo transplantation surgery. The following statements from donor interviews could be representative of him:

> I felt I was obliged to do it. I wanted to do it. There was really no choice. It was all about trying to save my daughter. They could have whatever they needed.
>
> (Forsberg et al., 2004, p. 374)

> It's my daughter so ... there is really nothing to discuss.
>
> (Lennerling et al., 2003, p. 1244)

> As my responsibility as a family member .... I have to do it.
>
> (Majeske, Parker, & Frader, 1996, p. 94)[4]

Unfortunately, if James refuses to donate, Sarah will continue to suffer severely or even die, and so, he eventually consents. Is James' consent voluntary?

Al-Khader and others seem to think not. Al-Khader proposed that we 'determine the degree of willingness or unwillingness' (2005, p. 338) of potential donors in order to 'screen out donors who are acting under duress' (p. 338) and therefore fail to give their consent voluntarily. Thus, Al-Khader and those who followed him hold that consent is involuntary if a person's unwillingness to donate, that is, his reluctance, aversion, or fear, exceeds a certain threshold (Adams, 1987; Biller-Andorno, 2011;

A. L. Caplan, 1997; Otte, Janssen, Rosati, & Gonze, 2004; Valapour, 2008). Al-Khader and others made unwillingness central to their view because they consider unwillingness to indicate a conflict with important interests of a person, and they claim that, if such conflict is great enough, a person's decision ceases to be truly his own and becomes involuntary. Hence, if James' reluctance is too great, his consent is involuntary.

This view is influential in the debate on living organ donation and also aligns with common parlance, where the distinction between voluntary and involuntary is often explained in terms of a distinction between willing and reluctant. For instance, *The Oxford English Dictionary* presents 'reluctant' as synonymous with 'unwilling' and explains the latter as meaning 'involuntary'.[5] Moreover, this view also seems to have allies in other philosophical debates. For instance, in the debate on legal responsibility, Hart and Honoré claimed that 'when we take a step reluctantly, as the lesser of two evils, this is one way in which, for common sense and the law, our act is something less than fully voluntary' (1985, p. 156). And finally, in twentieth-century philosophy of action, both Anscombe and Kenny also contrasted voluntariness with reluctance (Anscombe, 2000, pp. 31–32; Kenny, 1985).

However, this view, which identifies voluntariness with willingness and involuntariness with reluctance, cannot be right. Suppose James' pressure comes from seeing himself under a moral obligation to donate. In such a case, James is strong-willed and self-determined. He does not let himself be carried away by his fear, but distances himself from it and acts on his moral decision to donate. To this extent, he is autonomous, and the reluctance that accompanies his acts does not diminish his autonomy. Quite the contrary, it is a sign of autonomous agency as it shows that he is able to manage different preferences.

But if reluctance does not undermine autonomy, it cannot undermine the voluntariness of consent either. This is because, in the context of consent, autonomy and voluntariness are closely linked: voluntariness is a condition of the validity of consent, and such conditions are supposed to protect the autonomy of the person giving consent. Hence, conditions of valid consent can only be violated if there is a flaw in the protection of a person's autonomy, but not otherwise. Therefore, for consent to be involuntary, there has to be an infringement of a person's autonomy. Thus, as reluctance is consistent with autonomy, it is also consistent with the voluntariness of consent.

Therefore, voluntariness is not the same as willingness, and involuntariness is not the same as reluctance. The voluntariness of consent cannot be understood as a purely psychological concept, reporting on the inner states, desires, or preferences of the consenting person. Any adequate account of voluntary consent needs to focus more closely on the ethical role that voluntariness plays, that is, the role of a necessary condition of making surgery permissible.

It is here where the debate on organ donation can learn from contemporary theorists of agency. For instance, as Hyman explained in his treatment of voluntariness and action:

> Whether someone does an act willingly and whether she does it voluntarily are different questions.
>
> (2015, p. 96)

> Being reluctant contrasts with being willing, and 'voluntary' does not mean the same as 'willing' .... An act is done willingly if it is done with a certain attitude or in a certain frame of mind, if the person welcomes doing it or at least does it without reluctance, whereas an act is done voluntarily if the agent does not do it out of ignorance or compulsion .... 'Voluntary' does not describe a person's attitude or state of mind, whereas 'reluctant' and 'willing' do exactly that. That is why an individual can be willing or reluctant but not voluntary or compulsory, whereas an option, such as second-year logic, can be voluntary or compulsory but not willing or reluctant.
>
> (p. 84)

In response to this critique, however, proponents of the willingness-view may argue that my assessment of James' willingness was incomplete. They could claim that, although James' first-order preference against donation decreased his willingness, he also had a second-order preference, or even moral commitment, not to let his fear determine his decision, and this preference *increased* his willingness. Moreover, since this was a higher-order preference and one that James seemed to have reflectively endorsed, James' decision was *authentically his own* and therefore, on balance, perfectly willing. Thus, by claiming that people consent willingly when their decision is 'authentic' in this sense, proponents of the willingness-view can explain James' consent as voluntary after all, despite his fear and great reluctance.

Unfortunately, this response comes at a price. Suppose James has always prioritised his own physical well-being over that of others and therefore lacks a reflectively endorsed second-order commitment in favour of donation. Yet, upon seeing his daughter suffer, James steps out of his usual character, experiences moral pressure, and decides to donate. In such a case, James' decision is not authentic, because it is not (already) supported by a reflectively endorsed second-order preference or commitment. However, it is not the result of some questionable moral compulsion either. His instant decision to break with his prior framework of values can still be deliberate, autonomous, voluntary, and worthy of respect. In fact, when people radically revise their value framework in unprecedented circumstances, they exercise what Rawls calls a 'moral power' (2005, p. 30). And doing so is an integral part of people's autonomy. Therefore, the requirement of authenticity may ask for too much: people need not always support their decision with an already reflectively endorsed second-order preference in order to make autonomous and voluntary decisions.

Hence, we should not only reject the simple equation of voluntariness and willingness but also avoid a more sophisticated view based on claims about authenticity. Although my argument against authenticity-views may not be decisive, given the comprehensive debate about them in the literature, it highlights a problem that is particularly relevant for the context of living organ donation: most living donors find themselves in situations that are unprecedented for them, and as scholars pointed out, these are exactly the situations that pose the greatest challenge to authenticity-views (cf. Nelson et al., 2011).

9.2 Voluntariness Does Not Require Exercising Relational Moral Agency

Mare Knibbe et al. might offer a better explanation as to why James' consent is voluntary. Knibbe et al. discuss the case of a fearful mother and says that the mother's consent to donating an organ for her child is voluntary because it 'is an expression of who she is *as a mother*' (2007, p. 438, emphasis added). Thus, they consider the woman in her *parental role* rather than seeing her only as an *isolated individual.* In fact, Knibbe et al. specifically argue that the flaw in many accounts is the adherence to a picture of the ' "moral agent" as being self-interested, independent and free from emotional bonds, commitment and duties' (p. 435). Such a picture, Knibbe et al. argue, must have necessarily led to the false view that any pressure opposing self-interests must reduce a person's autonomy and voluntariness.

Alternatively, Knibbe et al. suggest that 'the interpretation of living donor voluntary consent must be based on a *relational view of the moral agent*' (2007, pp. 436–437, emphasis added), as opposed to an unduly individualistic picture (see also Crouch & Elliott, 1999; Majeske et al., 1996; Spital, 2005). This relational view holds that 'relations are seen as constitutive of moral agency' (Knibbe et al., 2007, p. 436), which means that the capacity to act from moral reasons, and being autonomous for that matter, requires that individuals actually have and promote valuable relations with others (Majeske et al., 1996; Stoljar, 2011). Accordingly, the pressure which James and the mother experience does not negate voluntariness precisely because James' and the mother's consent expresses who they are *as parents* and promotes valuable relationships with their families.

Knibbe et al.'s account is insightful, and I agree with her that people who exercise their relational moral agency consent voluntarily. But I disagree that exercising relational moral agency, so understood, is necessary for voluntary consent. To see why, consider the following case:

> *Estranged Father.* Bob has a 16-year old daughter, Carry, whom he has not had contact with since she was born. Upon hearing that she

> needs a kidney, he feels great moral pressure to donate and consents to surgery. Donating a kidney will not promote the relationship to his daughter, as her family made clear that there would be no contact afterwards, and it will even worsen Bob's relation to his current family, as they would need him healthy to support another child.

In some respects, Bob is like James: his daughter needs an organ, he is frightened about surgery, and he feels morally compelled to donate. In other respects, Bob is unlike James: donation worsens rather than promotes valuable relationships, and Bob therefore fails to exercise his relational moral agency as Knibbe et al. describe it.

However, considering Bob's consent involuntary for this reason is false. The requirements of consent must allow people to pursue a variety of different conceptions of the good and not just one that requires the promotion of existing relationships. This is because respecting a person's autonomy requires respecting people's own and often unique values. In *Estranged Father*, Bob still acts from his firm moral conviction, pursues his own conception of the good, and genuinely exercises his autonomy. His decision may even be perfectly authentic and express what is most important to him. Hence, even if Bob experiences pressure that does not lead him to promoting valuable relationships, his consent can still be voluntary.

In response, however, Knibbe et al. could adjust her view and claim that actually promoting valuable relationships is not required as long as Bob discharges a genuine moral obligation owed to his daughter, Carry. Discharging such a parental obligation may be sufficient to fulfil one's role *as a parent* and live up to the standards of relational moral agency, more widely conceived. Thus, on this modified view, Bob's consent is voluntary as long as the pressure he experiences stems from sound moral reasoning.

To test this view, suppose Bob is mistaken. Although he still thinks he is morally obliged to donate, for example, because he still thinks that he ought to compensate for his past failings as Carry's father and therefore continues to feel moral pressure, he is in fact *not* morally obliged, say, because the interests of all people involved would be better served with another donor, and Bob would wrong his other family when being absent during the donation. If so, Knibbe et al.'s modified view would consider Bob's consent involuntary, as he fails to fulfil the standards of relational moral agency, and imply that just as factual mistakes invalidate consent, moral mistakes do so too.

I am doubtful about this modified version. Generally, a patient's false belief invalidates consent only if it is the kind of belief that the physician is obliged to prevent or correct. Consider factual mistakes, for example, false beliefs about significant risks of a medical procedure. Due to their medical expertise, physicians ought to correct these factual mistakes and disclose relevant medical information. If they fail to do so, such mistakes invalidate consent. By contrast, physicians do not have a comparable *moral* expertise and thus are not in a position, let alone under an obligation, to ensure their patients' sound moral views. In fact, in several US legal cases, it was held that medical professionals only need to disclose what is 'inherent' in a medical procedure, where 'inherent' means 'inseparable from the procedure itself' (*Jones v. Papp*, 782 S.W.2d 236, 240 (Tex.App.1989)), and whether undergoing a procedure is morally required is certainly not 'inherent' in this sense. In addition, physicians will lack the required background information about their patient's life to make a moral judgement in the first place. Therefore, moral decisions, including potential mistakes, remain within the patient's own responsibility rather than the physician's responsibility and therefore do not determine whether the physician can permissibly perform a medical procedure. But if so, these mistakes cannot invalidate consent either, as validity is precisely about determining the permissibility of a medical procedure.

However, even if one remains unconvinced about my argument and still thinks that moral mistakes do invalidate consent, one should still not assume that they render consent *involuntary*. Generally, mistakes undermine consent by violating the requirement that consent be *informed* rather than the requirement that consent be *voluntary*. As Wertheimer (2012) pointed out, we achieve greater conceptual clarity when we separate voluntariness (as the requirement concerning the absence of controlling influences and certain types of pressure) from information (as the requirement concerning the absence of false beliefs).

Hence, I conclude: exercising relational moral agency is not necessary for voluntary consent, and moral mistakes, if they are relevant at all, should be seen as affecting the requirement of information rather than the requirement of voluntariness.

9.3 Voluntariness Is Consistent with Implicit Social Pressure

Now, consider a different scenario. Suppose Sarah needs *two* living donors, each giving part of their lungs, and both James and Debby are suitable donors. Debby instantly decided to donate and the family is now waiting for James to make a decision too. James believes that waiting for an organ from a dead donor would be an acceptable option and that he is therefore no longer morally obliged to donate. Yet, he feels unable to provide a justification for non-donation that his family would find convincing,[6] and the prospect of failing to provide such justification, to be perceived as a coward or failing father, or even to be blamed for non-donation exerts considerable pressure. It makes it seem impossible for James to act on his actual preference against surgery. As Crouch and Elliot, and Caplan explained:

> Some parents may not want to donate, in fact, may not even feel morally obligated to donate, but would be ashamed to have this attitude

> revealed to anyone else, especially to family. The opinions of others can be powerful motivating forces.
>
> (Crouch & Elliott, 1999, p. 277)

> Family members will ordinarily feel extraordinary pressure to 'volunteer'. The realization that one could be blamed for the failure to help a spouse, a sibling, or a child may be so frightening that potential donors see themselves as having no choice.
>
> (Caplan, 1997, p. 118; see also Mazaris & Papalois, 2006, p. 488)

Let us assume that there is just *implicit* social pressure, and no one *explicitly* pressures James. Even then, however, the situation could be problematic and potentially incompatible with the voluntariness of James' consent for two main reasons.

Firstly, the situation can be problematic because giving James the choice of donation could already harm him as it allows others to blame James if he declines donation.[7] By way of explanation: before Sarah's condition worsened and James became a suitable donor, donation was not an option. Thus, James could not *choose* but only *accept* his situation as a non-donor, and others could not ask James to justify any aspect of it. But after Sarah's condition worsened and James became a suitable donor, not undergoing surgery ceased to be the *non-chosen* default. Whatever James does now will be seen as his *choice* and as something he can be called on to justify. In Velleman's words: 'He can now choose the status quo [i.e. no surgery] or choose the alternative [i.e. surgery], but he can no longer *have* the status quo without *choosing* it' (2015, p. 10). Thus, James is harmed because he lost non-donation as his *non-chosen* default situation and because he may now be blamed for anything he decides to do.

But even if this account is right, it does not show that James' consent would be involuntary. Velleman addresses a question of policy, not a question concerning the validity of consent. He asks whether we should give people a choice to consent to something and not whether they can still consent validly, *if* they have that choice. Moreover, Velleman presents his argument as being based on the 'policy of nonmalfeasance rather than on the policy of paternalism' (2015, p. 15). Velleman's claim is that 'we must not harm others by giving them choices, not that we must withhold the choices from them lest they harm themselves' (p. 15). After all, James could be an infallible decision-maker and choose what is best for him. But even in such cases, Velleman argues, we will have reasons not to give him a choice about whether to undergo a certain procedure if the harm of giving him that choice is too high. It seems that this is also the position of the Council of Europe when it states that, in cases of extreme emergency, living organ donation 'should not be recommended' (The Council of Europe, 1997, Recommendation No. R (97) 16, (i). Otte et al. [2004] echo this position).

Therefore, even if Velleman is right and people should not be given the choice of donation in certain situations, for reasons based on a policy of non-malfeasance, this view does not imply that people lose the capacity to give voluntary and valid consent *if* they have that choice. One may accept that people may strongly prefer not to face a certain choice. One may even accept that it is not valuable for them to have that choice and that, as a matter of policy, people should not have that choice. However, this does not affect the claim that, *if* they are given the choice, they still have the *ability* to consent validly and voluntarily. Hence, even if James is harmed, he can retain his ability to give voluntary consent.

The second reason why James' situation of implicit social pressure could be problematic is that James may be unable to continue the relationship with his family as before if he does not donate. His wife and daughter may be greatly disappointed and change their attitudes towards James, even if they do not explicitly say so or threaten James. Thus, not consenting can be very costly, and although there is not explicit threat from others, this could be seen as 'coercive' and thereby negate the voluntariness of consent.

So, suppose James consents because he wants to avoid the risk of damaging his family relationships, which he values much more than avoiding surgery. After talking to the surgeon about his situation, James requests to proceed with donation. To evaluate James' situation, it is useful to consider Enoch's distinction between two different values underpinning a person's autonomy:

> You're autonomous in the sense of non-alienation vis-à-vis an action or a decision that concerns you to the extent that the relevant matter is determined by your values, or your deep commitments. You're autonomous in the sense of sovereignty if the matter is up to you, if you have a choice—that is, if you can actually make a choice, and furthermore if that choice will be the last word regarding the relevant matter, if it will be effective.
>
> (2022, p. 144)

For the present purpose, I will focus on sovereignty. Enoch explains that, in certain contexts, autonomy as sovereignty requires accepting a person's word as conclusive on a matter. He provides the following example:

> If you're hosting a departmental event, then your colleagues' reports about their dietary constraints should be treated as conclusive evidence for their respective dietary constraints ... *seeking further evidence* here would be unacceptable. But it runs deeper than that – even if the further, countervailing evidence presents itself, you should still ignore it. It is just not for you to second-guess my report that I keep kosher.
>
> (2022, p. 156–157, original emphasis)

The reason why we need to accept people's word here (and in certain other contexts), if we are to respect their autonomy, is because 'in treating people as sovereign in the relevant way we treat them more fully as agents and citizens. For respecting people's sovereignty ... constitutes respecting *them*, as *responsible active agents*' (Enoch, 2022, p. 159). And Enoch adds that second-guessing certain choices or decisions 'can be so offensive' (p. 159) precisely because it fails to give them the kind of respect they deserve as moral and responsible agents.

I argue that what Enoch says about the department event also apply, maybe with even greater force in James' case and the specific patient–physician relationship he is involved in. James will have made a judgement about what is most important for him. He has not been explicitly forced or coerced by anyone, but the situation is such that he has to choose between two undesirable options: surgery or damaging his family relations. In this case, the surgeon may be entitled to assist James' decision-making and also inquire into his value to some extent. Yet, respect for James' autonomy as sovereignty requires that the surgeon eventually accepts James' decision to donate. Rejecting James as a donor would disrespect him as a moral agent.

But if this is correct, namely that respect for James' autonomy requires accepting him as a donor, then this has implications for the voluntariness of James' consent. A satisfactory account of voluntariness should not conflict with respecting a person's autonomy. This is because, as previously explained, autonomy is the key behind consent, and the conditions of valid consent, including voluntariness, must therefore be understood in accordance with the requirements from autonomy. In other words, a satisfactory account of voluntary consent would not consider certain influences as negating voluntariness if doing so conflicts with important aspects of the value of autonomy, including autonomy as sovereignty. Hence, and applied to James' case, the correct account of voluntariness aligns with autonomy as sovereignty and thereby holds that implicit social pressure does not negate voluntariness.

Thus, James' consent will remain voluntary even in cases of implicit social pressure. Physicians may be obliged to assist their prospective donors, offer counselling, and help them in other ways to navigate such stressful situations. Yet, they are not entitled to reject people like James as a donor and must acknowledge that James can still give voluntary consent in such cases.

9.4 In Cases of Third-Party Pressure, Voluntariness Depends on the Role of the Surgeon and the Medical Team

Finally, let me move on to a more direct form of pressure. Suppose James considers waiting for a cadaveric organ an acceptable option and therefore no longer feels morally obliged to donate. However, James' wife Debby tells him that she will divorce him and fire him from the family company unless he donates. Divorce and unemployment would leave James in a very poor financial situation and even make him homeless. James eventually consents but only to prevent Debby from carrying out her threat.

In such cases, scholars in the literature all hold that the voluntariness of consent depends solely on Debby's influence: if Debby's influence is sufficiently severe, consent is involuntary and invalid (Adams, 1987, p. 568; A. L. Caplan, 1997, p. 123; Chessa, 2014; Hays, 2014; McGee & Fox, 1996, p. 106; Otte et al., 2004, p. 318; Valapour, 2008, p. 198).

But I think this view is mistaken, and I will defend the claim that in cases of explicit third-party pressure, the voluntariness of James' consent depends on how the surgeon and the transplant team react to the situation. However, to defend this claim, I will firstly need to focus on a slightly different question, namely whether the surgeon and their team could ever permissibly proceed with surgery in such a case. Consider the following case.

> *Respect.* James' family knows about his physiological compatibility as a donor and keeps pressuring him. After James informed the surgeon about his situation, the latter agrees with James to contact his family. They meet for a family conversation where the surgeon explains the viability of cadaveric donation and emphasises the importance of making the decision to donate free of pressure. Yet, the family cannot settle the issue, and the medical team is unable to alleviate James' situation. James eventually requests that the surgeon proceed with the donation. On the basis of the overall situation, he says donating is best for him. He insists that the surgeon no longer offer any help, contact his family, or interfere with his private decision.

Refusing James as a donor would disrespect James' part or role in deciding how to proceed. It would give short shrift to his perspective and unduly impose standards on him he does not share. It would thereby also put him in a situation that is, according to his own evaluation, worse for him. Accepting James' decision to donate, on the other hand, would respect his part in deciding what to do, at least in the interaction between him and the medical team, and it would allow him to pick the option he considers best for him under the circumstances. Furthermore, having offered any possible help for James, the surgeon and their team did not fail to discharge obligations owed to James. For these reasons, I argue, the surgeon can permissibly proceed with the surgery. Contrast this scenario with another case:

> *No Help.* According to the hospital's policy, a person will be identified as an incompatible donor due to physiological, psychological, or other reasons. 'Other reasons' are broadly understood and include people's requests to be identified as incompatible when

> pressured by others. The exact reasons for incompatibility will be kept confidential within the medical team and not released to anyone except the tested person. At the moment, only James knows about his physiological compatibility as a donor. His family has not been informed yet, and James does not want them to know. He asks for a general statement of incompatibility. Issuing this statement would be in line with the hospital's policy, and James' family would subsequently withdraw their pressure. Yet, the surgeon, although knowing about James' situation, deviates from the usual policy and only issues a specific statement on physiological donor compatibility. James' family keeps pressuring him and he subsequently consents to donation.

In this case, the surgeon could have helped James very easily. It was possible and feasible for him to provide James with a general statement of incompatibility. Yet, the surgeon decided to deny James this opportunity to escape the threats from his family. The surgeon thereby unduly controlled the circumstances in which James had to make his decision and made him worse off, compared to an otherwise possible scenario. For these reasons, it would be impermissible for the surgeon to perform the surgery.

No Help and *Respect* do *not* differ in terms of third-party pressure. In both scenarios, James consents to surgery only because Debby pressured him. However, they differ in terms of the surgeon's reaction: whereas the surgeon and their team did everything he could in *Respect*, the surgeon in *No Help* failed to help James where doing so was possible and feasible. Therefore, if my evaluation is correct and performing surgery is impermissible in *No Help* but permissible in *Respect*, permissibility cannot always depend on third-party pressure. The permissibility of surgery can depend on the surgeon's reaction to the situation.

This result can inform judgements about the voluntariness of James' consent. This is because the debate on living organ donation unanimously accepts what we can call the *Permissibility Principle*, that is, the view that performing donation surgery can only be permissible if consent is voluntary (see also Chapter 6). Thus, if permissibility requires voluntariness, and if performing surgery is found permissible, then James' consent must have been voluntary. This line of reasoning can be described a simple *modus ponens*: (1) X is a necessary condition of Y (e.g. voluntary consent is a necessary condition for permissible surgery). (2) Y is given (e.g. surgery is permissible). (3) Therefore, X (e.g. James' consent is voluntary).

In order to account for the conclusion in (3), we need to adopt a certain account of voluntary consent. Such an account can start with the premise that voluntary consent requires that the person's decision-making is not controlled by others. But then, one needs to claim that control over a person's consent can take different forms: *global control* is that coming from outside the interaction between the person giving consent and the person receiving it, for example, pressure from third parties like Debby. By contrast, *transactional control* is that coming from within the interaction between the person receiving consent and the person giving it (including the medical team more generally), for example, if the recipient of consent or their team threatens the consenter, or if he keeps him in his predicament where it would be possible and feasible to help, as was the case in *No Help*.

In order to accept the *Permissibility Principle* and the evaluation of the different scenarios of James' situation, we need to adopt the view that the voluntariness of consent depends on *transactional control* rather than on *global control*. In *Respect*, James' consent is voluntary because it was not transactionally controlled, whereas James' consent is involuntary in *No Help* because it was in fact transactionally controlled.

Hence, the voluntariness of consent depends on how the recipient(s) of consent, for example, the surgeon and their team, react(s) to the situation and not just on the influence exerted by third parties. The influence of third parties, and their strength and illegitimacy, may inform what the person receiving consent is obliged to do, but may not directly negate the voluntariness of consent.

9.5 ICCJ on Living Organ Donation

Having rejected widespread views in the literature on organ donation, I now defend my own proposal, ICCJ, as the correct approach to the voluntariness of consent in this context. According to ICCJ, a person's consent is voluntary if and only if the surgeon can interpersonally justify that he tolerated the pressure on a person's decision-making when obtaining this person's consent. ICCJ provides a distinct view by focusing on the interaction between the surgeon and the prospective donor rather than, as other views do, directly on psychological distress or social pressure. But this feature not only sets ICCJ apart from other views, it also makes it superior to them.

ICCJ can explain why moral and implicit social pressure do not invalidate consent. ICCJ's principle of *Assisted Decision-Making* is satisfied in cases of moral and implicit social pressure because the surgeon, when obtaining consent, would not compromise a person's ability or opportunity to make a free decision. He would neither threaten to harm a patient if he did not consent, nor render non-consent costly in some way, nor prevent the donor from taking part in some aspects of the decision-making, nor weaken a donor's emotional or cognitive capacities for decision-making. In fact, the surgeon could still actively assist the prospective donor by means of a shared process of deliberation. Moreover, simply allowing moral and implicit social pressure to be consistent with voluntary consent already enhances the process of shared decision-making: it refrains from encouraging people to hide their feelings out of fear of being rejected as a donor, and it creates a safe space for an open discussion. Finally, *Assisted Decision-Making* explicitly explains that consent can sometimes be ill-judged but still voluntary and thereby accounts for cases like *Estranged Father.*

ICCJ's principle of *Equal Moral Standing* explicitly requires the surgeon not to interfere when the donor pursues his conception of the good. Thus, even if people experience distress or consent with great reluctance, they may still engage in what *Equal Moral Standing* highlights as worthy of protection. As already mentioned, people can valuably pursue a conception of the good even when they eventually consent to something with great reluctance or when they see themselves without acceptable alternatives. In fact, once the situation has become like that, it may be particularly important for a person to be able to select what aligns best with his values and preferences. Therefore, tolerating moral and implicit social pressure can be interpersonally justified.

In addition, ICCJ's principle of *Trusted Partner* is also satisfied. A surgeon would rely on neither non-transparency nor his superior position of power to dominate rather than assist a person's decision-making. In fact, there is no concern over transparency at all, and the surgeon is not in any relevant position of power with regard to moral or implicit social pressure.

Hence, accepting consent given under moral pressure can be interpersonally justified, and therefore both James' and Bob's consent is voluntary in the examples described earlier. Thus, ICCJ is superior to other views by accounting not only for the voluntariness of James' consent but also for the voluntariness of Bob's consent in *Estranged Father.*

In addition, ICCJ also presents a more convincing proposal regarding third-party pressure because it can explain the difference between the scenarios mentioned earlier. In *No Help*, the surgeon *cannot* interpersonally justify his failure to help James. He deliberately deviates from clinical routine and makes the statement more specific so that James will run into the threats of his family. Providing the general documents would have required neither considerable effort nor the violation of any general medical obligation. By not providing the statement, the surgeon compromises the decision-making process: he deliberately prevents James from making a decision free from pressure and thereby violates *Assisted Decision-Making*. Moreover, the surgeon violates *Trusted Partner*: he fails to use his position of professional power to help James and alleviate the pressure on his decision-making. Hence, ICCJ explains why performing the surgery in *No Help* is impermissible and bases this explanation on the claim that consent is involuntary due to the illegitimate transactional control exerted by the surgeon.

By contrast, in *Final Say*, the surgeon *can* interpersonally justify that he tolerates the influence and obtains consent. He talks to James about this situation, offers advice, acknowledges James as the final decision-maker, and thereby satisfies *Assisted Decision-Making*. Moreover, he accepts

James' request, avoids imposing his own opinion on him, and allows James to pursue his conception of the good, thereby satisfying *Equal Moral Standing*. Finally, he relies on neither non-transparency nor his superior position of power to dominate James' decision in any way and thereby satisfies *Trusted Partner*. Hence, ICCJ explains why performing the surgery in *Final Say* is permissible and bases this explanation on the claim that consent is voluntary because the surgeon did not exert undue transactional control over James' decision.

Thus, ICCJ provides a distinct and novel position: unlike other views, it focuses on how the recipient of consent deals with third-party pressure, rather than on the features of the third-party influence. This position is also superior to other accounts because, unlike them, ICCJ aligns with the Permissibility Principle, the evaluation of *Final Say* and *No Help*, and the view that links voluntariness to transactional rather than global control.

Before I conclude, I want to explore one very unorthodox potential implication of my view, namely that *Assisted Decision-Making* could oblige a physician to provide *false* documentation on donor incompatibility; and if a physician fails to discharge such an obligation when it arises, consent will be involuntary for that reason.[8]

Suppose James' brother-in-law threatens him with severe physical injury if he does not donate and the only way for James to escape this threat is to provide false documentation on his incompatibility. ICCJ could imply that, in some of these cases, it is not only *permissible* for the physician to fake documentation but it is *obligatory* for her to do so.

According to ICCJ, there is a presumption in favour of providing false documentation in these cases, and if such a presumption cannot be defeated, it will be obligatory for the physician to provide false documentation. The presumption arises because providing false documentation serves the two fundamental principles of ICCJ. It serves the principle of beneficence by saving James from severe harm, that is, either physical injury or undergoing an intrusive operation that he does not want to undergo. And it serves the principle of respect for autonomy as it allows James to regain control over his situation and diminishes the influence of his brother-in-law.

This presumption can be defeated if the physician, *qua physician*, is under an obligation *not* to provide false documentation; and in fact, truthfulness is an important value in the medical context and among professional obligations. Such professional obligations limit the scope to which physicians are obliged to act beneficently and promote their patients' autonomy. However, to see whether this obligation of truthfulness defeats the presumption in favour of providing fake documents in the scenario under consideration, we need to put this obligation into context.

The obligation of truthfulness primarily purports to enable people's self-determination when they decide whether to undergo a medical procedure. A physician needs to tell the truth so that a person can base his decision about medical procedures on correct information. In addition, the norm of truthfulness also purports to maintain trust in the medical profession more generally. It is important that the public can rely on expert statements from physicians.

In the case at hand, telling the truth about donor compatibility would weaken James' self-determination, that is, it would weaken the self-determination of the person who is about to decide whether to undergo a medical procedure. By contrast, providing false documents would enhance James' self-determination. Hence, following the obligation of truthfulness would not fulfil its primary purpose, while deviating from it would promote such purpose.

In addition, if made public afterwards, having provided false documentation is unlikely to undermine public trust in the medical profession. After all, the physician will only have produced fake documentation to prevent great harm to a prospective donor. However, confirming this point may require further empirical evidence.

Furthermore, deceiving the coercing party does not seem to be of great concern insofar as it amounts to a loss of the the coercer's control over the situation. James' brother-in-law may even have forfeited his right to receive correct information.

But there may be some concern about the deception of the potential recipient of the organ. Even though this person may not be entitled to receive information about other people's compatibility, she might make the claim that *if* she is given information, it must be true information so that she can base her deliberation on facts.

Hence, the question arises as to whether the stakes for the prospective donor can be so high that a physician becomes obliged to provide false documents and override the potential entitlement of the prospective recipient of an organ to receive correct information.

According to ICCJ, the physician's decision has to be interpersonally justifiable *to the person giving consent*, and such interpersonal justification requires providing fake documentation under the following conditions: if the obligation of truthfulness does not serve its primary purpose, if deviating from such an obligation greatly enhances the control and self-determination of the prospective donor, if there is no other way of helping him, and if there is an immediate threat of severe harm that greatly outweighs the concern for the harm done to the potential recipient of the organ by not telling her the truth. Not providing fake documents would be unjustifiable under these conditions because it would unduly prioritise the norm of truthfulness and the perspective of the potential recipient of the organ over the severe third-party coercion that the prospective donor is subject to and cannot escape in any other way.

Although this implication does not present a precise formula for when physicians become obliged to provide false documentation, it provides guidance on how to evaluate such a situation: ICCJ identifies a presumption in favour of faking documents, relates to the purpose of the obligation of truthfulness, and requires the balancing of harms on the side of the prospective donor and those on the side of the patient waiting for an organ.

This potential implication of ICCJ sets my view apart from McGee & Fox as well as Mazaris & Papalois, who all reject an obligation to provide false documentation:

> Offering medical reasons when none exist is problematic, however, because it requires deliberately misleading the patient and this undermines the trust essential to the physician-patient relationship. Perhaps even more important, deception undermines the integrity of the family unit.
>
> (McGee & Fox, 1996, p. 108)

> Physicians ... must avoid lying or falsifying medical documents, both of which can result in catastrophic consequences.
>
> (Mazaris & Papalois, 2006, p. 488)

However, ICCJ's potential implication resembles Caplan's position, who argued:

> Transplant teams must even be prepared to lie to protect the ability of prospective donors to make voluntary choices ... transplant centers ought to be willing to offer a prospective donor the option of disqualification on medical grounds, even when none exists, in order to ensure that donors understand that they can choose not to participate without being stigmatized, ostracized, or penalized.
>
> (Caplan, 1993, p. 1999; see also Caplan, 1997, pp. 123–124; Kallich & Merz, 1994, p. 152)

ICCJ resembles Caplan's position as the latter also allows for an obligation to provide false documentation in certain cases. Yet, ICCJ's potential implication is also more stringent because being socially stigmatised would not be enough for ICCJ unlike for Caplan, to oblige physicians to provide false medical documentation. According to ICCJ, it has to be a severe and immediate threat against which there is no other means of protection. Hence, the pressure people experience when facing implicit social expectations, as discussed earlier, would not justify providing false documents.

9.6 Conclusion

This chapter discussed three types of pressure which people like James can be subject to when considering donating an organ to a family member: moral pressure, implicit social pressure, and third-party pressure. I defended my proposal, ICCJ, as the correct approach to voluntary consent. ICCJ provided a distinct view by focusing on the interaction between the surgeon and the prospective donor rather than, as all other views do, directly on psychological distress or social pressure. This feature not only sets ICCJ apart from other views but also makes it superior to them: it allows ICCJ to account for the distinction between voluntariness and willingness, to respect people's autonomy as sovereignty, and to accommodate the *Permissibility Principle* in cases of third-party pressure. Therefore, ICCJ's most distinct feature, that is, the focus on the interaction between the person giving and the person receiving consent, proved to be appropriate even in cases where strong influences come from psychological distress or from the influence of third parties, and not from the person receiving consent. These results are particularly important for two reasons: firstly, they explain voluntariness in situations where a person consents to something that offers no medical or financial benefit to him at all, but only aims to benefit another person. Secondly, they explain voluntariness in an area that is, from the perspective of the donor, neither treatment nor research, but rather a third class of medical procedures which I have not considered before. Hence, understanding voluntariness in this area was required to complete a comprehensive picture of the practical challenges to the voluntariness of consent.

Conclusion of Bottom-Up Defence of ICCJ

This brings my Bottom-Up defence of ICCJ to an end. I hope to have shown how the proper assessment of three key challenges from clinical practice, that is, nudging and manipulation, payment in clinical trials, and living organ donation, supports not only the general idea of interpersonal justification in assessing voluntary consent but also the more specific principles that my proposal, ICCJ, is based on. On this basis, I confirm ICCJ's view that voluntary consent is neither a 'psychological' concept indicative of the inner states of a person's mind (e.g. willingness or reluctance) nor a 'circumstantial' concept indicative of a person's set of options. Rather, it is an 'interpersonal' concept focusing on the interaction between the person giving consent and the person receiving it and requiring the absence of illegitimate control by the consent-receiver.

Notes

1 Parts of this chapter are reproduced from Kiener, Maximilian (2021) "Consent and living organ donation", The *Journal of Medical Ethics*, 47(12), e50–e50. Copyright notice year 2022. With permission from BMJ Publishing Group Ltd.
2 This is a case from actual clinical practice, reported by McGee and Fox (1996, p. 104). The parents' names are fictitious.
3 Further interview statements from frightened people can be found in Knibbe et al. (2007, p. 437).

4 Similar statements can be found in Fujita et al. (2004, p. 1426) and Knibbe et al. (2007, pp. 437–438).
5 See *Oxford English Dictionary*: 'voluntary' 7a; 'involuntary' 1a; 'willing' 3; 'unwilling' 2a and 5.
6 These situations seem well documented in clinical practice. For instance, in her interview research, Brown documented a case where a donor understood that their 'reservations about ... donation were valid' (2014, p. 278), but that she 'did not perceive that others in the family would find them as a justification for not proceeding with donation' (p. 278).
7 This section draws on some of Velleman's claims. In his discussion of a right to euthanasia, Velleman claims that giving people an additional option (e.g. whether to consent to a procedure such as euthanasia) can sometimes be harmful to them, even if they are infallible decision-makers. Therefore, we may have good reasons not to allow people to consent to certain procedures (Velleman, 2015).
8 To remind the reader: I use the terms 'surgeon' and 'physician' interchangeably. I will refer to the 'physician' in the rest of this chapter as it is the more general term and better suited to the claims I will make. However, nothing substantial depends on this terminological choice.

References

Adams, R. K. (1987). Live organ donors and informed consent: A difficult minuet. *Journal of Legal Medicine, 8*(4), 555–586.

Al-Khader, A. A. (2005). A model for scoring and grading willingness of a potential living related donor. *Journal of Medical Ethics, 31*(6), 338. doi:10.1136/jme.2004.009282.

Anscombe, G. (2000). *Intention* (2nd ed.). Cambridge, MA: Harvard University Press.

Biller-Andorno, N. (2011). Voluntariness in living-related organ donation. *Transplantation, 92*(6), 617–619. doi:10.1097/TP.0b013e3182279120.

Brown, C. (2014). Pressure and coercion. In J. Steel (Ed.), *Living donor advocacy. An evolving role within transplantation* (pp. 275–291). New York; Heidelberg; Dordrecht; London: Springer.

Caplan, A. (1993). *Must I be my brother's keeper? Ethical issues in the use of living donors as sources of liver and other solid organs. Transplantation Proceedings, 25*(2), 1997–2000.

Caplan, A. L. (1997). *Am I my brother's keeper? The ethical frontiers of biomedicine.* Bloomington: Indiana University Press.

Chessa, F. (2014). Informed consent for living organ donation. In J. Steel (Ed.), *Living donor advocacy. An evolving role within transplantation* (pp. 261–274). New York; Heidelberg; Dordrecht; London: Springer.

Crouch, R. A., & Elliott, C. (1999). Moral agency and the family: The case of living related organ transplantation. *Cambridge Q. Healthcare Ethics, 8*(3), 275–287.

Crowley-Matoka, M., Siegler, M., & Cronin, D. C. (2004). Long-term quality of life issues among adult-to-pediatric living liver donors: A qualitative exploration. *American Journal of Transplantation, 4*(5), 744–750. doi:10.1111/j.1600-6143.2004.00377.x.

Eggeling, C. (1999). The psychosocial implications of live-related kidney donation. *EDTNA/ERCA Journal, 25*(3), 17–20. doi:10.1111/j.1755-6686.1999.tb00042.x.

Enoch, D. (2022). Autonomy as non-alienation, autonomy as sovereignty, and politics. *Journal of Political Philosophy, 30*(2), 143–165.

Forsberg, A., Nilsson, M., Krantz, M., & Olausson, M. (2004). The essence of living parental liver donation: Donors' lived experiences of donation to their children. *Pediatric Transplantation, 8*(4), 372–380. doi:10.1111/j.1399-3046.2004.00187.x.

Fujita, M., Slingsby, B. T., & Akabayashi, A. (2004). Three patterns of voluntary consent in the case of adult-to-adult living related liver transplantation in Japan. *Transplantation Proceedings, 36*(5), 1425–1428. doi:10.1016/j.transproceed.2004.04.088.

Hart, H. L. A., & Honoré, T. (1985). *Causation in the law* (2nd ed.). Oxford: Clarendon.

Hays, R. (2014). Contraindication to living donation from an ILDA perspective. In J. Steel (Ed.), *Living donor advocacy: An evolving role within transplantation* (pp. 205–219). New York; Heidelberg; Dordrecht; London: Springer.

Hyman, J. (2015). *Action, knowledge, and will* (1st ed.). Oxford: Oxford University Press.

Kallich, J. D., & Merz, J. F. (1994). The transplant imperative: Protecting living donors from the pressure to donate. *Journal of Corporation Law, 20(1),* 139–154.

Kenny, A. (1985). *The ivory tower: Essays in philosophy and public policy.* Oxford: Blackwell.

Kiener, M. (2020). Consent and living organ donation. *Journal of Medical Ethics, 47*(12), E50.

Knibbe, M., Maeckelberghe, E., & Verkerk, M. (2007). Confounders in voluntary consent about living parental liver donation: No choice and emotions. *A European Journal, 10*(4), 433–440. doi:10.1007/s11019-007-9075-1.

Lennerling, A., Forsberg, A., & Nyberg, G. (2003). Becoming a living kidney donor. *Transplantation, 76*(8), 1243–1247. doi:10.1097/01.TP.0000087832.27092.4F.

Majeske, R. A., Parker, L., & Frader, J. (1996). In search of an ethical framework for consideration of decisions regarding live donation. In B. Spielman (Ed.), *Organ and tissue donation: Ethical, legal, and policy issues* (pp. 89–101). Carbondale: Southern Illinois University Press.

Mazaris, E., & Papalois, V. E. (2006). Ethical issues in living donor kidney transplantation. *Experimental and Clinical Transplantation, 4*(2), 485–497.

McGee, C., & Fox, M. (1996). Bilateral lung transplantation from living donors. In B. Spielman (Ed.), *Organ and tissue donation: Ethical, legal, and policy issues* (pp. 103–109). Carbondale: Southern Illinois University Press.

Nelson, R. M., Beauchamp, T., Miller, V. A., Reynolds, W., Ittenbach, R. F., & Luce, M. F. (2011). The concept of voluntary consent. *American Journal of Bioethics, 11*(8), 6–16.

Otte, J. B., Janssen, M., Rosati, M. R., & Gonze, D. (2004). Parental experience with living-related donor liver transplantation. *Pediatric Transplantation, 8*(4), 317–321. doi:10.1111/j.1399-3046.2004.00205.x.

Rawls, J. (2005). *Political liberalism.* New York: Columbia University Press.

Spital, A. (2005). More on parental living liver donation for children with fulminant hepatic failure: Addressing concerns about competing interests, coercion, consent and balancing acts. *American Journal of Transplantation, 5*(11), 2619–2622. doi:10.1111/j.1600-6143.2005.01083.x.
Stoljar, N. (2011). Informed consent and relational conceptions of autonomy. *Journal of Medicine and Philosophy, 36*(4), 375–384. doi:10.1093/jmp/jhr029.
Valapour, M. (2008). The live organ donor's consent: Is it informed and voluntary? *Transplantation Reviews (Philadelphia, Pa.), 22*(3), 196–199. doi:10.1016/j.trre.2008.02.004.
Velleman, J. D. (2015). *Beyond price: Essays on birth and death*. Cambridge: Open Book Publishers.
Wertheimer, A. (2012). Voluntary consent: Why a value-neutral concept won't work. *Journal of Medicine and Philosophy, 37*(3), 226–254.

Legal Case

- *Jones v. Papp* [1989] 782 S.W.2d 236 (Tex.App.) (9).

International Legal Document

- The Council of Europe/Committee of Ministers (1997) Recommendation No. R (97) 16. https://rm.coe.int/CoERMPublicCommonSearchServices/DisplayDCTMContent?documentId=0900001680505d5b (9).

10 Conclusion

Consent protects self-determination: it empowers people to decide how others can permissibly interact with them. But consent can protect self-determination only if people consent *voluntarily*. Being competent and informed does not suffice.

In this book, I focused on consent to medical procedures, and developing my proposal of *Interpersonal Consenter–Consentee Justification* (ICCJ), I claimed that consent is voluntary unless it is motivated by an influence that cannot be interpersonally justified. I explained that interpersonal justification requires that the consentee (i.e. the person receiving consent) can justify to the consenter (i.e. the person giving consent) that he exerted these influences or – when influences had a different source – tolerated their presence. The principles fundamental to the consenter–consentee relationship provided the basis for such a justification.

ICCJ introduced the concept of interpersonal justification to the debate on consent and most clearly differs from other views by (1) focusing on the reasons or motivation for which a person consents, instead of mere causal links or counterfactuals, (2) allowing the moral legitimacy and not just the strength of an influence to have a bearing on the voluntariness of consent, and (3) making the behaviour of the person receiving consent (the consentee) central to its approach.

On this basis, ICCJ is lenient in some respects: it considers consent voluntary in situations of great reluctance, psychological distress, lack of acceptable alternatives, and even some cases of third-party pressure. ICCJ is strict in other respects, however: it considers consent involuntary when the consentee fails to discharge certain obligations owed to the consenter, for example, in the case of third-party pressure, even if the consentee does not collaborate with the pressuring third party at all. Moreover, ICCJ acknowledges that certain influences invalidate consent, for example, the threat to abandon a patient, even if the extent to which it affects a particular patient is rather low.

I hope to have demonstrated that ICCJ can be supported on the basis of a *Top-Down* approach as well as a *Bottom-Up* approach. Both theoretical considerations around causation, morality, and coercion and

DOI: 10.4324/9781003301417-13

practical consideration concerning key challenges from clinical practice support ICCJ as the correct approach to voluntary consent.

However, over and above contributing to a topic in practical ethics, ICCJ also contributes to the more general debate on voluntariness that started in twentieth-century philosophy of action and cut ties with theories postulating volitions. In fact, many of my results contribute to the modern post-volitional understanding of voluntariness, for example, the rejection of counterfactual models of causation and the emphasis on the reasons behind people's consent. Likewise, my view on the relation between intentional action and voluntariness of consent, my account of how the voluntariness of consent can depend on the morality of another person's influence, and the disambiguation of what I term the *Coercion Principle* have also contributed to the understanding of voluntariness more generally.

Finally, ICCJ identifies three areas for further research. First, ICCJ encourages the transfer of the idea of interpersonal justification from the context of medical procedures to other areas of consent, for example, consent to sexual relations. Second, ICCJ opens new paths for investigating liability and responsibility. As I argued in the chapter on 'Voluntariness and Morality', there is key connection between consent and responsibility, allowing us to learn about one by looking at the other. And third, ICCJ connects and contrasts voluntariness with many other concepts (e.g. autonomy, reluctance, willingness, intentions, causation, moral legitimacy, and coercion) and allows us to understand the place of voluntariness within a wider web of concepts.

For these reasons, I hope that this book provides a contribution not only to the ethics of (medical) consent but also to related areas in moral and legal philosophy.

Index

Note: Endnotes are indicated by the page number followed by 'n' and the endnote number e.g., 20n1 refers to endnote 1 on page 20.

For Product Safety Concerns and Information please contact our EU
representative GPSR@taylorandfrancis.com
Taylor & Francis Verlag GmbH, Kaufingerstraße 24, 80331 München, Germany

www.ingramcontent.com/pod-product-compliance
Ingram Content Group UK Ltd.
Pitfield, Milton Keynes, MK11 3LW, UK
UKHW020135200926
475702UK00005B/754
* 9 7 8 1 0 3 2 2 9 3 8 8 2 *